George Moberly

Administration of the Holy Spirit in the body of Christ : eight lectures preached before the University of Oxford in the year 1868

Second Edition

George Moberly

Administration of the Holy Spirit in the body of Christ : eight lectures preached before the University of Oxford in the year 1868
Second Edition

ISBN/EAN: 9783337263515

Printed in Europe, USA, Canada, Australia, Japan

Cover: Foto ©Lupo / pixelio.de

More available books at **www.hansebooks.com**

THE
BAMPTON LECTURES

FOR M.DCCC.LXVIII.

The Administration of the
Holy Spirit in the Body of Christ.

EIGHT LECTURES

PREACHED BEFORE THE UNIVERSITY OF OXFORD,

IN THE YEAR 1868,

ON THE FOUNDATION OF THE LATE REV. JOHN BAMPTON, M.A.
Canon of Salisbury.

BY GEORGE MOBERLY, D.C.L.

FORMERLY HEAD MASTER OF WINCHESTER COLLEGE;
NOW LORD BISHOP OF SALISBURY.

SECOND EDITION.

Oxford and London:
JAMES PARKER AND CO.
1870.

OXFORD:
BY T. COMBE, M.A., E. B. GARDNER, E. P. HALL, AND H. LATHAM, M.A.,
PRINTERS TO THE UNIVERSITY.

EXTRACT

FROM THE LAST WILL AND TESTAMENT

OF THE LATE

REV. JOHN BAMPTON,

CANON OF SALISBURY.

—— " I give and bequeath my Lands and Estates to the
" Chancellor, Masters, and Scholars of the University of
" Oxford for ever, to have and to hold all and singular the
" said Lands or Estates upon trust, and to the intents and
" purposes hereinafter mentioned ; that is to say, I will and
" appoint that the Vice-Chancellor of the University of Ox-
" ford for the time being shall take and receive all the rents,
" issues, and profits thereof, and (after all taxes, reparations,
" and necessary deductions made) that he pay all the re-
" mainder to the endowment of eight Divinity Lecture Ser-
" mons, to be established for ever in the said University, and
" to be performed in the manner following :

" I direct and appoint, that, upon the first Tuesday in
" Easter Term, a Lecturer be yearly chosen by the Heads
" of Colleges only, and by no others, in the room adjoining
" to the Printing-House, between the hours of ten in the
" morning and two in the afternoon, to preach eight Divinity
" Lecture Sermons, the year following, at St. Mary's in
" Oxford, between the commencement of the last month in
" Lent Term, and the end of the third week in Act Term.

Extract from Canon Bampton's Will.

"Also I direct and appoint, that the eight Divinity Lecture Sermons shall be preached on either of the following Subjects—to confirm and establish the Christian Faith, and to confute all heretics and schismatics—upon the divine authority of the holy Scriptures—upon the authority of the writings of the primitive Fathers, as to the faith and practice of the primitive Church—upon the Divinity of our Lord and Saviour Jesus Christ—upon the Divinity of the Holy Ghost—upon the Articles of the Christian Faith, as comprehended in the Apostles' and Nicene Creeds.

"Also .I direct, that thirty copies of the eight Divinity Lecture Sermons shall be always printed, within two months after they are preached; and one copy shall be given to the Chancellor of the University, and one copy to the Head of every College, and one copy to the Mayor of the city of Oxford, and one copy to be put into the Bodleian Library; and the expense of printing them shall be paid out of the revenue of the Land or Estates given for establishing the Divinity Lecture Sermons; and the Preacher shall not be paid, nor be entitled to the revenue, before they are printed.

"Also I direct and appoint, that no person shall be qualified to preach the Divinity Lecture Sermons, unless he hath taken the degree of Master of Arts at least, in one of the two Universities of Oxford or Cambridge; and that the same person shall never preach the Divinity Lecture Sermons twice."

TO

THE REV. THE HEADS OF COLLEGES

IN THE

UNIVERSITY OF OXFORD,

THESE LECTURES,

PREACHED BY THEIR APPOINTMENT, ARE RESPECTFULLY

DEDICATED.

PREFACE

TO THE SECOND EDITION.

In publishing a Second Edition of these Lectures, I am anxious to say a few words of Preface which may tend to explain some points in them which I cannot but fear have been somewhat misunderstood.

I do not attempt to explain more fully or to defend more completely the main thesis of the Lectures, namely, the maintenance of the twofold theory of the Collective and the Personal Priesthood, or, which is the same thing put into a different shape, the Compatibility of the Plenary Powers of the Universal Church dating from the great Pentecost, with the Organic or Representative Powers of the Priesthood, dating from the gift of the Holy Spirit by the breath of Christ, as recorded in the twentieth chapter of St. John.

Well aware as I am that the subject is most imperfectly and superficially discussed in the Lectures, I must yet leave it as it stands, believing the view which I have taken to be just and true in the main, and if just and true, certainly important, particularly at this time and in regard to the present circumstances and needs of the Church.

But those circumstances bring one point of the theory into very particular and exceptional prominence,—I mean the position and authority of lay-people in Church

Councils; and I feel very anxious to state more precisely than has been stated in the Lectures the view which I have intended to take.

I have no idea that the lay-people ever had a distinctly consultative, still less a decisive, voice in Church Synods. The learned argument of Mr. Joyce in his recent letter to the Bishop of Derry establishes, what I never doubted, the contrary. It has been no part of my object to insinuate the opposite to his conclusions; but I have endeavoured, beginning at the beginning, and tracing the course of Church proceedings synthetically, to shew that the lay element, anciently recognized as real, even in respect of matters of faith, was gradually, in the course of ages, shut out more and more, until the theory, propounded in its breadth by Archbishop Manning, of an exclusive revelation to the clergy 'united to their centre' the Bishop of Rome, became the recognized view of the Ultramontane party in the Church.

It has been generally held by theologians (excepting always those of the high Roman School) that the retrospective acceptance of the whole Church, including lay-people as well as clergy, is necessary in order to give Conciliar decrees their full Œcumenical character and weight. This view,—the view of Gerson, and his friends at Constance, and of the Gallican Church,—of Archbishop Laud, and the Anglican High Church, of 'Janus' in modern Catholic Germany, involves the truth for which I desire to contend; and borrowing the sentiment of my dear friend the late Rev. John Keble, I venture to say that if the assent of the lay-people is thus necessary even in the highest of all instances, the settlement of the faith, it is matter not of principle, but of convenience and wisdom to decide at what point, and in what proportion, this Christian counsel shall be listened to and acknowledged.

My argument in the Fourth Lecture goes no further than this. I have urged, and I feel very deeply the importance of the view, that the full co-operation of the laity of the Church,—not as matter of benevolence or bounty, but as matter of debt and duty, is not more absolutely necessary in practice, than it is indispensable in theory to the full powers and efficacy of the Church.

It formed no part of my plan,—indeed, it was impossible in so short a sketch to deal with such things,—to suggest when, or where, or in what proportion the lay element should mingle with the clerical in synod or council.

No doubt, since the publication of the Lectures, the march of events has exhibited in a very marked way the opposite danger; and we are now called upon, not so much to prove the propriety of admitting the lay element into some proportion of counsel, as to protest against its swallowing up and overwhelming the clerical by mere superiority of numbers and social weight. God forbid that any words of mine should seem to sanction or assist so fatal a danger. If the encroachment of sacerdotalism is full of evil on the one hand, the tyranny of lay usurpation is certainly not less to be dreaded on the other.

Our brethren in Ireland are called upon to deal with the practical questions arising out of this subject very suddenly, and under circumstances of great difficulty and discouragement. May the Holy Spirit of God direct and sanctify their counsels, so that the grace and wisdom of the whole body, clerical and lay, may be united in due proportion to guide and govern its anxious course, suddenly deprived, as it has been, of the orderly but somewhat enervating direction of State control.

What that due proportion is, and by what means it is to be established, it is not for me to define; but I will venture to say, looking to the theory as well as to the earliest practice of the Church of Christ, that while the office of teaching belongs specially to the ordained clergy, giving them the ' prerogative' voice in matters of faith, the authority, even in those great things, belongs in such sort to the universal body, as that the lay people too, in their place and degree, have the right and duty of sanctioning (and therefore, of course, of refusing to sanction) the determinations of the ordained clergy; while in other subjects, more or less secular, their influence and counsel is of the greatest importance and necessity.

That they should be freely elected by the members of the Church; that they should themselves be not members only, but communicants; that they should have authority, real in all cases, but graduated according to the nature of the cases; that they should, at least when required, vote separately in their own order,—all these seem to be of the nature of principles, secondary no doubt to the main principle, but fundamental and necessary. Into further detail it is not my plan or duty to enter. The great and pressing object,—painfully pressing and immediate in Ireland, hardly less pressing though less immediate in England, is that the Church should prepare itself to act as an united body, gathering together its entire corporate strength, clerical and lay alike, in due proportion, so as to be ready, whether established or unestablished, to work with the full powers of the Holy Spirit who, dwelling in the Church as the soul dwells in the body, giveth to every man severally as He willeth.

SALISBURY, *Dec.* 22, 1869.

CONTENTS.

LECTURE I.

The Gradual Development of the Doctrine of the Holy Spirit.

REVELATION i. 4, 5.

Grace be unto you, and peace, from Him which is, and which was, and which is to come; and from the seven Spirits which are before His throne; and from Jesus Christ, who is the faithful witness, and the first begotten of the dead, and the prince of the kings of the earth . . . . Page 1

LECTURE II.

The Spirit-bearing Church with its Divinely constituted Organs.

ST. JOHN i. 32, 33.

And John bear record, saying, I saw the Spirit descending from heaven like a dove, and it abode upon Him. And I knew Him not: but He that sent me to baptize with water, the same said unto me, Upon whom thou shalt see the Spirit descending, and remaining on Him, the same is He which baptizeth with the Holy Ghost 33

LECTURE III.

The Teaching and Authority of the Apostles.

1 CORINTHIANS iii. 21–23.

Therefore let no man glory in men. For all things are yours; whether Paul, or Apollos, or Cephas, or the world, or life, or death, or things present, or things to come; all are yours; and ye are Christ's; and Christ is God's 62

LECTURE IV.

The Ecclesiastical, or Post-apostolic Teaching of the Church.

1 TIMOTHY iii. 15.

The Church of the living God, the pillar and ground of the truth 94

LECTURE V.

Holy Baptism.

ST. MATTHEW xxviii. 18–20.

And Jesus came and spake unto them, saying, All power is given unto Me in heaven and in earth. Go ye therefore, and teach all nations, baptizing them in the name of the Father, and of the Son, and of the Holy Ghost: teaching them to observe all things whatsoever I have commanded you: and, lo, I am with you alway, even unto the end of the world 128

LECTURE VI.

The Holy Communion.

1 CORINTHIANS x. 17.

For we being many are one bread, and one body: for we are all partakers of that one bread 159

LECTURE VII.

Ordination and Absolution.

St. LUKE xii. 41, 42.

Then Peter said unto Him, Lord, speakest Thou this parable unto us, or even to all? And the Lord said, Who then is that faithful and wise steward, whom his lord shall make ruler over his household, to give them their portion of meat in due season? . . . 192

LECTURE VIII.

The Personal Priesthood.

1 CORINTHIANS xii. 13.

For by one Spirit we are all baptized into one body, whether we be Jews or Gentiles, whether we be bond or free; and have been all made to drink into one Spirit 225

LECTURE I.

THE GRADUAL DEVELOPMENT OF THE DOCTRINE OF THE HOLY SPIRIT.

Grace be unto you, and peace, from him which is, and which was, and which is to come; and from the seven Spirits which are before his throne; and from Jesus Christ, who is the faithful witness, and the first begotten of the dead, and the prince of the kings of the earth.— Rev. i. 4, 5.

GOD, the object of human worship, the Creator and Governor of the worlds, and the Author and Giver of all good, is naturally conceived of by the human understanding as One.

Whether we regard the religion of the nations exterior to the chosen people as derived from primitive knowledge, or in any way evolved by human thought from man's natural instinct, or by his argument from the observation of nature, alike the religious conviction at which he originally, essentially, and naturally arrives, is that the supreme God is One. Primitive *knowledge* of course can know but of one, and the philosophy of causes stops irrationally short of its own necessary conclusion if it fails to reach one. Even the existence of evil, embarrassing as it is to the natural religionist, is, in itself, rather a difficulty to be accounted for than any kind of counter-argument or disproof of the Oneness of God.

Polytheism is the corruption—it may probably have begun by being the fanciful deduction—from Monotheism. Even in the classical Polytheism there is a deep central Monotheism which underlies the whole fanciful system of gods many and lords many. Unidentified into distinct doctrine, more or less lost sight of amid the names, natures, and offices assigned to separate deities—God, as distinct from Jupiter, Apollo, or Minerva—God, the Maker, Disposer, and Governor of all things, the Being whose utterance is Fate, is an idea, half seen as it were, and so to say, looking out from curtains, yet not unfamiliar to the minds of the great writers of antiquity.

God in His Unity, One God, and none other equal or co-ordinate with Him, is the basis of all real religion, natural or revealed.

If religion is to rule and govern the whole heart of man, so that no part nor portion of his complex being is to lack its due relation to God and heaven; if, again, true religion can be but one to all men, so that all men ought to bear one only relation, of worship, love, and obedience to Him,—there cannot be conceived to be any plurality, any diversity in God the object of that universal worship, love, and obedience. If the allegiance be one and utterly the same that is required from all men in all their nature, the object of that allegiance must be utterly one. The moment that the mind conceives more than a single object of religious allegiance, the allegiance itself is shattered, the aim divided; it becomes a duty to serve two masters; the entire consecration of the heart to God is made impossible.

That which we thus regard as the basis of all true worship whatever, was also, as a matter of history, the beginning of the worship of the True God in that chosen portion of mankind among whom the traditions of original religion were retained, and to whom the subsequent revelations of God's truth and will were made.

It has pleased God to make Himself known among them in three ages.

The first age of Divine knowledge and worship, beginning at the creation of man, may be understood to have extended up to the coming of Christ. If a more exact date be required, it may be found in the birth of the Baptist[a], or his preaching ('the Law and the Prophets were until John, since then the kingdom of God is preached[b]'), or in the Incarnation of our Lord, or His Crucifixion, or His Resurrection, or His Ascen-

---

[a] Ἀρχὴ τοῦ εὐαγγελίου Ἰησοῦ Χριστοῦ, Υἱοῦ τοῦ Θεοῦ ..... ἐγένετο Ἰωάννης βαπτίζων κ.τ.λ. St. Mark i. 1.

[b] St. Luke xvi. 16.

sion, or in the descent of the Holy Ghost, or rather, in all these dates together—for inchoate in the first of them, and growing more complete in each that succeeds, it was not finally established till the last of them was fulfilled.

One God—'The Lord thy God, O Israel, is One God' —One God amid the gods many and lords many whom the nations had devised and were bowing down to, was the God of Adam, of Seth, of Enoch, of Noah, of Melchizedech—the God of Abraham, Isaac, and Jacob, the 'I am' of Moses and Aaron, the memorial, the boast, and the defence of the nation that was called by His Name.

To believe in One God, eternal, self-being, almighty, to trust in His love and providence, to pray to Him for help and forgiveness, to obey His laws, to keep His commandments, to submit in resignation and conformity to His will, to refrain from all idea of dividing the worship and duty, of right His, to any other being, whether as rival or mediator—this drawn out into moral details by the traditional law of primitive religion, and into a multitude of ceremonial details by the Law of Moses, may be understood as the summary of all religion during the first age. The object of religion was the one, undivided, undistinguished Godhead. True religion, whether more or less enlightened by immediate direction from heaven, consisted in the due relation of man to that one, undistinguished, undivided Godhead.

It is conceivable that this simple knowledge, and with it this simple worship of God in His absolute and undistinguished unity, might have been all that man in his life on earth might have needed, if he had remained in his original uprightness, and had never fallen. That which sufficed for unfallen Adam might probably have sufficed for all his unfallen progeny.

It is a deep and just thought that as the fall of man necessitated the separate operation of the Three Persons of the most holy Trinity to restore him to the favour of God and salvation, so the doctrine of the most holy Trinity, first in its anticipations supporting the hopeful faith of patriarchs, and afterwards in its full development, became also the basis—more than the basis, the summary—of all Divine revelation, in the faith of which mankind should obtain that favour and that salvation[c].

Accordingly, from the very time of the fall of man, there begin to appear in the records of inspiration indications, dim indeed, casual as it were and indistinct, which read by the light of after-knowledge, are seen to indicate the future development of the unity of the Godhead into more than a single Person.

These nevertheless were for the most part (perhaps it may be truly said *altogether*) understood by those to whom they were addressed, perhaps by those by whose lips they were spoken, without any such meaning. If, for example, Moses wrote 'God said, let us make man

[c] Vide Note A.

in our own image^d,' we cannot suppose that either Moses or the Jews divined the deep and naturally undiscoverable meaning in them, which the Christian revelation illuminating makes visible to our eyes.

In like manner, if it is recorded that three [men] stood by Abraham at his tent door^e, and that he bowed himself toward the door, and said, 'My Lord, if now I have found favour in Thy sight, pass not away I pray Thee from Thy servant'—although the Patriarch's words, spoken no doubt by the Spirit of God, indicated a truth which they did not declare, of Three in One, yet we may not imagine that either Abraham who spoke them, or the Jews who read them, conceived accurately the profound meaning of the words which his tongue was thus guided to utter.

Gradually however, as the great promise of a Redeemer came to be more fully given, particulars were added by prophet after prophet which brought out with more and more clearness—at least to our eyes, looking back upon the words, and reading them by the light of our own knowledge—the idea of a distinction of Persons in the sacred unity of God.

'The Lord said unto my Lord, Sit thou on My right hand, until I make thine enemies thy footstool^f.' No doubt the Jews had not thought out the problem, 'If David call Him Lord, how is He then his Son?' yet there lay the Divine doctrine all but apparent, like

^d Gen. i. 26.   ^e Ibid. xviii. 2.   ^f Ps. cx. 1; St. Matt. xxii. 45.

a diamond in a mine, waiting only for the ray from heaven to make it reflect the Divine truth with unmistaken brightness.

The Child to be born, whose Name should be called 'Wonderful, Counsellor, the Mighty God, the Everlasting Father, the Prince of Peace [g]'—the 'Son of the Virgin whose Name should be called Immanuel, which being interpreted is, God with us [h]'—the 'Rod out of the stem of Jesse [i],' on whom the sevenfold Spirit of Jehovah should abide—the Branch of righteousness to grow up unto David, who should bear the name of Jehovah our Righteousness [k], He whom the Angels of God should worship, whose throne is for ever and ever, who in the beginning laid the foundation of the earth, and the heavens are the work of His hands [l];—the Person, I say, whom these and many other such passages of the Prophets designated in such terms, must needs, we might have thought, have been looked forward to (had not the veil lain upon the hearts of the people and their teachers) as God, and yet not as utterly identical, or to be confused with the Divine Father.

All these sayings however, clear as they seem in the retrospect, assuredly did not, even if they conceivably could have done so, set clearly before the minds of the Jews that which they speak with unquestionable distinctness to ours. Nor when the actual fulfilment

[g] Isa. ix. 6.   [h] Ibid. vii. 14.   [i] Ibid. xi. 1, 2.
[k] Jer. xxiii. 5, 6.   [l] Heb. i. 6, 8, 10.

began, and the Son of God, having taken man's nature upon Him in the womb of the Blessed Virgin, of her substance, came among men, the anciently predicted Immanuel, did the doctrine of God in more than a single Person present itself to the possessors of the ancient Scriptures as one for which they were at all prepared by the study of the prophecies. It is true of course that they wished and hoped for a temporal Messiah, and it is correspondingly true that the low estate and personal meekness of the Messiah when He came set them upon blaspheming, and at last putting to death, the Son of Man, who seemed to disappoint those hopes and wishes. But independently of all this, sayings such as 'I and My Father are One;' 'My Father worketh hitherto, and I work;' 'Hereafter shall ye see the Son of Man coming in the clouds of Heaven;' 'The Son of Man which is in Heaven;' 'What and if ye shall see the Son of Man ascend up where He was before;' 'Say ye of Him whom the Father hath sanctified and sent into the world, Thou blasphemest, because I said I am the Son of God;' 'The Father is in Me, and I in Him [m];'— certainly did not strike on the minds of the hearers as being what they were prepared by the prophecies to hear from the lips of any one, whoever he might be, and of whatever dignity or power.

[m] St. John x. 30, v. 17; St. Matt. xxvi. 64; St. John iii. 13, vi. 62, x. 34, xvii. 21.

No; the truth seems to be this:—Till the second age of the development of the doctrine of God had actually taken place; nay more, till the Lord Himself was on the point of leaving the earth in the flesh, and spoke the words which alone, so far as I know, contain in a collected form the doctrine of the separate Persons in the Godhead—'Baptizing them into the Name of the Father, and of the Son, and of the Holy Ghost [n];' and till the actual descent of the Holy Ghost on the day of Pentecost, bringing all things to the Apostles' minds which the Lord had said unto them, taught them the meaning of these things and thereby guided them into all truth,—none knew fully, not even the Apostles themselves (as we may judge from a multitude of instances both of their conduct and their sayings even to the last), that God had revealed Himself to them in another Person, and that He with whom they had companied in those years when He went in and out among them, was the Eternal Son, by whom all things were made, of one substance, power, and eternity with the Father, true Jehovah.

It is beside my present purpose to enter more fully into the consideration of this, which I have called the second age of the development of the doctrine of God—the age of Immanuel, God among men. It was necessary that Christ should be born, and suffer, and rise again from the dead the third day [o]. It was neces-

[n] St. Matt. xxviii. 9.   [o] St. Luke xxiv. 26, 46.

sary that He should not only give us the pattern of sinless obedience and perfect holiness, but that He should also bear our sins in His own body on the tree, giving His life a ransom for many, reconciling God to sinners by reconciling sinners to God p, blotting out upon the Cross the handwriting that was against us q, the fatal indictment of our guilt. *It was necessary.* And God forbid that in our pride of shallow reasoning we should attempt to question the necessity of that Divine Sacrifice, or its efficacy for our salvation! If the atonement of Christ for sin, the purchase of the souls and bodies of men by His Blood shed upon the Cross, be not the truth, the very truth, of God, then is the Church of God mistaken from the beginning; nor is there any word or record of God safe from the arts of those who would elevate their own philosophy into the ultimate criterion of all truth, and the only reasonable rule of all belief.

As it was with the gradual announcements of the second age of the Divine development, so was it also with the third. Not in the same number indeed, nor with anything like the same fulness and distinctness, as in the case of the Person of the Son of God, but still neither unfrequently nor indistinctly when we come to look back upon them, the being of a third Person in the holy Godhead and the offices of the Holy Spirit had been indicated in the ancient Scriptures.

<p>p 1 St. Peter ii. 24; St. Matt. xx. 28; Rom. v. 6-11.
q Col. ii. 14.

I.]   *Indications of the Third Age.*   11

All expressions—and there are many such—signifying a plurality in God, still more such as give indication of three, may be taken as instances of the first kind. Some of these I have already referred to. When, again, we read that the Spirit of God moved upon the face of the waters; that God by His Spirit garnished the heavens [r]; that the hosts of heaven were made by the breath or spirit of His mouth; that the Lord God and His Spirit sent the Prophet Isaiah [s]; that the Spirit of the Lord departed from Saul [t]; that God put His Holy Spirit in Moses; that the Israelites rebelled and grieved the Holy Spirit [u]; that the Lord's Spirit should not always strive with men [x]; that it should come to pass afterwards that God should pour His Spirit upon the seed of Jacob [y]; that He should pour out His Spirit upon all flesh, so that their sons and their daughters should prophesy; and that upon the servants and the handmaids He should pour out His Spirit [z];—when, I say, we read expressions like these, and you well know how numerous they are in the Old Testament, while we acknowledge that the Jews understood them of God Himself, without conceiving the least idea of any distinction of Persons in the single Godhead, yet neither is it to be denied that such expressions read by the light of subsequent revelation do reflect the sacred Truth of

[r] Gen. i. 2; Job xxvi. 13.
[t] 1 Sam. xvi. 14. [u] Isa. lxiii. 10, 11.
[y] Isa. xliv. 3.
[s] Isa. xlviii. 16.
[x] Gen. vi 3.
[z] Joel ii. 28.

God, and show how from the beginning the development of the great doctrine of the three Persons in the one Godhead has been gradual and uniform.

The indications of the third age, the age of the Holy Spirit, occur more frequently and more decisively from the early part of our Lord's own history, and in the first three Gospels. They begin with the conception and birth of Christ: 'The Holy Ghost shall come upon thee, and the power of the Highest shall overshadow thee: therefore also the Holy Thing that shall be born of thee shall be called the Son of God [a];' 'Fear not to take unto thee Mary thy wife: for that which is conceived in her is of the Holy Ghost [b].' The preaching of the Baptist brings forcibly out the great contrast between his baptizing and the Lord's. 'I indeed baptize you with water; but One mightier than I cometh, the latchet of whose shoes I am not worthy to unloose: He shall baptize you with the Holy Ghost and with fire [c].' The separate personality of the Holy Spirit comes out with great clearness in the narrative of the Lord's baptism, giving indication at the same time of a future dispensation of the Spirit: 'Upon whom thou shalt see the Spirit descending, and remaining on Him, the same is He which baptizeth with the Holy Ghost [d].' His dignity, again, as well as His personality, is remarkably shown in the contrast taken by the Lord between the

[a] St. Luke i. 35.   [b] St. Matt. i. 20.
[c] St. Luke iii. 16.   [d] St. John i. 33.

degrees of sin incurred by blasphemy against the Son of Man and blasphemy against the Holy Ghost [e].

The commentary of St. John on the Lord's promise of the rivers of living water [f], given on the great day of the Feast of Tabernacles, is very much to my present point. For they show how words of the Lord in which no express mention is made of the Holy Spirit—'He that believeth on Me, as the Scripture hath said, out of his belly shall flow rivers of living water'—together with the whole set of passages of the Old Testament which are to be adduced as explaining the words [g] ('as the Scripture hath said'), when interpreted by the inspired Apostle, are found to have meant nothing less than the unquestionable declaration of the coming dispensation of the Holy Spirit. 'This spake He of the Spirit, which they that believe on Him should receive: for the Holy Ghost was not yet given; because that Jesus was not yet glorified.' And in the first commission of the Twelve, in words however which belong also to their ultimate mission as apostles into all the world, they are bidden to take no thought when they are delivered up, how or what they shall speak, 'for it shall be given you in that same hour, what ye shall speak. For it is not ye that speak, but the Spirit of your Father which speaketh in you [h].'

---

[e] St. Matt. xii. 32.   [f] St. John vii. 39.
[g] Isa. xii. 3, xxxv. 6, 7, xliii. 19, xliv. 3 ; Joel ii. 28 ; Zech. xii. 10, xiv. 8. Cf. St. John iv. 14.   [h] St. Matt. x. 20.

But all the previous intimations of the coming dispensation of the Holy Spirit are of minor importance in comparison with the full outpouring of information upon the subject given by our Lord Himself in that solemn discourse held on the eve of the Crucifixion, and recorded in the thirteenth and following chapters of St. John. It is not needful to quote at length such well-known words: let it suffice to say summarily that the Lord promises another Paraclete besides Himself, to comfort them when He is gone; that in the coming of that Paraclete, both the Father and the Son should dwell with and in the people of God, and that, so truly and closely that they might be said to *see* the Lord again in that indwelling, that He should teach them all things, even things to come, and bring all things to their remembrance whatsoever He had said unto them; that He should convict the world of sin, and fully teach them the great topics of righteousness and judgment, and that His own departure in the flesh was absolutely needful before this Paraclete could come, or 'that day' of peace, of comfort, and enlightenment dawn upon the inheritance of God[i].

With these preliminary announcements and preparations, after the Apostles had waited, in great uncertainty as it would seem, respecting the nature of that 'power from on high,' and 'the promise of the Father,' for ten days since the Lord's Ascension into heaven, the

[i] St. John xiv. 16, 19, 23, 26, xvi. 7, 8.

Holy Ghost descended on the great day of Pentecost. A sound from heaven as of a mighty rushing wind, an appearance of separate tongues, like as of fire, which sat upon each of them, and they were all filled with the Holy Ghost.

At that moment, the third age of the development of God for the restoration of the world finally began; never to come to an end or to be superseded upon the earth till the restitution of all things, when the Son of Man should come again in the clouds of Heaven, in like manner as the disciples had recently seen Him go into Heaven.

This third age crowns, but in no respect supersedes, the other two. God the Father is still the Creator, the great object of all true worship, the beginning of all things, the Father of Christians (being the Father of Christ), the Giver of the Holy Ghost. The Son is still our only Redeemer, our Lord, and our God. Though absent from us in the flesh for our good, He is still ever present with us. He walketh among us, and in our churches; when we meet, two or three, to pray in His name, He is in the midst of us. He is in our poor, in our sick, and in our suffering people. If any despise or persecute even His little ones, it is He who is despised and persecuted. He is with us even unto the end of the world.

But the most immediate, characteristic, and peculiar presence of God among us in this the third age, is His presence in the Holy Spirit.

The Holy Spirit dwelt in the Redeemer Himself without measure or degree, sanctifying and making holy in the most perfect manner the Man Christ Jesus. Of that fulness the Lord breathed upon the Apostles even before the Ascension. When on the day of Pentecost the Holy Spirit came down in the fuller and more peculiar manner that characterizes His presence in the Church, the Church received the full gift which her Lord had partially bestowed upon her before; and in that presence she retained His presence also. Thenceforward, the Spirit sanctifying the Church at large and the separate members of it, Christ walked in the Church, and the separate members became Christ-bearing; Christ being formed in them [j], according to the language of St. Paul in the Epistle to the Galatians, by the Holy Spirit.

Thenceforward, I say, the Holy Spirit dwelt in the Church of Christ, dwelling in the separate souls of Christian people. Great words these, brethren, and very wonderful words!—which, though they be the expression of the ordinary belief of Christians ever so slightly learned in the mysteries of the Christian faith, contain in them the germ of all the deep questions on the subject of God and man which have perplexed, and will no doubt continue to perplex, the minds of men till the end of time.

That God should create at all, and make a world—

[j] Gal. iv. 19.

obvious and undeniable as is the fact that He has done so—is a truth in which lie embedded all the endless controversies of the relation which the absolute bears to the finite.

That God who is a Spirit, should yet be three in Person, of whom one should be in some specific sense the Holy Spirit, is a mystery purely of Revelation, and therefore one which, when once stated in such terms as are made known to us, we can no further explain or elucidate.

That God who is a Spirit, almighty, original, eternal, should have created other spirits, as of angels and men, and created them free agents—agents capable of free obedience or free transgression—agents capable of counteracting His will, and doing what He would fain have not done,—is a mystery of natural religion and philosophy so profound as altogether to baffle, as it seems to me, all attempt to fathom or comprehend its marvellousness. It is the very wonder of omnipotence. If we could comprehend it as clearly as we necessarily and by the force of reason and instinct accept and believe it, we should have mastered in their very germ the endless questions of foreknowledge and freedom, predestination and free-will, which are not so properly questions of Revelation, as corollaries of the one great question, How it can be that the Supreme Spirit, unfettered by any conditions, or laws, or principles, save those of goodness and truth, which are part of His own essential

Being, can have created other beings, to be (under whatever conditions, laws, and principles) beings possessed of a freedom given and created by Himself, and yet in its exercise independent of Himself, beings capable of thinking and doing that which He would fain they did not do, and introducing evil into His world.

With most of these questions we have at present no concern. It is sufficient to have indicated where their sources lie. But in the last of them our present interest is nearer; for many of the points on which we shall have to speak in connexion with the subject of the administration of the Holy Spirit in the Church of Christ, become, I will not say more easy, but less liable to unnecessary and irrelevant difficulty, if we endeavour to fix our thoughts for a while on the original mystery—the mystery of the Omnipotent and Omnipresent Spirit creating subordinate spirits, localized in space, limited in capacities and powers, in the midst of all the conditions arising from their forming a part in a great and multifarious world, and *free*—free to obey, or disobey, to act out their Creator's design and will in creating them, or to run counter to it.

Let us think for a few moments of ourselves. I feel that whatever be the precise nature or powers of that which I call my spirit, it lives in this body. Though it be ever so diverse in its own kind from the nature of the body, yet strictly and absolutely within it it has its present necessary abode. From the body as from a centre, with the body as with an instrument, it sees, thinks, energizes. So subtle is the union which it has with the body, that I cannot by any delicacy of anatomy or self-inspection trace the frontier line at which actions in which body and spirit are both engaged pass from the one to the other. With the health of my body, my spirit is light, vigorous, lively; with the decay or sickness of my body, the functions of my spirit are languid and feeble, and unequal to their usual activity. My body is in all points such as other bodies are. It has no freedom. The blood which circulates in my veins, circulates by a force and under a law independent of my knowledge and will, and only recently discovered by my kind. The food that I eat, the motions of which my limbs are capable, the growth that I have reached, all the details of my bodily being, are part of the great irrational and unfree system of things which I see round about me in heaven and earth, in mineral, in plant, in animal, according to their various kinds. But within this body—*where* I know not, and *how* I know not— there dwells a being of a totally different kind and dignity from this outward frame which I call my body. Affected by the body, confined in the body, acting with the body so closely and subtilly that I cannot with any minute accuracy distinguish their operations, this spirit that is within me is a wonderful—the most wonderful— creation of the God of heaven and earth. I can do what no plant, nor mineral, nor animal, however great their so-called powers of instinct, can do. I can sin. I can rebel. I can fly in the face of the God that made me. There dwells in my body a free being—decayed, I am informed, and degenerate from the type in which God made my first father, and, as I feelingly know, much more inclined to sin than to obedience, to evil than to good, yet not so far altered from that primal type as to be otherwise than a free being,—sharing, therein, the kind of angels, sharing, if it may be said with reverence, the kind of God,—free, within limits, no doubt, and surrounded by all sorts of impassable and inevitable conditions, but *free*. God, the Omnipotent Spirit, who made me, who surrounds me with all the manifold conditions of my being, who is Himself round me, near me, watching me, trying me, does not naturally nor ordinarily interfere with my freedom. He might fill me with Himself. He might supersede all the powers and the powers of choice which He has given me. He might so far occupy with His operation my still uncoerced will, making my free soul beat so absolutely true to airs divine as that there should be only the possibility, not the likelihood, scarcely the danger, of its running counter to His own most good and holy will. How near to this perfection of a free creature He made our first parents I know not. Certainly I suppose that they in yielding to temptation departed more grossly, more sinfully, more wantonly from their naturally high and pure estate than their decayed descendants do when in their unfeebled and degenerate state they yield to the like temptations;—just as I imagine there never could be conceived to be any sin so utterly sinful and shocking as that of the rebel angels. But whatever was the primal condition of our first parents, and the relation in which their free spirits stood to the almighty creating Spirit who made them and pronounced them 'very good,' there can be no doubt that from the fall of man, and as regards the descendants of Adam, the state of things has been materially and grievously changed. The free spirits of men, visited as we know occasionally, and as we may suppose not unfrequently, by the influence of the Almighty Spirit, so as to think thoughts above their own thoughts, and speak words above their own words, were still in the main left to themselves. The temptations to which they were exposed had become heavier, nearer, more numerous by far than before. The strength was less. The simple directness of the will was warped. The free, created spirit fell continually. No longer harmonizing in all its movements with the almighty creating Spirit, it incurred extreme corruption of sin; and the habits of sin, growing on from father to son, pervaded large tracts of humankind with an awful degeneracy from which the spirit of man himself could in no wise rescue or restore itself.

It seems to me to be important to keep asunder in thought the natural energies of the spirit of man from the supernatural energies produced by the direct infusion or influence of the Holy Spirit of God. Difficult as it is, or impossible in particular cases to distinguish them, yet in reality they are different, and in thought may easily be kept unconfused. The free, created spirit of man, the wonderful work of God, has its own powers; and these, differing greatly in different individuals, are sometimes capable of extraordinary efforts, which nevertheless lie altogether within the scope of the natural powers of humankind. It seems to me to be a mere rhetorical confusion, capable however of leading to very mischievous consequences, to regard the intellectual achievements of great men, as of Homer, of Milton, or of Newton, as aught but natural achievements, or to attribute them in any strict sense to the infusion, or inspiration, or whatever other word be preferred, of the Holy Spirit of God.

However, it is, I suppose, to be believed, that the decayed moral nature of man after the Fall was saved by some interposition on the part of the Creator from exhibiting the full effects of corruption. It is difficult to reconcile the extreme and hideous sin which reigned far and wide in the heathen world with the high thoughts of moralists and poets, and the conscience of good and the loftier feelings which here and there we become aware of in the conduct and sentiments of individuals, unless we believe that while the decay was very great indeed, and the deflection from the original state of good, the merciful Creator, who among the Jews was preparing a restoration for the whole race, was upholding, beyond their nature, the heathen nations also from sinking, like the evil spirits, to a depth of debasement which should be too low to be restored.

However this may be, there can be no doubt that even in the first age, as I have called it, of the development of the doctrine of God, when He was hitherto known among men only as the single creating Spirit, it pleased Him, in some way not natural but supernatural, to infuse into the spirits of some men a light or power which was not their own, nor part nor consequence of their own originally-bestowed faculties, but God's. 'The holy men of old in the Jewish Church, speaking as they were moved by the Holy Ghost[k], not improbably sibyls and priests of the heathens, uttering unconsciously words not their own, passed over the limits of the natural powers of their kind, and with more or less of unconsciousness gave utterance to that which was put into their mouths by the almighty Spirit who created them, and at other times left them to the natural operation of their own powers.

Now what I wish particularly to observe at this point of my argument is, that the uninfluenced freedom of the spirit of a man is a considerably more difficult thought than that such spirit should receive from the almighty creating Spirit help, or influence, or direction.

[k] 2 St. Pet. i. 21.

It is more hard to conceive that the created spirit of a man, particularly in its decayed and degenerate state, when the imaginations of his heart are only evil continually, should be absolutely left to the free working of its own natural powers, than that the Creator-Spirit should in some way occupy, enlighten, strengthen, straighten it. His work it is, even in its decay. He designs and wills its restoration. He is round it, with it, entirely conscious of its inmost secrets. He can, if He will, pervade it wholly. If He will, He can by a mere act of power replace or recreate it in its pristine perfection. Surely supernatural aid from the Creating Spirit is not a thought which ought to be considered a strange, still less an incredible one. On the contrary, looking, as we are looking, at the original relation of the creating and created spirits, it would seem to be a very credible and likely thing that, beyond and above the natural powers of the *kind*, God should 'inspire' some or many of them, according to His will, in such ways as might tend to keep the race to which He was continually adding multitudes of fresh souls, all debased and at enmity with Himself, from falling utterly and hopelessly away, and so should prepare the restoration which in His infinite mercy He had always designed.

But while we speak of the Divine Spirit, omnipotent and omnipresent, as able to impart of His own powers, strength, light, knowledge not their own into the free spirits of men whom He created, whereby He may more or less completely occupy them, dwell in them, and fill them with Himself, let it not be supposed for a moment that any portion of such power belongs to any created spirits whatever, whether obedient and retaining still their first estate [1], or disobedient and fallen. No angel nor devil has any gift of ubiquity. If any created spirit be in one place, he is not in another. If he is busy protecting or endangering the soul of one, he is not with another. Moreover, no created spirit can penetrate, or enter into, or fill, or possess by actual indwelling the spirit of a man. The good spirits derive their holiness from the Holy Spirit. As to the evil spirits, from whom all such aid has been wholly withdrawn, and who are thereby left to the unmitigated badness and misery of free spirits in rebellion, we know indeed that they have been allowed to dwell in the bodies of men, as Satan entered into Judas Iscariot, inflaming desires, suggesting thoughts, creating opportunities and offering excuses for sin. But the free spirit of a man is not liable to direct invasion or occupation by any created spirit whatever [m]. It may, no doubt, enslave itself. It may yield and yield till it is in no sense its own master any longer. The evil spirit may thus have mastered it and reduced it to hopeless captivity. Yet even then, in this consummation of the victory of evil, it is a victory from without. The free spirit has put on bondage. But the Holy, Omnipotent, Omnipresent Spirit of the

[1] Vide Note B.   [m] Vide Note C.

Most High God can if He will, and as He will, inspire and sanctify, or occupy and utterly fill the spirits of all, men and angels, whom He has created. If He be in one Spirit, He is not less in another. If it be true that He is still, in these days, far from the spirits of the heathen, or dealing with them only in occasional visitations as with the heathen in the days before Christ, He is not the less dwelling in the Church and the members of the Church, not less in the souls of the departed just than in those who are still fighting in His strength the battle of God against the world, the flesh, and the devil.

And this we believe that the Holy Spirit of God doeth, in this the third age of the development of the doctrine of God, to the Church of God in general, and to the separate souls of Christian men and women. We believe that as He dwelt in Christ without measure, so, but in measure, He dwelleth in the souls of Christian people, whereby they are no longer in the simple natural state in which they were born, but in a new and supernatural state. What the powers and what the privileges are of this new state, and how they are communicated to Christ's people, I propose to discuss in the succeeding discourses. Suffice it for the present to say, that in this indwelling, and in all the great things that belong to it, consists the operation whereby mankind, lost in Adam, are to be restored in Christ. Innocent and unfallen, man only knew the Father. What other revelations might have been designed for him, and when and how to be made, we know not. It was in the course of his restoration from the state of loss and ruin that he came to know of the other holy Persons, and of their separate action on his behalf. 'The upward course of the knowledge of God,' says the great St. Basil, 'begins from the One Spirit, and through the One Son, reaches to the One Father. And reversely, the downward course of goodness, and the natural order of sanctification, and the kingly dignity, beginning from the Father, reaches through the Son, to the Spirit[n].'

Thus has God, who before the Fall was at one with His human children, filling them with His Holy Spirit, and keeping them in all innocent goodness, so that their will was altogether at one with His will, since the Fall gradually brought them near to Himself, bringing thereby Himself near to them;—in the first age their distant Father, accepting their worship through priests, giving to His chosen people, and perhaps to others, occasional indications of His will, keeping mankind from total ruin and the condition of devils, sustaining hopes more and less distinct of a restoration to be wrought afterwards; —in the second age, their Brother, their Friend, their Example, their Atoning Sacrifice, their Risen Lord and King;—in the third age, their close, inward, heart-sanctifying Inmate, the source of all Divine strength, and all acceptable service. And so, restored and sanctified man returns by gradual ascent upward to the

[n] Vide Note D.

Father. 'For,' as St. Basil says again, ' receiving the gifts, we first meet Him who distributeth them [the Spirit] : next we apprehend Him who sent Him [the Son]; and so we lift our thought to the first Fountain and Cause of all good things' [the Father] º.

I forbear all attempt to speculate on the mysterious language of the Holy Scriptures respecting the sevenfold nature of the Holy Spirit, so remarkably foreshown in the golden candlestick of the seven lamps in the tabernacle P, in the prophecies of Isaiah and Zechariah, and referred to over and over again in the Book of the Revelation of St. John, indicating, as it might seem, yet some further mystery—to be revealed, it may be, hereafter—in the being of God. Nor will I endeavour to come to any clear understanding of the manner or way in which we may conceive the Holy Omnipotent Spirit to act upon the free subordinate spirits which He has created. What is the precise meaning, for example, of being born of the Spirit, I suppose we cannot discover; nor is it important to enquire. We can understand with sufficient clearness what would be the condition of a free subordinate spirit left absolutely to the workings of its own will. We can understand how, if the will be warped, or evil, it might sink down into utter and unlimited ruin and despite of God. On the

º Vide Note E.
P Exod. xxv. 31, 37 ; Isa. xi. 2 ; Zech. iv. 2 ; Rev. i. 4, iii. 1, iv. 5, v. 6.

other hand, we can conceive, sufficiently at least for our purpose, that God may, if He will, repair it anew in its original goodness and strength; or how, short of this, He may, if He will, fortify it with powers not its own in its feebleness and danger; that He may do so in degrees varying from the faintest whispers of good, the slightest and most occasional help, to the fullest occupation and, so to speak, repletion with Himself, making man not less man, but as it were Divine[q]. We can sufficiently understand the difference between such help as is occasional and uncovenanted, and such as is permanent and promised. Nor is there any difficulty in conceiving that help given in the permanent and promised way may be gradually taken away if misused and neglected, and so, the Divine and supernatural element once infused into the spirit of man, gradually and totally withdrawn. And such general conceptions will suffice to enable us to understand practically the expressions of Holy Scripture, when we read of the birth of the Spirit, being filled with the Spirit, speaking by the Spirit, the Spirit speaking in men, grieving or quenching the Spirit, or the Spirit not always striving with man.

The operations of the Holy Spirit, whether in the Church at large or in the separate hearts of Christians, are secret, invisible, and at least ordinarily undistinguishable by any inward consciousness from the natural working of the mind of man. But lest that which is thus

[q] 2 St. Pet. i. 4.

invisible should for that reason be disbelieved, or counterfeited, or in any of the various ways in which human incredulity or human enthusiasm might do it wrong, abused to the injury of man, it has pleased God to bind His invisible operations to outward and visible methods, which give assurance of that of which otherwise we might be uncertain. The great channel whereby the invisible Spirit is communicated to men is the Holy Catholic Church, the Communion of Saints, visible, to be recognized of all men, a city set upon a hill. The assurance of the first gift of the invisible Spirit to the separate human spirit, is to be seen in the water and the sacred words which by Christ's institution convey and accompany the birth of the Spirit. The assurance of the life and growth of the Holy Spirit, of the continuing love and favour of God, and of our being very members incorporate in the body of Christ which is the blessed company of all faithful people, is in the faithful partaking of the blessed eucharistic bread and wine, which communicate the spiritual food of the body and blood of Christ, and unite us more closely than anything else on earth with God. The proof that we are not under delusion in believing ourselves thus helped by the invisible Spirit, and gradually drawing nearer to God and heaven, is to be found in the fruits of the Spirit, in love, joy, peace, long-suffering, gentleness, goodness, faith, meekness, temperance[r]. So mercifully is the

[r] Gal. v. 22.

viewless operation of the Spirit, invisible to others, unfelt in ourselves, bound to things which we can hear and see, and surely know, in order that the humble spirit of a Christian man, walking before God in patient and orderly ways, may receive the blessed assurance that by the working of God he is being drawn up to high and heavenly things, and gradually becoming more assimilated to the likeness of his Lord.

I propose in the ensuing Lectures to trace in some degree the administration of the Holy Spirit in the body of Christ, to trace it from the unmeasured fulness with the Holy Spirit dwelling in Christ Himself to the measured and divided sufficiency with which the same gift was imparted to the Apostles and through them to the Church at large.

It will be my object to show that, compatibly with the existence by successive ordination of persons expressly empowered to administer the life-giving and life-supporting rites of the Church, the real and ultimate possessor of all the power and privilege, under Christ, is the Church itself; the Church entire; not apostles, not bishops, not clergy alone; but the entire body of Christ, comprising apostles, bishops, clergy, and lay-people,—all in their respective places contributing, and bound to contribute, to the great work of diffusing more widely, and deepening where it is diffused, the living energy of the Holy Spirit, so far as it is given to human agency to aid in diffusing and deepening it.

It is obvious that so great a subject must necessarily be dealt with in a very slight and superficial way in the course of eight Lectures, and I am painfully aware that what is necessarily and in itself slight and superficial will be still more so in my hands. But I have wished to descend upon various great questions of Church constitution and administration from the height of a great principle; and for this purpose a superficial and somewhat hasty view may not be without advantage. Many great things are more capable thus of being seen in their mutual relation to each other, than if the details of each were more thoroughly searched into.

I shall endeavour, if it please God, in the next Lecture to speak of the general doctrine of the Spirit-bearing Church with its divinely constituted and ordained organs, that is to say the Priesthood. The two following Lectures will deal with the subject of apostolical and ecclesiastical teaching and authority. Then will follow three Lectures on the two Sacraments of the Gospel and the two great sacramentals, Ordination and Absolution. The concluding Lecture will be devoted to the subject of the Personal Priesthood, by which every member of Christ is permitted to draw near to the Father, and present himself in his body and soul a living sacrifice, holy and acceptable to God for Christ's sake, rendering thereby his own rational and intelligent service.

LECTURE II.

THE SPIRIT-BEARING CHURCH WITH ITS DIVINELY CONSTITUTED ORGANS.

And John bare record, saying, I saw the Spirit descending from heaven like a dove, and it abode upon Him. And I knew Him not: but He that sent me to baptize with water, the same said unto me, Upon whom thou shalt see the Spirit descending, and remaining on Him, the same is He which baptizeth with the Holy Ghost.—St. John i. 32, 33.

THE event recorded by St. John the Evangelist in these two verses forms, I apprehend, an epoch of the greatest possible importance in the history of the Church of God.

With the proper relation of being borne by the second and third Persons of the Holy Trinity to one another in their own eternal and equal Godhead, we have at present no concern. Nor is it of any importance to our present discussion to speculate upon the degree or manner in which the Holy Spirit dwelt in and with the Man Christ Jesus for His own sanctification while He 'grew, and waxed strong in spirit, and the grace of

God was upon Him [a],' from His conception in the womb of the Blessed Virgin Mother till the day of His baptism in the river Jordan. But when that baptism was completely done [b], and the Lord had gone up out of the water, having fulfilled all righteousness [c] by accepting the ministrations of the Baptist, the descent of the Holy Spirit as here recorded, and His remaining upon the Lord, seem to mark the precise commencement of that with which I am more immediately concerned, the administration of the Holy Spirit for the restoration of mankind. The visible descent of the dove not only designated, but empowered also, the Man Christ Jesus to be in all time to His Church the sole baptizer with the Holy Ghost [d], the one and single Source through whom, by such channels and media as He should choose and empower, the Holy Spirit should pass in an orderly and covenanted way for the sanctification and salvation of men.

In like manner, when we read, two chapters later in St. John's Gospel, that God giveth not His Holy Spirit by measure [unto Christ] [e], and that He consequently speaketh the words of God, we are, no doubt, to understand that in the Man Christ Jesus, ' whom God hath sent,' the Holy Spirit dwelleth, not as in other men, divided severally according to the will of God, but

[a] St. Luke ii. 40. [b] Vide Note F.
[c] St. Matt. iii. 15. [d] St. John i. 33.
[e] St. John iii. 34.

entirely, absolutely, without separation of office or distinction of gift. Not only did His human spirit altogether conspire and agree according to its human powers with the Holy Spirit, but it was also made to be so much greater in capacity than that of other men, so superhuman in ability to receive, to entertain, and to impart, that no gift, no power, no fulness, nor largeness of divine and spiritual influence can be conceived but such as He possessed in the most unlimited and complete abundance, and could bestow on others. Out of His fulness have all we received. The gift was in Him entire. He had the spring, the fountain, the very source of the welling waters of the Holy Spirit of God.

This gift of the Holy Spirit was, no doubt, imparted thus to the Man Christ Jesus for our sake. Blending with the fulness of His own personal sanctification, it was yet not identical with it. He needed it not for Himself, we may be sure. It was given to supply these 'differences of administration [f]' which all proceed from the same Lord. It was to be communicated from Himself to His people. But this communication was not to take place instantly and at once. It was necessary that He should first live for a while in the flesh upon the earth, teaching, preparing, and fulfilling prophecy, proving Himself, by all the wonderful works that He did [g], to be the expected Messiah, the hope

[f] 1 Cor. xii. 5.   [g] Vide Note G.

of Israel. It was necessary that He should transact on the earth all the work of His glorification—the glorification as of the corn of wheat which dies and is buried before it rises to its new and multiplied life [h]. It was necessary that He should give His life upon the cross a ransom for many, and rising from the dead after preaching to the spirits in prison, should be exalted to His Father's right hand in heaven.

Then, when all this was duly done, and the glorification of the Lord consummated by His ascension in the flesh, everything preliminary to the full effusion of the Holy Spirit was completed. Ten days more of solemn waiting, and then at length, in visible form as of divided tongues of fire, and with the sound of a mighty rushing wind, He descended on the great day of Pentecost. It was from the Father that the dove had come forth and remained upon the head of the Son on the banks of Jordan. It was by the Son that the tongues of fire were sent down which sat upon the head of twelve in one of the chambers, if it be so, of the Temple of Jerusalem. I say, brethren, upon the head of twelve; for though I am aware that many of the greatest ancient writers speak of the tongues as one hundred and twenty, the number of the disciples who were together at the election of St. Matthias, yet even these appear to acknowledge at other times that, for the purpose of succession and

[h] St. John xii. 23, 24.

derived authority, the gift was in the apostles alone. So, for instance, St. Augustine, who at other times speaks confidently of there having been a hundred and twenty tongues, says, 'He thoroughly bathed the apostles with the spring of living light, so that they afterwards, like twelve rays of the sun, and as many torches of truth, should illuminate the whole world, and inebriated, should fill it with new wine, and should water the thirsty hearts of the nations i.' I wish, therefore, to be understood, not as denying that the number of those on whom the tongues rested exceeded twelve — though I confess that I doubt it — but as meaning that on twelve, and twelve only, they rested in such sort as to make them the patriarchs of the family of Christ, the channels for the communication of the graces of the Holy Spirit, in His orderly and covenanted methods, to the sons of men.

In this great event, then, the Holy Spirit, who had dwelt without measure in the Lord Himself, was by Him imparted to twelve men, in order to be imparted to others. The Twelve were become, for purposes of spiritual administration, the living and life-giving Church. They were become the Spirit-bearing and Spirit-transmitting body of Christ; He in them, and they in Him; one in the oneness of the Holy Spirit, in some sort, as He was one with the Father. All the great things said in the seventeenth chapter of

i Vide Note H.

St. John were now fully true of them. They, in their spiritual being and aspect, were not of this world—that is, they did not owe their origin to this world—even as their Lord was not of this world.

It seems to me to be important to dwell for a short time on this point—I mean the condition of the Twelve during the short time that elapsed before they began to teach or baptize or bring others into the communion of the body of Christ. In them, conjointly, dwelt for the present the fulness of the Holy Spirit, in so far forth as He was given from Christ to be transmitted for the sanctification of mankind. Personal graces, administrative graces, all the diversities of gifts to be given in many divisions to men in the Church through human agency, were to issue from that great gift which, hitherto undivided, except to twelve holders, rested for such transmission upon them alone. As in the case of the miraculous feeding of the multitudes of four or five thousand,[j] the Lord gave to the disciples, and the disciples to the multitude, so the gifts which were to sanctify the innumerable company of the members of the body of Christ in all future ages should flow down from one single source through twelve channels. Governors and governed, teachers and taught, graces inward and graces outward — all Christians should derive the orderly communication of the covenanted indwelling of the Holy Spirit through the

[j] St. Matt. xix. 19, xv. 36.

agency of these twelve men on whom the tongues sat, like as of fire, on that great day.

As I must not be understood to deny that the gift of Pentecost was extended, except for purposes of transmission and derivation, to others besides the apostles, so neither do I mean to signify that the gift bestowed on the apostles at Pentecost was the first and only aid of the Holy Spirit which they had received. On the contrary, during all the time of their companionship with the Lord from their first believing, they always undoubtedly possessed—'pro modulo tamen et mensurâ,' to adopt the words of St. Jerome speaking on this very point [k]—the gift of the Holy Spirit. Without Him they could not have believed originally. By Him they had wrought miracles. By Him they had confessed Christ, and clung to Him under the pressure of difficulties of doctrine of no slight magnitude—'Lord, to whom shall we go?'—and not wholly deserted Him, even when for a while they forsook Him and fled in the moment of extreme danger in the Garden of Gethsemane. Moreover the breath of the Lord, as recorded in the twentieth of St. John [l], had been a further and most signal step in that 'profectus apostolicus' of the same St. Jerome, the growth and progress of the apostles, before the last great effusion gave them the real 'baptism of the Holy Ghost,' which, completing their own graces, enabled

[k] St. Hieron. Epist. cxx. ad Hedibiam, vol. i. pp. 835, 836.
[l] St. John xx. 22.

them to become the channel divinely appointed for diffusing those graces to other men.

And not to the apostles only is it to be believed that occasional and partial gifts of the Holy Spirit were given before Pentecost[m]. We cannot doubt that to the same Holy Spirit we must attribute all that is good in angels or men, all the special influences by which holy men spake at any time as they were moved by the Holy Ghost, all the imperfect yet hopeful feeling after God, if haply they might find Him, among the heathen, all the zeal of God which St. Paul acknowledges even in the midst of error and blindness among the Jews, all the willingness and eagerness to receive the message of salvation, when once it was preached, whether in Jews or Gentiles.

But all this, true as it is, does not in any degree interfere with the statement which I have ventured to lay broadly down—namely, that the covenanted graces of the Holy Spirit, those of which Christian men were orderly to drink in the body of Christ, those which were to issue from the great gift of Pentecost, were all for the present moment centred, under Christ, in the Twelve.

If then we were to endeavour to speak with exactness respecting the position held by the Twelve, we seem to be able to distinguish three several aspects in which they are to be regarded as recipients of the Holy Spirit.

First, as Christian men, receiving the inward sanctify-

[m] Vide Note I.

ing graces, the like of which all Christians partake of in the body of Christ. These graces, which in the case of ordinary Christians, inchoate and uncovenanted before baptism, have their covenanted beginning in baptism the sacrament of the heavenly birth of water and of the Holy Spirit, began to the Twelve in a manner exceptional and different from that in which they begin to Christians in general, as the beginning of a series must always be different from the continuance of it. None can point definitely to the time at which the apostles were baptized. Perhaps the truest answer to the question when were they baptized would be to say that in the ordinary sense and regular manner they were never baptized at all. Yet in saying this, there are two or three points that should not be forgotten. First, that they surely received John's baptism, that is, they were solemnly washed with water as persons repenting of sin, and looking forward to receive forgiveness in Christ; secondly, that the Lord Himself said to Peter, 'He that hath been bathed, needeth not save to wash his feet[n],' and although the main scope of these words was no doubt referrible to the times in which the Gospel should be fully preached, and the 'bath' regularly received as the outward means and pledge of the new birth, yet we can hardly suppose that they had no personal application to the apostle to whom they were spoken at the very moment when he sought to decline the washing of his feet by the Lord's

[n] St. John xiii. 20.

hands. Indeed, St. Augustine[o] and Thomas Aquinas conclude from this verse that the apostles had certainly received the bath of regeneration from the hands of the Lord Himself. And thirdly, that they were expressly told by the Lord immediately before the Ascension that 'not many days hence[p],' they should be baptized with the Holy Ghost, and that, in terms which by the contrast with John's baptism seem unquestionably to denote Christ's baptism properly so called. Putting all these things together, it seems most in accordance with the language of Holy Scripture to conclude that either the fulness of the gift of Pentecost superseded the 'bath' of water indispensable in all other cases, or more probably that, superadded to the bath of Jordan, and completing and crowning the gradual increase of that 'apostolic growth' of which St. Jerome speaks, it filled up the sacrament, and completed to those who, being themselves the first could not receive it by the agency of any other men, the administered birth of water and the Spirit. Certainly in all other cases, even in so remarkable instances as those of Cornelius the first Gentile convert, and Saul the persecutor, separated as he was from his mother's womb to be an apostle[q], and called by the miraculous appearance and voice of the Lord Himself on the road to Damascus, the water could not be, and was not, dispensed with. 'Can any man forbid *the* water,' (τὸ ὕδωρ) asked St. Peter at Cæsarea, 'that these

[o] Vide Note J.   [p] Acts i. 5.   [q] Gal. i. 15; Rom. i. 1.

should not be baptized, which have received the Holy Ghost as well as we[r]?' 'Arise, and be baptized, and wash away thy sins, calling on the Name of the Lord[s],' said Ananias, sent by God to restore the sight of the trembling and astonished persecutor and called apostle, and to admit him to the full sacrament of Holy Baptism.

But whatever were the baptism, or the equivalent of baptism, in the case of the apostles, there can be no doubt that they received all those ordinary graces which to other Christian people have their covenanted beginning in baptism, and are continued and cherished by the use of prayer and the other means of obtaining the help of the Holy Spirit. Whatever they were besides, they were Christian men as we are—planted into the body of their Lord, looking forward therein to their divine inheritance, liable to sin, requiring the continual help and support of the Spirit, unassured of final safety until the day when death coming upon them in the stedfastness of their repentance and faith should 'bind them fast' for ever

'To the bright shore of love[t].'

This first. And secondly, they were Christian men holding personally extraordinary gifts for external service, such as the gift of tongues, and others of a like

---

[r] Acts x. 47.   [s] Acts xxii. 16.
[t] Christian Year—Eighth Sunday after Trinity.

kind. Probably they were endowed with these in different measures and degrees,—perhaps each of them with some more than with others; perhaps all in a higher degree than other gifted Christians,—yet were these not different in kind from those which were given to others, for the edifying of the Body of Christ—gifts given according to the will of the Spirit to every man to profit withal. And eminently among these high gifts was the inward vision of the revealed truth of God, divinely qualifying them to be the sacred prophets of that truth to all generations of mankind.

And, thirdly, they had what no other men ever had, or could have after them—the full gift of the Holy Spirit for diffusion by the use of outward means among the countless multitudes of Christian people who should come after them. 'As out of the twelve patriarchs,' says Hooker, 'issued the whole multitude of Israel according to the flesh,' so 'according to the mystery of heavenly birth our Lord's apostles we all acknowledge to be the patriarchs of the whole Church[u].' They were, for the time, the Church; not members only, not governors or teachers only—others in all time should be these—but comprising in themselves, as in the first *reservoir* from the sacred spring, all membership, and all governorship, the whole of which in all subsequent generations of the Church should trace its descent, so

---

[u] Eccl. Polity, Bk. V. ch. lxxvii.

far as it should be legitimate, through them to the Holy Spirit of Christ Himself.

No sooner, however, had the Twelve received the power from on high for which they had been bidden by the Lord to tarry in the city of Jerusalem[x], than they began to impart of it to others. Perhaps we may not unduly generalize here, and drawing a Christian universal from this particular, say that the true fire of the Holy Spirit can never be present in any man without its setting him instantly upon endeavouring to diffuse that light and heat to others beside himself. However, on that very morning they began to baptize, and baptizing, whether by their own unassisted hands or no, not fewer than two hundred and fifty people apiece between nine o'clock in the forenoon and night, had already exhibited the beginning of that irrepressible growth of the sacred body of Christ, which should cause it to resemble the grain of mustard-seed in its enlargement, and the multiplication of the buried corn of wheat. To the three thousand men and women that day planted into the body of Christ the Holy Spirit was given. One and all they received the ordinary graces of Holy Baptism, the birth of water and the Holy Ghost. Nothing was wanting to them, in order to the making of their calling and election sure, except to keep, to strengthen, to cherish and increase in their hearts the Divine grace which, together with the means of cherishing and increasing it,

[x] Acts i. 3.

was already theirs. Thus began—to be continued to the whole multitude of Christian people in every age of the Church—the transmitted graces of personal holiness and acceptableness in Christ, the precious personal graces, by means of which men and women planted into Christ are to reach salvation.

If then what I have said be true, and on the morning of the first great Whit Sunday the Twelve constituted the Church, so as to have become, so to speak, the body of Christ visible upon the earth, how stood the case on the evening of that same day, when now three thousand men and women were already baptized [y], and so had been made to drink into that one Spirit whose presence constitutes and binds into one that great and sacred body? And how stood the case when the Lord went on to add daily, as we read, to the Church such as were in process of salvation, and multitudes of men and women, to the number of many thousands more, were brought into the body [z]?

It seems to me to be very important indeed to endeavour to realize the state of things, in respect, I mean, of the divine and spiritual powers and privileges of the body, which was necessarily brought about by this change.

There can, I suppose, be no doubt that in the language of Holy Scripture it is the Church, entire and complete, not any class, or rank, or caste of persons

[y] Acts ii. 41, 47. [z] Acts iv. 4, v. 14, vi. 7.

within it, which is spoken of as the Spirit-bearing body of Christ, the successor of Christ, the holder of power and privilege in Christ,—nay, even as Christ Himself upon the earth.

'As the body of a man is one and hath many members, and all the members of that one body, though they be many' and have various offices of duty and degrees of strength and honour, 'are one body, so also is Christ[a].' No person can, I suppose, have any doubt that this great saying applies to the Church at large, not to the apostles or clergy within the Church only, but to the entire Church, including all its members whether clerical or lay. In like manner we believe, with St. Cyprian and St. Augustine[b], that when Christ promised to St. Peter the keys of the kingdom of heaven[c], He promised them to the Church at large, whose faith and whose unity St. Peter on that occasion represented. We believe that in the case of the admission of a child or a converted heathen into the body of Christ by Holy Baptism, it is the Church at large, the common parent of Christians[d], who bears as a mother the newly made member of the body. We believe that in Holy Communion it is the whole Church, the body of Christ, which commemorates the life-giving sacrifice of the Lord, feeding its unity and its holiness by feeding on the meat indeed and the drink indeed of His spiritual body and blood[e]. We

[a] 1 Cor. xii. 12. [b] Vide Note K. [c] St. Matt. xiv. 18.
[d] Gal. vi. 26. [e] 1 Cor. x. 17, xi. 29; St. John vi. 55.

believe that in absolution it is the Church's peace that is given; that in excommunication the sentence is to be pronounced upon such as, when their sin has been told to the Church, refuse to hear the Church f. If a council makes decrees in matters of faith, it does so not as overruling the Church, nor as issuing laws of faith to the Church upon its own authority, but as representing more or less faithfully the entire Church, and speaking in its name, so that its decrees are really binding in exact proportion to that faithfulness. All these things speak plainly to the great truth that in the Church in its entireness, in all its members, not in some only, dwells the fulness of the Holy Spirit, and so the ultimate authority which nothing but the indwelling of the Holy Spirit can give. If an ordinary parish priest teaches his people, he still speaks as the *parson*, that is, as bearing in his small sphere the *person* g of the Church.

This is one great half of the truth, never to be forgotten. But all this is entirely compatible with that other not less important half, namely, that there exists in this Spirit-bearing body a divinely descended priesthood, who, ordained by imposition of hands in due succession from the apostles, are divinely authorized to represent the entire Church in these various functions, reserving some of them entirely in their own hands to administer, yet even in these wielding powers which are ultimately the powers of the whole body, and in others

---

f St. Matt. xviii. 17. g Gerens *personam* Ecclesiæ.

asking, in various degrees, the joint action of other members of the body besides themselves.

It is not necessary in order to constitute a true representation either that the representatives should be selected and empowered in the first place by universal choice and delegation, or that they should require, in order to be continued in their representative position, any renewal of reference to the universal will. It is however, I imagine, essential to a faithful representation, considering that the representatives are only men, and therefore liable to the infirmities of human feeling and passion, that the whole body should in some manner and degree that should be real, however small, have a certain amount of power to act; that it should not be absolutely and entirely excluded, I do not say from any participation in the actual administration of such powers, but at least from contributing its sanction (and if its sanction, then by obvious consequence its possible refusal of sanction) in such ways and degrees as to constitute a reality however subordinate, or indirect, or retrospective, even in the highest and most sacred instances of the exercise of such powers. And herein the view which I have stated differs from that of the Roman Catholic writers, who, admitting the representative character of the clergy, and carrying it further, so as to maintain the virtual representation of the whole Church in the single person of the Bishop of Rome, do really destroy in fact what they acknowledge in terms, while they entirely disallow that amount of real participation which appears to be absolutely essential to any real representation at all [h]. This then is the position which I desire to take, and this is indeed the very thesis which it is my purpose to illustrate in these Lectures—namely, that while on the one hand the Spirit-bearing Church in all its members is the ultimate possessor of every sort of divine power and privilege in and under Christ the Head, so that the persons who exercise spiritual office and authority within it are, in strictness of speech, real representatives of the body of which they are thus made to be the organs,—on the other hand it is most true, and most earnestly to be maintained, that they also hold by direct descent from the apostles the gift of the Holy Spirit, conferred in the apostolic laying on of hands, which gift empowers, enables, and authorizes them, as nothing else can do, to discharge those offices and exercise those powers which thus in the name and on the behalf of the whole Church they discharge and execute towards the separate members of it.

It is obvious, I trust, that I am speaking now, not of the personal graces bestowed upon the single souls of Christians for their separate growth in holiness, but of the official graces, if I may so call them, which, inherent in the whole body, are exercised within it representatively by the clergy.

[h] Vide Note L.

Perhaps it is necessary, in order to distinguish these things clearly from one another, to add a few more words of explanation.

We believe, then, that there are ministered to every person once made a member of the body of Christ personal graces of inestimable value, whereby he has within him the birth of the Holy Ghost, the privilege of sonship, and the right of personal prayer and unimpeded access to the throne of the mercy of God, so that even if he were alone in the world it would be possible for him (though, no doubt, in his isolation deprived of many great blessings and comforts in the Church) yet to make his divine calling and election sure in Christ to the end. But each individual person needs for his perfection to come, in a multitude of ways, under the operation of the collective graces, so to call them, which dwell in the Church of God as such, beyond and above those personal ones which dwell in himself and in all his brethren and neighbours in the Church together. For the body of Christ is not a mere aggregate of sanctified individuals. Consisting as it does of all the members, yet it is more than all the members together. It possesses gifts which are not merely the united gifts of the aggregated members, but gifts of the body as such. The individuals only derive their life from the life of the body. They do not draw the life of their baptism from the ministering priest or from their godparents. The Church is their mother in Christ, and the priest and the godparents are in their respective offices representatives of the Church, as the Church is the representative of her Lord. It is with the Church, and the separate Christians who compose the Church, as it is with the natural body to which St. Paul so often compares them. It is not the life that is in the hand, the life that is in the eye, the life that is in the ear, which, together with the life of all the other members, make up the life which is in the body. On the contrary, it is the life which is in the body which is the principle of the life that is in each and all of them. If the body should die, they die of course, and all together. They cannot club together their derivative lives, and make a joint-stock of life to supersede, or be equivalent to, or outlive the life that is in the body. And extremely parallel to the case of the members of the natural body, is that of the members of the Body of Christ. They have, no doubt, a life in them which once derived from the life of the body is truly their own, and not dependent, so far as regards themselves and the absolute necessities of their own personal salvation, upon the life that is in others; yet even for their own perfection it is in many ways necessary that graces different from those which are determined to the growth of individuals should dwell among them, while for the continuance of the succession of Christian people in other generations, and for the performance of such works upon individuals as they need for their full perfection, it is necessary that some persons should be qualified by express qualification to exercise upon them those powers which ultimately reside in the body at large, so as to be the organs of the body for these purposes, the channels of those graces which may be called collective rather than personal, official rather than directly sanctifying.

But returning to what is my more immediate subject, the official graces or powers, I repeat that the holders of them are, when properly regarded, to be considered as divinely descended representatives, exercising within the body the powers which essentially and ultimately belong to the body itself at large.

I must repeat that these two things are not in any degree inconsistent in themselves, or incompatible with one another; and that no reason whatever is to be alleged, drawn from the nature of the case, why a true representation of others should not be intrusted to an hereditary or long descended class of holders, or why a succession of men inheriting authority for the purpose from such a long descent, sufficiently authorized in its beginning and its subsequent steps, should not at the same time be true representatives of the whole body to which they belong. If the case were one of merely human institution, such as the civil polity of a state, there would, no doubt, be a great likelihood of their being found to be practically incompatible; for the hereditary holders of power might very probably forget their representative character altogether, and those whom they claimed to represent might come to find that their mind and wish, however universal and undoubted, was entirely ignored and lost sight of by their so-called representatives. Usurpation and tyranny gradually growing up would probably issue in their natural consequence of revolution and disunion. Yet even in this case the evil would not be really inherent in the nature of the case, but in the passions of men.

That such ill consequences may occur even in the case of the Church is, alas! only too clearly proved by the course of its history. Usurpation has, in that case, also proved to be the fruitful source of every sort of division and disunion.

But the Church has within it the secret of restoration. The primitive constitution of the Church, fairly studied and obediently followed, would seem to point out, if men would honestly and faithfully adopt it, the true remedy. In the recognition of the due relation of the separate members of the Spirit-bearing body to each other, and of the whole to Christ, lies the rule which is to reconcile in all time interests, so to call them, and actions which might otherwise be liable to conflict. The powers of all are derived, none are original. The Holy Spirit is alike the source of all, and the primitive usage and practice of the Church of Christ seem to assign to all the true and perfectly intelligible limits of their respective authority. There is assuredly reserved to the Church at large, at least in its primitive constitution, authority to remonstrate and to overrule tyrannical pretensions on the part of those who hold the official powers, as the holders of these official powers have also the right in their respective places and degrees to rebuke and repress the extravagances of individual fancy, or of congregational caprice and self-will.

If either of these two essential principles of the constitution of the Church should be omitted or forgotten (as indeed each has been woefully forgotten in some portion of the Church), extreme evil cannot fail to be the consequence. If the holders of ministerial office and power come to be regarded merely as representatives of their brethren, deriving all authority to exercise their functions from the express or implied delegation of the multitude in each successive generation —which is, I presume, more or less the extreme Protestant view—one of two consequences can hardly fail to follow: either there will be a mere congregationalism, in which every community, either great or small (and communities will gradually, by the continued operation of the same cause, become smaller and smaller), will feel itself at liberty to elect and depose its ministers, to determine without appeal upon the truth for itself, and to institute laws and rites of worship according to its own judgment—a consequence which would involve innumerable varieties of teaching and practice, and divisions and subdivisions without end—or, if it were attempted to set up any central and general authority, it would be impossible to establish, or, if it were impugned, to prove, the universal consent on which alone it could be intelligibly based, and extremely difficult to displace it, if, in consequence of its becoming corrupt or tyrannical, or for any other adequate reason, that universal consent, once given, should be withheld or changed. The case would not be very unlike the instances with which we are familiar in political life, of irresponsible power based upon a factitious universal suffrage. On the other hand, if the holders of such offices were to be regarded merely as descendants and inheritors of powers originally confined to twelve men, and subsequently handed down from them by direct and exclusive succession to themselves, I do not see how they could be regarded otherwise as a body, than a separate, irresponsible, supreme company, as compared with the mass of lay Christians. They would be, not indeed by blood, but by clear separation and difference, a caste in the Church, in whom would absolutely reside all the power, all the knowledge, all the prerogatives of authority of all kinds, while the large mass of men and women who constituted the immense numerical majority in the Church would have no duty but to listen, submit, and obey—no voice in counsel, no share in power, no right of judging, criticising, or objecting. In short, on this theory the clergy would be the real Church, and the lay-people simply dumb recipients of whatever the clerisy—that is the Church—chose to lay upon them. But in the joint and true theory, both these inconveniences are avoided. The powers inherited by the whole body are determined for administration to such as, holding by direct succession from the apostles, receive not the personal designation only, but the personal grace and empowerment also by the gift of the Holy Spirit conveyed by the imposition of apostolic hands, which authorizes and enables them to exercise upon the members of the body various sorts of authority which are really inherent in the body itself. They are for public purposes the organs of the body's life; but the great life itself, the great deposit of the spiritual life, remains in the body at large. There is the true inheritor of Christ, the real agent which, instinct with the Holy Ghost, mighty in numbers, mighty in diverse gifts, mighty in faith, mighty in holiness, irresistible and all-powerful if it were as perfect as it might be in holiness, still more irresistible and all-powerful if it were at full and entire unity in itself— unity of doctrine, unity of love, and unity of action—contains in itself the real principle of absolute conquest and mastery over the whole world. The analogy so much presented to us in Holy Scripture, of the natural body of a man, can hardly, as it seems to me, be pressed too far in its strong and close bearing upon my present point. One vitality diffused over the whole, special organs for special services of general and indispensable use, all needful for each, each needful for all;—does not the likeness seem to fit in every particular, shewing by an example of which every one of us is fully capable of judging how 'the whole' spiritual 'body fitly framed together and compacted by means of every joint of the supply, according to the working in the measure of each several part, maketh the growth of the body unto the building up of itself in love[i]?' The strength and health of the whole natural body is needed to enable each separate member and limb, each bodily organ and faculty, to discharge its own proper functions successfully; and yet no one of these separate members or organs derives its own peculiar functions nor the power to exercise them in the first place from that strength and health. The nervous sensibility helpful to the eye as the organ of sight, or to the ear as the organ of hearing, or to the other organs for the discharge of their respective offices, is diffused over the whole body; yet not only do these organs not derive their peculiar powers from that diffused sensibility, but if the organs themselves be from any cause inoperative, no such diffused sensibility can restore them. The body is absolutely blind if the eye cannot see, and entirely deaf if the ear cannot hear. The case appears to be closely, I might say singularly, parallel to that of the spiritual body, and may very justly, as it does most forcibly, illustrate the case of a priesthood, strictly

[i] Eph. iv. 16.

representative in its own proper being, yet receiving personal designation and powers, not by original derivation from the body which it represents, or continual reference to it, but by perpetual succession from a divine source and spring of authorizing grace.

No doubt very many practical questions of no slight importance and difficulty may arise under peculiar circumstances. It may happen that the succession requisite for the due transmission, and so for the full inheritance of the priestly powers, may by various accidents be broken. Casual occurrences, like that of the throwing of the survivors of the crew of the 'Bounty' upon Pitcairn's Island, or political complications like those which led to the discontinuance of the episcopate in Protestant Germany, may cause either the inevitable interruption or the practical stoppage of functions which we believe to be essential to the full and perfect constitution of the body. Yet even in such cases as these, the analogy of the natural body does not fail to suggest the true solution of the difficulty. The whole body with its diffused vital sensibility, the whole body with its large and manifold powers, can do a great deal, if not to supply, at least to compensate for the loss—the temporary loss or deficiency of power in a single organ. We know how much more acute and sensitive than is ordinarily natural to them some of our senses are wont to become when others are for a long time interrupted in their exercise; how keen, for instance, hearing and touch are wont to become to those who have been very long deprived of the use of sight or are born blind. We know how abnormal the sensitive powers which pervade the whole body sometimes become in their acuteness in cases of natural or artificial somnambulism. Yet surprising as these powers are in the way of helpfulness or partial compensation when any special organ is long inactive or originally deficient, yet they cannot either restore the organ itself in its decay or be a full substitute for it if it be wanting. If the eye cannot see, circuitous methods may, no doubt, be adopted which may be more or less successful in conveying to the brain some idea of those impressions which sight would have imparted at once; yet these neither are nor can be the same, nor nearly equivalent to the ideas of real sight. And exactly so it may probably be with the organs of the spiritual body. The life that is in all the members may suffice in some degree to supply something that in particular places is wanting, and under special circumstances may offer a practical substitute for the interrupted graces which should have flowed down in orderly succession from the ordaining apostles, so that we may well believe that personal life in the Spirit may still be maintained even there and then; and yet it is necessary for the perfect condition even of the personal life, at least to future generations, that the locally or partially interrupted succession should be restored as soon and as completely as possible. Not all the nervous power and health of all the rest of the natural body can make an eye, nor enable the man who is blind, to see; nor can all the lay people together either be or make a priest.

It only now remains to endeavour to trace, through the main ordinances of the Christian Church, the joint operation of these co-ordinate and closely related powers. Each has, in its turn in the course of the history of the Church, been greatly obscured; each is, by many Christian people, still held with such narrow and one-sided strength as to exclude practically, if not theoretically, the other. But in the maintenance of both—the real and effective maintenance of both, in their respective places, and with their respective authority — lie the strength, the weight, the stability, and the effectiveness of the Church in every part of its divine work. And so it must needs be, if, as we believe, both alike are the gift of the Holy Spirit of God, in whom alone man can hope to affect the soul of man, or help or guide, in any the least degree, himself or his brethren forward on the road that leads to holiness and salvation.

LECTURE III.

THE TEACHING AND AUTHORITY OF THE APOSTLES.

Therefore let no man glory in men. For all things are your's; whether Paul, or Apollos, or Cephas, or the world, or life, or death, or things present, or things to come; all are your's; and ye are Christ's; and Christ is God's.—1 Corinthians iii. 21–23.

IT is the peculiarity of the Christian religion, as contrasted with all other systems which have at various times claimed the religious respect of men, that it is based on certain truths exterior to man, the belief of which is necessary as a qualification for the admission in the first place, and afterwards for the continuance of men in the brotherhood and privileges of the Christian body. These truths are of two kinds: first, abstract truths, as of the nature of God; and secondly, concrete truths, or facts, as of His doings towards men in the course of their history. The former class comprises those truths which, though unassisted reason might in some degree have discovered or guessed at them, as at the being and attributes of God, yet require the enlightening and informing help of God in order to become fully and correctly known. The latter class comprises those which, though as facts which have been transacted on the earth they belong to a great degree to the class of things to be witnessed by historical and human evidence, are yet much blended with the former class in respect of all those particulars which give them religious significance and import. Of the former kind is the truth of the doctrine of the Holy Trinity, in all its details; of the latter are the facts of the Crucifixion and the Resurrection, which have their peculiar religious importance in the divine greatness and dignity of Him who suffered and rose again.

These truths are, according to the Christian scheme, not only to be generally recognized by Christian men, but are to be closely, faithfully, and, if I may so say, affectionately, believed and accepted by each several one of them. Such distinct personal belief of them is one of the necessary qualifications for participating in the blessings of the Christian religion. It is not enough to adhere and to worship; but a rational and intelligent belief in these truths (proportionate, no doubt, in point of intellectual fulness and accuracy to a man's opportunities and capacity of forming it), is requisite for every individual Christian. Such faith is one of the necessary cords or links of the great union which is allowed to bind man to God in Christ.

It being thus essential to the existence and continuance of the Christian Church that these truths and facts should be certainly known and correctly believed by every individual partaking in the life of the Church, and it being also clear that the nature of these truths and the significance of these facts require a divine aid and help—that is, the aid of the Holy Spirit of God—in order to their being correctly known and believed by Christian people, it follows to enquire what methods it has pleased God to institute for this purpose, and by what provision of means His saving truths are to be brought home and assured to the faithful conscience of believers in every age of the Church.

We believe that one very signal and special gift conferred on the twelve apostles in the descent of the Holy Spirit on the day of Pentecost, was the knowledge of all truth, according to the promise made to them by the Lord in the sixteenth chapter of St. John's Gospel [a], whereby they individually and collectively became, first possessors, and secondly, as possessors, imparters of the divine truths to the Church and to the world. In them, we believe, and in them at first alone, resided that divinely communicated knowledge which should prove sufficient, as knowledge, for the salvation of men. We are not told in what way it was made known to their minds, whether in words, or in vision, or in any other objective way, or whether it was that the actual infusion or presence of the Holy Spirit in their spirits lifted them

[a] St. John xvi. 13.

subjectively, so to speak, to an elevation of remembrance and understanding of the words which the Lord had spoken to them, of sight, judgment, or of knowledge in matters of sacred truth, greater and higher than could have been attained by the natural powers of man. There are passages of Holy Scripture which would seem to suggest each of these methods. Perhaps the idea most expressly suggested by the language of St. John is that of *guidance*[b], and by guidance I suppose we may understand, not the superseding of their own powers so much as the enabling and directing them—the presence of the Holy Spirit in the spirit of men, not only pointing the way, but also strengthening and enabling them by divine help, so as to make their own spirits capable of discerning the way of sacred truth.

It is not necessary to attribute to them any larger measure of such knowledge, or any different kind of it than might, in God's wisdom, suffice to effect the purpose for which it was given. The nature and the extent, and along with the extent the limit of their divine knowledge, may well be understood from those words of St. John, in which he tells us why some only of the signs which Jesus did are recorded in his Gospel: 'Many other signs truly did Jesus in the presence of His disciples, which are not written in this book: but these are written, that ye might believe that Jesus is the Christ, the Son of God; and that believing ye might

[b] Vide Note M.

have life through His Name ᶜ.' A like limit, fixed in reference to a like object, we may, I suppose, understand to have bounded the divinely-imparted knowledge of the apostles. That which should suffice for the full life of the Church, that which should furnish the full matter of necessary faith, that which should be enough when faithfully believed to bring all mankind to salvation in Christ, they possessed, we cannot doubt, abundantly; and with it they had the duty, and with the duty the power, of making it known by word of mouth and by pen, while they lived and laboured personally upon the earth, and of transmitting it afterwards by adequate though not identical ways to the generations that should come after them, even to the end of the world.

It is also, I suppose, not improbable (according to the analogy of the free and, if I may so call it, the arbitrary effusion of the Spirit, who giveth to every man severally as He will ᵈ) that there may have been diversities, possibly not insignificant ones, in the communication of the great gift to the Twelve. He who 'at sundry times and in divers manners spake in time past unto the fathers by the prophets ᵉ,' may not improbably have given to one of the Twelve a fuller participation of some one gift and less of another, whilst another of the same company may have had the latter gift in a higher degree, and the former in a lower one. There may have been equality

ᶜ St. John xx. 30, 31.   ᵈ 1 Cor. xii. 11.   ᵉ Heb. i. 1.

in diversity, or there may possibly have been inequality. Certainly, though we know nothing of all this, yet it cannot be denied that the general analogy of divine gifts as witnessed in the inspiration of ancient prophets, and in the language and imagery of parables, would lead us to expect that such was probably the case.

But even if the actual gift were supposed to be absolutely equal, or identical to all the Twelve, we must not forget that there certainly were diversities, and these in all probability of no inconsiderable magnitude and consequence in the men themselves—diversities of character, of temper, of natural ability, strength and weakness, and the like; and these, certainly not annulled by the presence of the divine gift, would of necessity have had the effect of modifying the use and application, and so, practically, it may be said, the *possession* of it so far as regards the communication of it to other men, even if it were supposed to be in itself entirely identical to them all.

Now when we put these things together—when, I mean, we consider that the great gift of the Holy Spirit was thus possessed by twelve men; that it was possessed by them with such limitations in respect of the object for which it was given; that it was probably possessed by them in different degrees of fulness, or at least with diversities of detail; that it was certainly possessed in combination with different natural powers and characters by each; that it was possessed by men who not only could not read each others hearts, but also had their own independent mind and thought blended more or less undistinguishably with it,—when, I say, we consider all these things, and endeavour to give them the weight which they undoubtedly ought to carry, it seems plain that they not only suggest the idea of the interchange of counsel, of comparison of mind and mutual support and advice among the holders of the great divided gift, but shew such mutual counsel to have been essential to them in theory and indispensable in practice. The conciliar action of the Church seems to follow as an inevitable consequence from the fact of the twelvefold division of the tongues of fire upon the heads of twelve equal men at Pentecost.

And it is to be very particularly observed that the apostles, though singly possessed of this great gift, did uniformly act and speak with full acknowledgment of such necessity. On the occasion of the first very serious question, involving in a high degree both doctrine and discipline, which arose in the infant Church—the question whether it was to be held necessary that Gentile converts should be circumcised—that is to say, whether every person, whether born a Jew or no, should pass through Judaism as through an indispensable portal into the Church—the apostles and elders assembled together in council 'for to consider of this matter [f].' Now let us reflect upon the signal significancy of this fact as going

[f] Acts xv. 6.

far towards determining the original basis of the constitution of the Church in respect of the possession of divine truth and authority. Who are they who assemble 'to consider' respecting this great and vital question, this question which is eminently one in which both sacred truth and divine authority of discipline are so much engaged?—the apostles and the elders. What need, I ask, to assemble, if the voice of one apostle singly—what need to call the elders into council, if the voice of the Twelve jointly—was to be esteemed in such sort the actual voice of the Holy Spirit, as that none others could either confirm or gainsay it? 'And when there had been much disputing' (debating, examining, inquiring, πολλῆς συζητήσεως γενομένης—which undoubtedly indicates the possibility, at least, of different views and opinions, and that on the part not of apostles only, but elders also), St. Peter rose,—not to allege his own personal or Apostolic authority as final on the subject, but to *argue*, on common grounds which all could appreciate, and to explain his own forwardness by speaking on the ground of his having been selected by God to be the one by whose mouth the word of the Gospel was first preached to the Gentiles. And when, after the narrative of the successful mission of St. Paul and St. Barnabas, St. James, referring to the argument of St. Peter, and confirming it by quotation from the prophet Amos, had pronounced the conciliar decree, they did not hesitate, in the name of the apostles and elders and brethren, to say that 'it seemed good to the Holy Ghost, and to us,' not to lay upon the Gentile converts the burden, with which some, even in the days of apostolic inspiration, were desirous to load them g.

Surely it ought to be never forgotten how in this the greatest instance of all,—greatest because it was the first, because the subject was one of fundamental consequence, and because of the probable presence of the whole Twelve in the council,—how, I say, personal privilege and class power within the body, even of the apostles themselves, merge in the privilege and power of the entire body. No one apostle claims, even for a single moment, to be the single depositary of divine truth, nor to be commissioned to know and teach it independently of the fraternal and parallel gifts of the whole apostolic college. Nor does the whole apostolic college consider and determine the question alone. Not even so; but now that the divine gift which was once in themselves alone, has by their agency been imparted beyond themselves to many others, at once the counsel of the others, according to their degree and position, becomes requisite in order to give to decree or doctrine the plenary authority of the Holy Ghost, who dwelleth in the whole body. The decree of Jerusalem does not issue from one apostle as from a monarch, nor from the college of the apostles as from an oligarchy, but from the apostles and elders and brethren, as from a great

g Acts xv. 28.

constitutional body which must all speak, according to its position and degree, before the full voice of the Holy Spirit can be held to have spoken through its empowered human organs with authority unquestionable.

Thus the divine knowledge of each apostle, and by consequence his authority in teaching (for be it observed that knowledge and authority in matters of this kind are practically identical), is seen to have two important and different characteristics. It is derived directly from the gift of God: but though so derived, it is not independent of the support, counsel, and brotherly unanimity of the others, in their degree, in whom any part of that great gift of God also resides. It is authoritative, and sufficient in itself for unhesitating and efficient teaching; but for plenary and universal power it demands the consentient agreement, not of the other apostles only, but of the whole body of the Church at large. So, from the first, a direct descent of special gifts is seen to be compatible with a wide diffusion of ultimate authority, and the first recipients of divine light are not recipients of divine light only, but representatives also of the body, in which, through their own agency, the divine light has been diffused.

The narrative of the Acts of the Apostles, and the indications of others of their acts contained in the Epistles, seem to bear out this statement in both its parts with perfect fulness. In the first nine chapters of the book of Acts, the apostles are represented as acting, singly or jointly as the case may be, but everywhere with full authority, unopposed and unquestioned, in all that they do. St. Peter and St. John at the Beautiful Gate of the Temple, and before the kinsmen of the high priest; St. Peter in the matter of Ananias and Sapphira; all the Twelve in the case of the ordination of the deacons; St. Peter and St. John in the laying on of hands at Samaria; all the Twelve in the acknowledgment of St. Paul when introduced by Barnabas; St. Peter at Lydda and Joppa,—in all these instances, as I say, the Twelve, singly or jointly as the case might be, acted with authority unopposed and unquestioned in the first years of the Church.

When however the great case of Cornelius the centurion had occurred at Cæsarea, and St. Peter (strangely, as we might think, needing—even after the words of the Lord in the tenth of St. John, and the twenty-eighth of St. Matthew, and the enlightenment of the day of Pentecost—the further instruction of a miraculous vision [h]) had ventured, on the strength of the visible effusion of the Holy Spirit, to baptize Cornelius and his kinsmen and near friends, the great and novel act stirred, as we read, the Church in Jerusalem greatly. 'The apostles and brethren that were in Judea heard that the Gentiles had also received the word of God. And when Peter was come up to Jerusalem, they that were of the circumcision contended with him [i].' Is not

[h] St. John x. 16; St. Matt. xxviii. 19; St. Mark xvi. 15.   [i] Acts xi. 1.

the mere fact of their contending with him—an apostle, and the first of the apostles—full of significance? Who were the contenders? Hardly, we can suppose, apostles; more probably some of the brethren; some perhaps of the great company of the priests who had recently submitted to the faith. Any way, there were found those who publicly withstood the leading apostle in the greatest and most signal step yet taken in the history of the Church. How then did St. Peter reply? Did he allege his own single inspired authority? Did he ask a rescript from the other eleven, still apparently unscattered, laying down the inspired law from the apostolic college? Far from it. He rehearsed the whole matter from the beginning. He laid before the apostles and brethren the grounds of his conduct. He satisfied them of its propriety by argument; so that 'when they heard these things they held their peace and glorified God, saying, Then hath God also to the Gentiles granted repentance unto life [k].'

I consider that these cases establish beyond question the points which I am now urging: first, that in their acts and in their oral teaching the apostles, separately or jointly, acted and spoke with an authority which was complete, ample, and unquestioned; but secondly, that for absolute and plenary power—for such power as belongs to the undoubted utterances of the Holy Ghost by the mouth of man—they needed the universal con-

[k] Acts xi. 18.

sent and agreement of all those in whom, according to their various degrees, the Holy Spirit, the only source of divine truth, resided.

The apostles however did not only teach orally, with such powers as I have described, but some of them also wrote books, and the body of their writings, together with three books written by apostolic men, not apostles, constitute a most important portion of the sacred teaching which the inheriting Church possesses. How then do the principles which have been hitherto laid down bear upon these writings, and what aspect do they give to the great controversies which have agitated the Church of late years, respecting their divine character and authority?

Let us consider.

If an apostle, travelling alone, preached the word of God orally in some heathen town, as in Corinth, Philippi, or Ephesus, we have already seen that his words were authoritative as coming from one of those upon whom either the Holy Spirit had rested at Pentecost, or had been specially given since, for the teaching and conversion of the world: yet that at the same time they were not so finally authoritative as not to be conceivably capable of error (witness the case of St. Peter and St. Barnabas at Antioch) nor to be absolutely independent of the joint and confirming authority of the other apostles and of the Church at large (witness, as I have already quoted, the history of the Council of

Jerusalem, and the language of St. Paul in the Epistle to the Galatians[1]). If then, after having left such a town, the apostle should write a letter, whether of doctrine, encouragement, or additional advice and counsel to those whom his preaching had converted to Christ, is there, in the nature of the case, any reason to suppose that his written words differed in point of authority from his spoken ones? or that any *infallibility*, so to call it, attaches in any especial way to his writings beyond what attached to everything that he did or said?

And here, brethren, bear with me while I venture to protest against the use of the words 'infallible' and 'infallibility' in such an application altogether. It seems to me to be mere confusion of thought to attribute infallibility to books or statements, or propositions in words of any kind. I understand what is meant when I am told that a Gospel by St. John or an Epistle by St. Paul is certainly true and authoritative, because the apostles were infallible; but I can attach no meaning at all to the words that the Gospel or Epistle are themselves infallible. They are true or not true, authoritative or not authoritative. But 'infallibility' seems to me to be a word without meaning as applied to them. Infallibility, in any intelligible sense, is surely a quality of *persons*. Persons may be said to be infallible who are in such sort possessed of the truth as to be incapable of being

[1] Gal. ii. 2.

deceived themselves, or of deceiving others; so that they may be consulted without possible risk of error arising from them: but a book, an answer, a proposition or statement in words, surely cannot in any intelligible sense be called infallible. It is, as I said, true or untrue, authoritative or not authoritative. I cannot see how it can be more. No doubt it may be held to be true because written or spoken by a person who is infallible, and so, by an impropriety of speech, be said to be infallible itself; but if this be, as I suppose it is, the only meaning with which the word is applied to the books of Holy Scripture, the impropriety is surely one which requires to be pointed out and to be guarded against. We are, then, driven back upon the 'infallibility' of the men themselves, and this is a point respecting which we are not wholly devoid of grounds for forming some judgment.

It may seem a slight thing to make this observation, but I hardly think that it is really without importance. For in truth this unfortunate word 'infallible' is in these controversies apt to be so lightly and incorrectly used, as to import a new and very perplexing element of obscurity and difficulty into a subject already sufficiently difficult in itself. Nor indeed do I see how the cause of truth would suffer, on any side or in any way, if we should be content to refrain from the use of it altogether [m].

[m] Vide Note N.

But to return. Is it, I ask, possible to assign to the letters of an apostle, written as I have supposed, any authority different in kind or greater in degree than that which we assign to his spoken words? I confess that I cannot imagine it to be possible. It is surely conceivable, *a priori*, that written words of an apostle may have been liable to the same extent of possible perverseness and error to which his spoken words and actions may have been liable. It is also conceivable that an apostle might have communicated his written words as well as his oral teaching to his brethren, lest at any time he should write or have written in vain [n]. Do we seem in any, even in the smallest degree, to depreciate or lessen the value of the apostolic writings by such sayings as these? Nay, brethren, I verily believe that we establish and uphold it, and set it on a basis which is quite unassailable by such attacks as it has recently been exposed to: for we shew that while the authority of these writings rests first upon the real apostolic authority of the single apostle, commissioned, enlightened, and empowered to teach, yet still a man, with his own character and circumstances, and one of several others as much commissioned, enlightened, and empowered as himself,—it rests secondly and ultimately upon the recognizing confirmation and acceptance of the whole Spirit-bearing body, whose seal finally sanctions, and gives plenary confirmation and authority to

[n] Vide Note O.

all that is therein written, recognizing it as the very voice of the Holy Spirit, and therefore absolutely true and absolutely authoritative. The authority in the matter of teaching, like all other authority in the body of Christ, is twofold in its source and in its kind: first personal, then universal; first sufficient, then plenary; first unresisted, then irresistible.

If it were possible to imagine the discovery of an original letter[o] by St. Paul or St. John or any other of the Twelve, a discovery which should leave no doubt whatever of its genuineness as being the real writing of the apostle, it would of course come to Christian people with all the weight that necessarily belongs to the writing of one of the inspired apostles, one of the original pillars of the Church; and such weight we should acknowledge *a priori*, before we had opened a page of the book or read a line of its contents.

But I apprehend that we have St. Paul's own authority for saying that we—that is, the members of the Church of Christ, both lay and clerical—must exercise a distinct and undoubted judgment upon the book and its contents when once we have opened it and read them. 'Though we, or an angel from heaven, should preach any other gospel unto you than (or beyond) that which we have preached unto you, let him be accursed. As we said before, so say I now again, If any one preach any other gospel unto you than that ye have received,

[o] Vide Note P.

let him be accursed ᵖ.' Observe the repetition, brethren, —which is indeed not by any means a mere repetition, but a fuller and completer statement, adding another most important particular to what had been said before. The apostle does not only say, 'any other gospel than that which *we have preached.*' Had he stopped there, he might have seemed to set the authority of Christian teaching altogether and exclusively upon the personal preaching of the apostles,—but he adds, 'than that *ye have received.*' Surely it cannot be denied that he here invokes the Christian judgment of the members of the Church in general to pronounce upon the identity of any teaching supposed to be new with that which the apostles have authoritatively taught, and which the Church at large is conscious of having received. He sets up the validity and authority of Christian teaching upon two pillars which are not identical. It must, in order to be accepted as true and authoritative, harmonize with what the apostles have taught the Church, and what the Church knows that she has received. In other words, St. Paul must be understood, I apprehend, to recognize in respect to the all-important subject of Christian truth the very same two co-ordinate principles which I have endeavoured to maintain—the Divine descent of gifts determined to their special holders, and the great supporting, upholding authority of the universal body, of which these specially endowed men are

ᵖ Gal. i. 8, 9.

the representatives. Precisely the same inference is to be drawn from the language of St. John in his First General Epistle. 'These things have I written unto you,' he says, 'concerning them that seduce you. But the anointing which ye have received of Him abideth in you, and ye need not that any man teach you: but as the same anointing teacheth you of all things, and is truth, and is no lie, and even as *it hath taught you*, ye shall abide in Him q.' It can hardly be denied that St. John here, in an epistle addressed to the whole Church, attributes to all whom he addresses the possession of divinely imparted truth, founded upon a previous teaching, and now fully theirs by the anointing of the Holy Spirit, in which possession of truth they all, in the strength of that anointing, are to take care to abide. And all this, it will be observed, belongs to the age in which the apostles were still living, and teaching upon the earth.

As to the actual writings of the apostles themselves, therefore, it seems to me to be a clear case that their authority, when carefully looked into, will be seen to rest upon two separate and distinct grounds. First, such as may be termed *a priori*, if I may so describe them, inasmuch as they are the writings of men specially and personally endued with the gift of the Holy Ghost for the teaching of the world. And this, in their case, might well be considered to be

q 1 St. John ii. 26, 27.

sufficient even if it were alone; for it might be reasonably and very forcibly argued that, even if there were a conceivable liability of error in the oral communications of men who, though assisted by the Holy Spirit, were yet of like passions as ourselves, their written and enduring words might well be expected to be kept free from the possibility of incurring any such danger. But it is not alone; for in strong and, as it seems to me, incontrovertible confirmation of this *a priori* ground for accepting the apostolic writings as the utterances of the Holy Spirit, we have the full and unquestioning recognition of the fact by the whole Spirit-bearing Church of their own and succeeding ages. If the former or *a priori* argument established almost beyond the reach of question that *whatever* the apostles wrote for the teaching of the Churches was reasonably to be held to be Divine, the latter or *a posteriori* argument proves that these special writings are Divine as a matter of fact, and that all that they contain is absolutely true, and lacking in no point the full and entire authority of the Holy Spirit, under whose guidance and direction they were written.

I have hitherto spoken only of the actual writings of the apostles themselves; but the view which I am urging comes out with considerably greater force and clearness when we turn to the three books of the New Testament which were not written by apostles—the Gospels of St. Mark and St. Luke, and the history of the Acts. Whence do these books derive the authority which the Church has always assigned to them? What grounds have we for believing that they come to us with the same Divine weight which we attribute to the apostolic books?

We shall probably be told that St. Mark was the disciple and interpreter of St. Peter, and St. Luke the companion of St. Paul. And both these facts are established upon good evidence, and possess no inconsiderable significance in the argument. But are they sufficient to carry the conclusion we require? I own that I greatly dread the thinness of the logic which would rest so important a doctrine upon such slender grounds. If, even in the case of the apostles themselves, we have not rested the final weight of the authority of their writings upon their own separate and personal infallibility, how is it possible to strain the same argument to prove the Divine authority of writers —an authority that we believe to extend to every single fact that they record, and every single word that they have written—of whom we do not know with any certainty whatever how much or how little they communicated with those apostles whose names are quoted to supply authority to their narratives? No, surely; while these facts, fairly proved, go far enough to establish for these books a strong *a priori* claim to reverence and respect, the real ground on which we must ultimately base their Divine character, and therefore their absolute authority, must be that they were recognized as such by the early Church. In respect of the really apostolic books the *a priori* argument may seem to be so strong, even at this distant date, as to balance, if not to outweigh, the *a posteriori* recognition. But in regard to these books the *a priori* argument is comparatively so feeble as to throw out into especial prominence and force the importance of the *a posteriori* recognition or seal of the Church. This is the case still more strongly in the case of the two books of St. Luke than in that of St. Mark, not only because there is more express evidence of tradition for connecting St. Peter—an actual companion of the Lord—with the Gospel of St. Mark than St. Paul with the writings of St. Luke, but also because St. Luke in the preface to the Gospel seems to refer the authority of his narrative altogether to a different source. What that authority is, and how the preface to St. Luke's Gospel is to be interpreted, I will not detain you now by examining[r]. Suffice it for the present to say that the ordinary interpretation of it seems to me to be very superficial and incorrect, and that, so far as I can judge, it appears when duly examined rather to put St. Luke into the position of one of the eyewitnesses of the facts which he relates, than to disclaim that position for him.

But however this may be—whether St. Luke's autho-

[r] Vide Note Q.

rity be derived from the eyewitness of others, or, as I rather believe him to signify, from his own, alike the *a priori* grounds on which the two books which he has contributed to the body of the New Testament are esteemed divine and therefore incontrovertible, whatever and however strong they once were, must be considered to have almost wholly perished by lapse of time and the consequent loss of information respecting them. Consequently little, if anything, now remains to us on which we can ground the strong and assured certainty which we feel upon the point, except the uniform and consentient testimony of the ancient Church, which in its Spirit-bearing multitude of all ranks and degrees, pronounced it to be a true and authoritative record of the evangelical history, Divine, and one which might not be in any respect questioned or gainsayed.

Considerations such as these which I have suggested, appear to me, brethren, to be helpful as enabling us to put the Scriptures of the New Testament into their proper position of relation to the general knowledge and teaching of the apostolic age, and so indirectly to supply the true answers to a multitude of embarrassing questions and difficulties which otherwise appear to be extremely hard of solution. For these writings, no otherwise than the oral teachings of the apostles, form an integral part of that great inheritance of the Church, which the Church from the early days has recognized, acknowledged, and submitted to, as the divine and authoritative teaching of the Holy Spirit. They had their place in the first age, as confirming and supplementing the oral teaching, and I suppose that it is not difficult to understand the feeling with which a man might have expressed a preference for the oral over the written teaching in words like those of Papias: 'If ever any one came who had kept company with the elders, I used to ask him the words of the elders, what Andrew or Peter said, or Philip, or Thomas, or James, or John, or Matthew, or any other of the Lord's disciples. For I did not think that the things written in books did me so much good as those that came from the living and abiding voice[s].' And it is not to be forgotten that the living tradition of the first age must, in the nature of things, have retained a very large number indeed of memories — memories of words, acts, even of looks and gestures of the Lord—of infinite interest to those who heard them from the lips of living witnesses, the total disappearance of which from the inherited treasure of the Church gives no inconsiderable addition of weight to the written record, which, after all that is lost, still, by God's merciful providence, contains enough to enable us to believe that Jesus is the Christ, the Son of God, and believing, to have life through His Name.

But by degrees, under the same wonderful superintending providence of God, these writings, of which

[s] Papias ap. Euseb. Hist. Eccl. iii. 39. p. 222. Vide Routh's Reliq. Sacrae, vol. i. p. 39.

the greater part were, so to speak, occasional, and referring to the particular needs and circumstances of particular Churches, began to shew themselves as a connected body. One Gospel, whether with the consciousness of the writer, or no, supplemented another. Doctrines taught, or referred to, or omitted in one Epistle, were found to have their confirmation, or explanation, or completion, in another; until at last, and by degrees, the Church came to recognize what neither the inspired authors themselves, nor the Church which had received them as Divine, had before known, that they all formed parts of a Divine whole, and that while individual writers, under the help and direction of the Holy Spirit of God, had been compiling narratives or writing letters according to the separate needs which they had themselves felt, the Holy Spirit of God had been unawares preparing a vast code of truth and doctrine which should become the full and undeniable written law of the Church to all future ages.

It might, as I just now said, be possible for individual Christians to prefer the orally delivered recollections of the apostles to written books. It was more than possible for the Church in the days when these writings were still incomplete, some of them still of uncertain authority, and some (by their being addressed to single Churches, or even individual Christians) still not universally known, to rest more upon the still strong and unquestioned tradition of oral teaching, than upon the gradually accumulating and gathering strength of written books; but as the Book of God by degrees gained its completeness, and the Church recognized in it not only the authority of its several portions, but also the entireness and self-supplemented character of the whole, the enduring nature of writings as distinguished from oral tradition necessarily and universally gave to 'THE BOOK' the first place in point of authority, as the source of the teaching of the later ages. Not but that even then and always the words of the book were to be explained, its doctrines gathered and interpreted, and its omissions (for omissions there still were) supplied by the strong and ever-descending stream of traditional teaching, which formed, as it were, a mighty code of the common law of the inheriting Church.

The very occasional character of the separate portions of the book, and its varied authorship, gave it a new and very peculiar value. For from its occasional character the interior life of Churches, the temptations to which the early converts were liable, the sins which they committed, and a multitude of particulars relating to their condition and its dangers, and the modes also in which the apostles dealt with special cases, mingling authority with persuasion, and tempering severity by gentleness, came out with a clearness and force which could hardly have been otherwise given; and from the varied authorship of the books, all reflecting in the clearest way the mental and moral peculiarities of their respective writers, we see how different schools, so to call them, of mind and thought (as of St. Paul, St. Peter, and St. John), under the shaping and governing influence of the Holy Spirit of God, are all made capable of combining in one harmonious record of faith and love.

In like manner the views which I have stated appear to me to suggest indirectly the true answers to many perplexing and embarrassing questions which otherwise would seem to be very difficult to answer. For if it be true that the Church in the first ages decided these books to be Divine, partly on *a priori* grounds, that is, upon arguments founded on the sanctity, or means of information, or proved possession of Divine help in the writers, or the like, a considerable part of which have, in the course of ages, necessarily perished; and partly on what I may call *a posteriori* grounds, that is to say, because they recognized in the books themselves the very truth of the holy Gospel given to the Church, and therefore yielded entire and devout acceptance and submission not to their general truth and divineness only, but to the very words, yes and to the very order of the words, in which that truth is conveyed; and if they who thus put the seal of such universal acceptance and submission, constituted the entire body of the Church in their generation, in the several members of which according to their various degrees and duties resided the fulness of the Holy Spirit, the only source of all Divine knowledge, —we seem not only to have full and adequate grounds for considering their authority established, but also to escape the necessity of going into very many perplexing questions which we could not avoid if the whole proof of the divineness of the books lay upon us, and we had in every generation to prove it anew with constantly decreasing means of investigation and knowledge.

We do not need, for example, any theory of inspiration. It is quite beside the mark that we should speculate as to the degree or manner or nature of the influence which the Holy Spirit saw fit to exercise upon the writers' minds. The primitive Church neither constructed nor transmitted any theory of the kind.

We do not require any subtle analysis to enable us to distinguish the Divine from the human elements, both confessedly present in the composition. The primitive Church neither denied the fact, nor attempted to search into it.

We do not care to ask or answer questions about verbal inspiration. The primitive Church was content to recognize the books as the utterance of the Holy Spirit, to be absolutely submitted to and acknowledged as Divine and true.

If questions like these were ever such as could be reasonably enquired into, or possibly answered, they are simply anachronisms now. The case is necessarily and very importantly altered in respect of the grounds of our belief by mere lapse of time. If we have lost on the one side much, very much indeed, of what I have called the *a priori* grounds on which the authority of the books was once rested, we have gained proportionally on the other. We seem to stand on a ground that is higher, and one which makes us independent of various questions like these which I have alluded to. It is sufficient for us,—it *must be* sufficient for us,—that the books have been pronounced by those who alone had the means, and therefore the power and duty to pronounce upon them, to be utterly true, authoritative, and Divine. They have upon them the seal of God in the Church, and they neither need nor can possibly have more. Not only is the time altogether passed by when we could have cross-examined evidence, or searched to the bottom the validity of the arguments on which the books were thus recognized, but also God did actually give to that age the duty of doing all this, and the means of doing it rightly, and He has withheld from us both the duty and the means. It was their precise work to pronounce with spiritual discrimination upon the writings which claimed to be Divine. They have pronounced;—some they have declared apocryphal; some they have with one voice, sometimes after longer or shorter delay, pronounced canonical. The seal of God in the Church is upon them, and they neither need nor can possibly have more. Criticism may, no doubt, discover difficulties in them—apparent discrepancies, apparent errors of this sort or that. We can but reply, that we *do not know*. We have not the knowledge necessary either to convict them of error or, at least in very many cases, to acquit them of it; and let it be observed that when any man claims to convict them of error, he is in fact claiming to possess a complete knowledge of the whole case, which he certainly has not, and which he cannot possibly have. If we had lived in those ages we should have known and should have been able to explain or reconcile many things which now seem difficulties to us, but now the knowledge requisite for reconciling them has perished. But this we know, that these books, their truth, authority, and divineness, are guaranteed to us by the Holy Spirit in the body of Christ from the earliest times, and that if that guarantee is capable of deceiving us, then there is no point of Christian truth or Christian hope on which we can rely.

I do not know, brethren, how far I have succeeded in making my meaning clear. I have wished and intended to exemplify in this the first and greatest instance of all —the teaching and authority of the apostles themselves —the general principle which I laid down in the earlier Lectures, namely, that not even in these twelve holy men themselves, highly exalted as they were above all other sons of men, as privileged to become the very channels by which it pleased God to communicate the covenanted graces of the Holy Spirit to those who came after them, did the sacred gifts reside in such sort as to exclude from the real participation of ultimate power and authority the whole of the Spirit-bearing body of Christ in all its members, in their due proportion; so that, whether they taught orally, or compiled narratives in writing of what they had seen and heard, or addressed letters to their converts, or whether they acted as fathers and governors in Christ either of the particular Churches which they planted, or of larger portions of the Church, or of the Church at large, they did all with a general acknowledgment, to be plainly gathered from their conduct and their language, that they were but the organic, representative voice of t e Spirit-bearing body, personally authorized and empowered by personal consecration of the Holy Spirit Himself to teach and govern all, in the name of all, and with the authority of all.

No one can be more conscious than I am, brethren, of the extreme slightness and imperfection of the way in which I have dealt with this subject. But you will, I trust, readily understand that I have meant my words to be suggestive only. I have wished to illustrate a very large theme by bringing it under the scope of a still larger principle, and for this purpose a slight and imperfect sketch is not without some advantage. To my own mind there appears to be some weight in the considerations I have urged. They seem to connect themselves intelligibly, and I think not unsatisfactorily with a great system of Church doctrine and authority; and to offer some help towards setting various incidental questions of no slight difficulty and importance upon a clear and sound basis.

Such as they are, I commend them, brethren, to your candid thought, earnestly hoping that nothing that I have said may infringe in any degree on either of the two great pillars of Christian truth and authority, the Divine descent of apostolic authority on the one hand, or the plenary possession of every sort of Divine power for the restoration of mankind in the whole Spirit-bearing body on the other.

LECTURE IV.

THE ECCLESIASTICAL, OR POST-APOSTOLIC TEACHING OF THE CHURCH.

The church of the living God, the pillar and ground of the truth.—
1 Timothy iii. 15.

WE considered in the last Lecture the subject of the teaching of the Church in the days of the apostles themselves, and endeavoured to point out, however briefly and imperfectly, that alike in oral and written teaching, even the individual holders of the great gift of the enlightening Spirit taught with a general acknowledgment that not in themselves singly, nor even in themselves conjointly, apart from the body, but in the whole community of believers, which is the body of Christ, dwelt that fulness of the Holy Spirit which alone could give the plenary and final authority of absolute and undeniable truth to Christian teaching.

It will be observed that herein is our first great example of the general theory stated in an earlier

Lecture: I mean the distinction to be taken and continually observed between the ultimate possession of spiritual power and authority, and the organic instrumentality provided to administer it. It will be observed that while the ultimate possession is with the Church at large, the representative organs of the Church derive their personal authority to teach and their right to be esteemed representatives of the Church in that regard, not from any act of election or empowerment done by the whole Church, but directly from the gift of God, which first constituted the apostles themselves and then those to whom they delivered the succession of the like authority, the teachers of the teaching Church, the tongue as of fire of the believing body, the legitimate and divinely authorized and empowered proclaimers to the Church and to the world of the mercies of God in Christ, and of the restoration of mankind to His love, and the hope of heaven.

I proceed, for the purpose of further illustrating this same great principle, to consider the post-apostolical or ecclesiastical teaching of the Church; and I would observe in the first place how impossible it is to draw a strong and definite line which shall divide exactly the apostolical from the ecclesiastical teaching. It is very worthy of particular remark how very early the ecclesiastical or corporate character and powers of the Church begin to exhibit themselves, and how soon the personal supremacy, so to call it, of apostles separately, and of the apostolic body in general, is seen to give place and merge itself in the orderly system which, by the overruling providence of God, was destined to last on, and to keep the Church together in its unity of faith and discipline through all the subsequent ages. I have already noticed the very remarkable absence of authoritative assertion on the part of the apostles (even though it is probable that all the Twelve were present together) at the Council of Jerusalem, and in the matter of the baptism of Cornelius the centurion at Cæsarea. Other indications of the same kind are to be found in various other parts of the early apostolic history as drawn from the Acts and the Epistles. But, passing over these, I would call particular attention as to a very striking and less obvious instance of the same thing, to the old age of St. John the beloved apostle. It appears to me to be very instructive indeed to observe the total, and I may almost say the surprising absence of any such authoritative assertion on the part of St. John, left behind for so many years, the sole survivor, as we believe, of the Twelve, certainly the sole survivor in the Churches adjacent to Europe. And this fact, which would have been very instructive if he had been any one of the least distinguished among the Twelve yet surviving all the rest for many years, becomes greatly more so when we remember how eminent he was among them all as the beloved apostle, as the one who had lain on the Lord's breast at the last supper, as one of the sons of thunder, as one of the two who should indeed drink of the Lord's cup and be baptized with the Lord's baptism, and as the one who should in some sense tarry till the Lord should come. If it be true that St. Peter was in some sense the first in order of the apostles, yet in many chief respects St. John stands out among the Twelve in a position as great and as highly honoured as any[a]. Nothing can be more beautiful, nor, in respect of the point which we are now considering, more instructive, than the gentle, loving old age of St. John during his last years at Ephesus. We might have expected that the whole Christian world, west and east, would have besieged him with questions of all sorts, with difficulties of doctrine and practice, with new perplexities continually emerging with the increased spread of the Church, and the complications arising from it, and have looked to receive from the lips of the last of the apostles—the only remaining one of those on whose head the Holy Spirit had rested in visible form on the great day of Pentecost—final and authoritative decision of them all. But instead of anything of this kind, the aged apostle is represented to us in the most trustworthy legends of his later life, as passing his old age in the utmost quietness of 'calm decay and peace divine,' as teaching the young, reclaiming the fallen, and with his dying words exhorting his children to love one another. Not a word is heard of supremacy,

[a] Vide Note R.

nor of any lapse to the sole survivor of the Twelve of any exclusive authority which might be conceived to have devolved upon the last of those on whom the tongues of Pentecost had rested. The Church in all the world had by this time been based upon its true and lasting foundations. Even Ephesus had its bishop, whom he recognizes even while he delivers in the letter of Christ contained in the Apocalypse the warning of the Holy Ghost to him and to his Church. And so the old man gently and simply passes away, his work sweetly, gently, lovingly done; leaving behind him the now firmly organized and established Church in well-nigh all the known world, the body of Christ with all its universal life and all its necessary organs, full of the Holy Ghost, to remain till the end of time, sufficiently furnished with all the graces and powers wherewith it is to operate throughout its whole history in the regeneration and salvation of mankind. There seems to me to be a very strong argument in the long old age of St. John as the sole survivor of the Twelve, in favour of the Church system both in its general outline and in its details; and be it remembered how definitely that outline and those details are given in the letters of Ignatius and Polycarp, the latter of whom may, not impossibly, have been the actual bishop of the Church of Smyrna addressed in the Book of the Revelation.

The apostles then had done their work. The space

of time which intervened between the death of the two sons of Zebedee (how remarkably they drank the Lord's cup, and shared His baptism, and as it were sat on His right hand and on His left in their deaths!) was probably not less than fifty years. In this time they had delivered the faith to the keeping of the Church; and they passed away one by one with what may well seem a strange silence of authoritative tradition respecting their separate works and sufferings. Consider how little we really know of the lives and labours of those among them of whom we know most—even of St. James the Greater, St. James the Less, and St. Peter—while of the greater number of the rest we really know nothing. And yet we cannot doubt that each one of them passed through years of laborious work, and of sufferings very notorious in their own time; so that St. Paul could say that God had seemed to set forth the apostles last, as it were appointed unto death, for that they were made a spectacle unto the world, and to angels, and to men[b], and that they mostly ended their course by martyrdom. But in spite of all that precious work—so precious that the wall of the city of God, as seen in the vision of St. John[c], had twelve foundations, and in them the names of the twelve apostles of the Lamb—how deep is the silence of history respecting it! It seems to me that the inference to be drawn from that silence is very closely

[b] 1 Cor. iv. 9.   [c] Rev. xxi. 14.

akin to that which I have already drawn from the gentle and long protracted old age of St. John, and that both give great additional confirmation to what has been said as to the way in which the apostolical authority and powers, under the good providence of God, merged themselves early and completely in the ecclesiastical.

The apostles died, some sooner, some later; but the Holy Spirit of Pentecost lived on in the Body to which they, under God, had been the means of communicating spiritual life. And in the continuing presence of the Holy Spirit the faith lived on unchecked and unimpaired, though the first great preachers of it were gradually taken to their rest. 'And that faith so preached,' to adopt the words of St. Irenæus, ' the Church, though scattered in all the world, diligently guards, as inhabiting one single house. Alike she believes these things, as having one soul and the same heart, and with harmonious voice preaches and teaches them, and hands them down as having a single mouth. For the languages of the world are various, but the power of the tradition is one and the same, and neither have the Churches in Germany believed otherwise, or delivered otherwise, nor those in Spain, nor among the Gauls, nor in the East, nor in Egypt, nor in Libya, nor those that are planted in the middle of the world. But as the sun, the creature of God, is one and the same in all the world, so everywhere doth the preaching of the truth shine and enlighten all men who desire to come to the knowledge of the truth ᵈ.'

Thus the Church had entered upon its inheritance. The sacred revealed truth faithfully handed down from the original sources, and maintained by the working of the Divine Spirit of God in the hearts of succeeding generations, was to be the inalienable possession of the organized body of Christ upon the earth; not to be added to, not to be changed, not to be diminished; to admit of no developments in doctrine altering or multiplying its essential characteristics, nor of any compromises of the original revelation to suit the fastidious criticism or pseudo-liberality of other times; a definite body of Divine dogmatic truth entrusted by God to the Spirit-bearing body to be His appointed means in regard to faith, for bringing mankind to salvation in Christ.

It was entrusted, I say, to the organized body; and by that expression I mean that while the possession of it, the ultimate and absolute possession of it, was in the whole body — in the bishops and clergy, in the faithful lay-people, in all without exception or exclusion, — yet according to their various degrees — who shared the Divine gift in which alone it had its being or existence, yet that such widely and orderly diffused possession was entirely compatible with the successive empowerment by divinely descended ordination, of special persons to be the organs of the body in the

ᵈ Vide Note S.

particular office of publicly uttering and declaring it.
In other words, the truth resided as a possession in
the universal body. The divinely authorized tongue for
its proclamation was the ordained clergy.

Not but that from the first it was the duty, as it was
also the practice, of others besides the ordained teachers
to spread the sacred truth which they, not less than the
ordained teachers themselves, believed and lived upon.
So they which were scattered abroad in the persecution
that followed upon the death of Stephen (and they are
expressly said to be 'all') went everywhere spreading
the good tidings of the Word. They surely could not
refrain from making known to others the Gospel which
their own souls had welcomed, nor was there, nor could
there ever be, any need to withhold it till some specially
commissioned preacher should arrive to give it authorized utterance. So Aquila and Priscilla took unto
them Apollos, who, himself unordained, spake and
taught diligently the things of the Lord, and expounded
unto him the way of God more perfectly. So we read [e]
in ancient Church historians that Frumentius and
Ædesius, two young men who had no external call or
commission to preach the Gospel, being carried captive
to India, converted the nation and settled several
Churches among them; and again, 'that the Iberians
were first converted by a captive woman who made the
king and queen of the nation preachers of the Gospel

[e] Vide Note T.

to their people.' And so in all Christian ages have pious lay-people, by private exhortation, by instruction as parents, as friends, as teachers, and where the case required, by more public methods[f], contributed to spread and keep alive among others that of which they as well as the clergy were in full possession; not by any means usurping the special office of the ordained teachers, but supplementing it in manifold ways which the actual voice of the ordained teachers could not reach. So again when learning became diffused, and the clergy were no longer the sole possessors of it, lay-people, by published books, by oral counsel and other such means, began to take larger and more influential part in the great work of keeping up and spreading the great inheritance of Gospel truth which belonged no less to them than to the clergy, whose commissioned and empowered duty of teaching they desired not in any degree to invade by such proceedings, but to assist and further it. The list of laymen who, from Hermas and Justin Martyr to the present generation, have written in support or illustration of Christian doctrine, is a very long and a very noble one, far too long to introduce in this place. And I will venture to say that these writers have furnished a very precious support, and one that could be ill dispensed with, to the cause of truth. The greater freeness of mind which lay-people have brought to the subject, even if it has occasionally been tinged with error, has

[f] Vide Note U.

enriched it. The greater intermixture of other knowledge, and the habits of mind engendered by other pursuits, have supported and strengthened it. The earnest adhesion of men who have not been bred to the profession (so to call it) of teachers has been no inconsiderable safeguard against the danger, by no means an unreal one, of confounding the priesthood with the Church, the organs with the body, and coming to consider the possession of the truth as the exclusive privilege, and, as it were, the vested interest of its authorized teachers. Indeed, I will venture to say broadly, that there is no department of learning or knowledge in which lay-people making real progress and advancement, and publishing the result of their studies for the benefit of others, are not doing clear and manifest, though indirect service to the truth of God. Whether they pursue science with a clear, bold, unhesitating step, extending the limits of human knowledge of the ways and works of God, I hail their progress as a distinct and unquestionable contribution to that store which brings man nearer to an intelligent and lofty appreciation of the greatness of Him who is to be read as undoubtedly, though in a different page of His works, in nature as in grace. Or if they dive into history and the antiquities of the human race, equally and alike undoubtedly—at least so long as their progress is real and not of guess—do they strengthen the foundations of that religion whose roots lie so deep in history, and which is never so intelligently believed as by those who can appreciate history, who know the value of ages, and can estimate the gradual unfolding of the designs of God in the long tale of the fate and fortunes of mankind upon the earth. Or, if they pursue philosophy, mental or political, or in any other real way reach farther and see more truly the essential methods whereby the real good and prosperity of mankind are increased—alike, I boldly say, that there is no department of human knowledge in which real progress—real, sound, true, and ascertained progress—can be anything but a real help to divine truth. It may be indirect, it may be distant. Those who pursue it may possibly not know what is the ultimate effect of what they do. They may perhaps not intend, nor wish to further any such effect. Those who more immediately study theological truth may possibly dread their words, and feel disposed to discourage their studies. But both alike are surely narrow and mistaken in their supposed antagonism. The only possible antagonism is when the one misinterprets or over-interprets some of the outlying and unessential expressions of the truth, and the other is in the state of guess. For God is alike the Author of the natural and moral world, and of the Gospel; and every true step by which the knowledge of any is advanced, is, in its ultimate consequence, a step in the wider, deeper, and truer knowledge of all. The laws of nature are but the uniformity of the doings of the creating and governing God in His world of nature. The laws which govern the wellbeing and prosperity of men in their political and economical relations, are but the principles which He has laid down for these purposes, gradually ascertained by men, and purged from the disturbing effects of selfishness and self-will. The truths of theology, perfectly compatible and entirely harmonious with these, are the supernatural helps whereby the spirit of man is trained in its aspect towards God, and its progress to the eternal kingdom. Far be it from a theologian to imagine that true science and true philosophy, pursued to the utmost limits of human powers, can be other than a real help to religious knowledge. Far be it from a Christian philosopher to doubt that however far he may be enabled to extend the borders of real knowledge in any department, there still needs the sacred cultivation of the immortal spirit in the revealed truths of God, in and by the Church, the body of Christ, the faithful reliance on the atoning blood of the Redeemer, and the cherished life of the Holy Spirit of sanctification in the heart of regenerated man.

But while we grant—nay, not only grant, but maintain that the gift of divine truth is so given to the Church in general, as that all, whether they be clerical or lay, have their respective share in the possession of it, so as to live upon it themselves, to illustrate and spread it in their own sphere, and to be able to render to others the reason of the faith that is in them, it is equally true and undeniable that to the ordained ministry, and to them alone, belongs the special duty of the public preaching and teaching of it. From the very first days it has been perfectly clear that God has given such a ministry of teaching,—that the apostles, and bishops after them, appointed such teachers by ordination given with imposition of hands, and that teachers claiming to teach without such mission and authority were not to be listened to. 'How then shall they call on him in whom they have not believed?' asks St. Paul of the Romans, 'and how shall they believe in Him of whom they have not heard? and how shall they hear without a preacher? And how shall they preach, except they be sent? as it is written, How beautiful are the feet of them that preach the gospel of peace, and bring glad tidings of good things [g].' And his words addressed to Timothy, Bishop of Ephesus, teach with the utmost plainness the same lesson on the other side, when, speaking of future evil days, he says that 'the time will come when men will not endure sound doctrine; but after their own lusts shall they heap to themselves teachers, having itching ears; and they shall turn away their ears from the truth [h].'

By such imposition of hands the Apostle Paul ordained elders in every Church [i], and elders so ordained he bade to take heed to all the flock over which the Holy Ghost had made them overseers, to feed—no doubt with the

[g] Rom. x. 14, 15. [h] 2 Tim. iv. 3, 4.
[i] Acts iv. 23; xx. 28.

food of holy truth—the Church of God which He hath purchased with His own blood. What St. Paul did he directed Timothy to do likewise [j], to lay hands, not suddenly, nor without adequate time of trial, on other men for the ministry of the Gospel. And Titus in like manner he bade to ordain elders—presbyters, teaching priests—in every city [k]. The point is too clear for argument. The universal Church has always considered the imposition of hands by the successors of the apostles as essential to ordination, and ordination essential to those who are to be the public and authorized teachers of the Christian truth.

To the ordained clergy then belongs, especially and peculiarly, by the divine descent of commission and power, the special office of teaching and preaching that sacred doctrine and truth of God of which the Church of God at large is the strong and sure foundation and pillar. It belongs to them, one by one, as separate teachers, each bearing the person or character of the Church in his own sphere; and it belongs to them jointly, and under due authority, in matters of counsel and mutual help. Representatives they are only and always, not lords, nor irresponsible authorities. Graduated into a great system, patriarchs, metropolitans, bishops, priests (and deacons, if they be thereto licensed by episcopal authority)—they are the voice of the Church for the public teaching of the truth of God.

---

[j] 1 Tim. v. 22.   [k] Titus i. 5.

From this constitution flowed directly, as an inevitable consequence, the system of councils, which, rooting itself as has been already observed, in the age of the personal presence of the Twelve, became, when they were taken away, the normal and constantly adopted practice of the Church in the ages which followed.

The first post-apostolic synods of which we have any express mention, are recorded by an anonymous author quoted in the fifth book of the history of Eusebius, as held about the years 160-170 against the heresy of Montanus; 'For the faithful in Asia,' he says, 'having come together often, and in many places in Asia, and having examined the new doctrines, and having declared them profane, and having disapproved of the heresy, so at last they were driven out of the Church, and excluded from communion.' And Tertullian, in the same century, testifies to the constant practice of holding councils 'per Græcias' from all the Churches, 'by which both certain deeper questions are handled for the general benefit, and the representation of the whole Christian name is celebrated with great veneration [l].' Eusebius also tells us of various synods of bishops held in the second century on the subject of the time of holding Easter—in Palestine under Theophilus of Cæsarea and Narcissus of Jerusalem, in Rome under Victor, in Pontus under Palmas, in Gaul under Irenæus and others [m].

---

[l] Vide Note V.

[m] Σύνοδοι δὴ καὶ συγκροτήσεις ἐπισκόπων ἐπὶ ταὐτὸν ἐγίνοντο. Eusebius, Hist. Eccl. v. 23.

The third century is chiefly remarkable for the Council of Carthage under Cyprian on the subject of re-baptizing such as had received heretical baptism. In the early years of the fourth century councils held in various parts of the Christian world, at Eliberis, at Arles, at Ancyra, at Neo-Cæsarea, at Laodicea are immediately followed by the great ecumenical council of Nicæa, by the fifth canon of which regular synodical assemblies are ordered to be held in every province twice a year.

Thus the corporate principle was recognized in all the Church from the beginning,—that corporate principle which, based upon the fact of a diffused life in all the Church, is directly opposed to the idea of a fixed local centre, or a single human head. According to this principle the whole spiritual life that is in the Church must, in its various degrees and methods, conspire and unite before any decision upon controverted truth can be held to be absolutely final and authoritative. The principle is entirely compatible with the existence of subordination and variety of position in the Church, and with very great corresponding difference in the weight and value of opinion in persons holding such various positions; but nevertheless it excludes none who partake in the life from partaking also in the possession of the powers which are the necessary incident and consequence of that life.

But what place, it must be asked, had lay-people in the councils, and so, in questions of doctrine and discipline in the Church? Is it not quite plain and clear, from the long history of such meetings in later days, that the consultative voice as well as the preaching voice of the Church remained with the bishops almost exclusively, only occasional notice being given even of the presence of presbyters, as in the first Council of Toledo, of Eliberis, and a few others? And again, if the principles which I have ventured to lay down in these Lectures be really sound and true, is their voice in consultation and counsel really to be silenced and pass for nothing? Can it be, if the ultimate possession of the truth be indeed the privilege of the entire body, that so large a majority of the members of the entire body should be devoid of all participation in pronouncing what that truth is, or that the organs for declaring it should be held to be also the sole authorities for determining it?

It is a question of very great importance in itself; and in reference to modern times and occasions it is one of the very highest consequence: and over and over again, brethren, I must beg you to remember that I can but touch these great questions in the slightest way, and can only hope to *suggest* thoughts which really require very much more extended investigation than I can give to them.

The reading of the text in Acts xv. 23[n] is so uncertain on critical grounds that we cannot safely infer from the

[n] Vide Note W.

mention of 'the brethren' in the letter of the Church that lay-brethren took any part in the decision of the Council of Jerusalem. True; but neither can we with any certainty deny the fact of their having done so. Indeed the presence of that reading at a time when certainly the tendency of things in the Church had begun to confine all government more and more exclusively to the clergy, may seem to throw the balance of critical weight rather in favour of these words. There surely has been no time since the fifth century in which we can imagine such a reading to have been voluntarily introduced into the text. However, whether the words 'the brethren' stand in the letter or no, the resolution to send it was come to by 'the apostles and elders with the whole Church,' and it was sent after they had been 'assembled with one accord;' 'so as to show,' says Chrysostom, 'that it is not done in a tyrannical way, that all take part in the resolution, and that they wrote the letter with careful consideration[o].'

The slight notices of councils in the second century by no means tend to establish the absolute exclusion of lay-people from them. According to the writer (perhaps Apollinarius of Hierapolis) quoted by Eusebius, 'the faithful' came together in Asia to condemn the heresy of Montanus; and Tertullian, speaking of frequent councils, uses the expression 'repraesentatio totius nominis Christiani,' and neither the words of Eusebius or Ter-

[o] Vide Note X.

tullian distinctly exclude, to say the least of them, any class of the members of the body of Christ.

The language of Tertullian too, in other places, respecting the inherent power of lay-people in their place in the Church in other respects, strongly confirmatory of the idea that he would not have regarded their voice as altogether powerless in matters of Christian counsel and joint decree [p].

From Tertullian we pass to Cyprian, who never passed a day without reading the writings of Tertullian, ever asking for them with the words 'Give me my master [q].' No person who reads the Epistles of Cyprian can be ignorant how constantly he recognizes the share of the 'plebs Christiana' in the essential powers of the body of the Church [r]. Take for example the following passages: 'For this thing is agreeable to the modesty, and discipline, and life of us all, that the bishops assembling with the clergy in the presence also of the standing (that is, the not lapsed) laity, to whom also themselves respect is to be paid for their faith and fear, we may be able to settle everything by the sacredness of united counsel?'— 'To that which our fellow-presbyters have written, I have not been able to write back anything alone, since I have resolved from the beginning of my episcopate to do nothing of my own private opinion without your counsel (the letter is addressed to the priests and deacons) and

[p] Vide Note Y.   [q] S. Hieron. de Viris Illustribus, c. 53.
[r] Vide Note Z.

without the consent of the lay-people.' Nay, the clergy of Rome, in writing back in reply to Cyprian, allege the same thing: 'In so important an affair,' they say, 'the same thing approves itself to us which you have already dealt with, namely that the peace of the Church (that is, the restoration of the lapsed) must be deferred; and that then a communication of counsels being made with the bishops, priests, deacons, and standing lay-people, the case of the lapsed be dealt with.' His practice in council was correspondent with these views. The record of the Council of Carthage begins thus: 'Very many bishops having assembled at Carthage on the Kalends of September from the province of Africa, Numidia, Mauritania, with the priests and deacons, a very great part of the lay-people being also present.' In like manner at the Council of Eliberis in the year 305, we read: 'When the holy and religious bishops had taken their seats in the church of Eliberis .... and likewise the elders' (whose names are also given), 'all sitting down, while the deacons and all the people stood by, the Bishop spoke.' And in the first Council of Toledo in the year 398: 'The bishops assembling, the presbyters sitting with them, the deacons standing by, and the others who were present at the council being collected.'

The presence of laity in councils is but rarely heard of in later times; but we read of it in some of our own Anglo-Saxon councils. In the Council of Pisa professors and doctors of theology were admitted to vote, and in the great Council of Constance doctors and canonists and others not in holy orders were admitted to a full share in consultation against the strenuous efforts of the Papal party, chiefly through the arguments of John Gerson, Chancellor of the University of Paris, and the Cardinal of Cambray [s].

If, bearing these things in mind, we endeavour to estimate the degree of influence exercised in primitive times by the laity on the counsels and decisions of the Church, we shall, I think, perceive that it was by no means small or insignificant. They had an unquestioned voice in the selection of the bishops, and even, as there is reason to suppose, of the presbyters; so that even those who sat in council were the men whom they had concurred in choosing. They were present, often if not always, in the same sort of position as the ordained deacons at the consultations and debates of councils. Their acquiescence and approbation were implied in their silent presence. No doubt the instance of St. Cyprian is the most striking one as applicable to my point to be found in Christian antiquity, but his principle and practice are distinctly acknowledged by the Roman clergy, and by the occasional indications that appear even through the deepening and gradually systematized sacerdotalism of later times.

That such influence gradually diminished there can, of course, be no doubt. It is a striking indication of

[s] Latin Christianity, viii. 257; Fleury, vol. xxi. p. 226.

the early diminution of it that there are two canons of the Council of Laodicea expressly depriving 'the multitude' of any voice in the election of bishops or priests, plainly showing, as is observed by the Greek commentator Zonaras, that they had possessed that privilege before [t].

Gradually the influence of the laity, as telling in any direct and legitimate way upon the counsels of the Church, diminished till it expired altogether. It is melancholy to read the struggles for reformation, the hopes, the good intentions of many, and the repeated disappointments of the age before Luther, while good men were doing their best to purify the Church from the terrible evils which had become inveterate in it. The history of the Councils of Constance and of Basle [u] is the history of good intentions, and often of bright hopes, fighting up in vain against a system which was too strong for them,—the sacerdotal system, the Roman system, the system which at this day some who were once our friends would fain press upon us, as they have accepted it themselves, in its corrupt and terrible simplicity,—a system that refused to be reformed from within, and was only driven into intenser and completer exclusiveness when reform took the shape of rebellion, and western Europe, in its most thoughtful and intelligent nations, incurred the ban of excommunication from the patriarchate of Rome. I suppose that no candid

[t] Vide Note AA.   [u] Vide Note BB.

reader of the history of the fifteenth century can doubt that if the councils of Christendom had been constantly conducted on the principles laid down in the Letters of Cyprian, the Church might have been saved the melancholy rent and separation of the next century; and I venture to think that the Erastianism which exists in the Church of England, and the fettered condition of the clergy under the control of a lay parliament, not necessarily even Christian, is but a natural reaction from the loss of a primitive principle, which would, if it had been duly developed according to the necessities of the Church and the greatly increased fitness of many of the lay-people, by education, learning, piety, and practice of life and business to partake in its consultations, and with the deepened sense of responsibility which such participation would naturally have produced, have contributed to give an immense increase of strength and freeness of union and power to all its movements, and have placed it in a position much more in accordance with its true spiritual constitution.

It is no doubt easy, if we assume as a first principle that the practice of the Church in its middle centuries is in these respects altogether right and apostolical, to frame retrospectively a fair-sounding argument to *account* for the same practice not being found in the records of the earlier ages. But endeavouring to take the other line, and trace synthetically the working of the Church from the Acts of the Apostles onwards in respect of its conciliar action, and its theory of the possession of divine truth, I find myself entirely at a loss to discover the beginning of the doctrine that the truth was in such sort delivered to the bishops, as that they alone (or even along with the presbyters) have the absolute and final right to consult or judge respecting it. I cannot find the beginning in the records of the ancient Church of that doctrine which in its extreme form teaches that 'the pastoral ministry [v] as a body cannot err, because the Holy Spirit, who is indissolubly united to the mystical body, is eminently and above all united to the hierarchy and body of its pastors,' or that 'the episcopate *united to its centre* is, in all ages, divinely sustained and divinely assisted to perpetuate and to enunciate the original revelation.' That such indwelling of the Holy Spirit in the body of Christ is the very truth of God, I thankfully and from the bottom of my heart acknowledge. That by a divine succession of authority and empowerment the priesthood are made to be the organs for imparting to the separate members of the body the efficacy of those powers which, by the presence of the Holy Spirit in the whole body, are those of the whole body, I fully and entirely believe. That the bishops are the chief governors of the Church; that to them belongs the highest and principal authority; that for the sake of that honour and authority, and for many reasons of convenience and necessity, bishops

[v] Vide Note CC.

should often meet alone, and their voice and judgment suffice to rule in questions of such kinds, all this I grant most freely and unhesitatingly; but I cannot consent to transfer absolutely to those who are rulers, because they are divinely appointed representatives of the Church, the possession, in such sort, of the truth, as that it should not be possessed by the whole Spirit-bearing body, capable in its various degrees of knowing, assenting to (and if of assenting to, then conceivably of differing from) the conclusions of those to whom the preaching voice, and the prerogative of place and priority in consultation and judgment unquestionably belong. And as for the episcopate being *united to its centre*, that is, to the Pope of Rome, and as such holding these exclusive powers of alone being possessed of the truth of God, such teaching seems to me but as the ingenious completion of an edifice of cards, built up by a thin logic in defiance of the most certain facts of history, and the most undoubted doctrine of the great writers of the primitive Church.

It is also no doubt right to represent, as is often represented, the conduct of St. Cyprian as that of a man raised by God in very stormy times to hold together, by the grace, wisdom, and love which God gave him, the conflicting elements in the Church. I ask no more. For there is no real wisdom except it be in truth, and other times are stormy, possibly not less stormy and dangerous than were those of the African Church in the age of Cyprian. We do not doubt that that great saint held a very high and eminent position, and that his episcopal powers were very great, so that even if he had acted alone, his acts would have been both wisely done, and done with sufficient authority; yet even then they would have been subject to the silent review of brother bishops and presbyters, and the silent approving acquiescence of the whole body of believers. And it is in the fact of that silent review, and of that silent approving acquiescence, that the 'wisdom' of the course which he took is to be seen. He was so meek and wise as to ascertain beforehand that he moved with the full consent and approval of his clergy and people, and while no doubt a bishop so acting may win so far upon the minds of men as that his own mind may be impressed upon all, it is also not impossible that he himself may receive suggestions, and derive not only much additional weight from such consultation, but perhaps a larger wisdom also than his own mind without that aid might supply.

The present age, and the circumstances of the Church of England, appear to me to make it of singular importance, and at the same time to offer a singularly favourable opportunity, to develope these principles anew in practice. A colonial diocese of the Church of England seems to afford a state of things rarely occurring among us at least for many ages past, in which it is not only possible to act out these principles in their integrity, but also in which it is nearly impossible without them to hope for any permanent or widely extended effects upon colonial populations. Here at home, surrounded as we are by a multitude of conditions, the result of centuries of political and ecclesiastical action of every various kind, hampered by difficulties too many and too intricate to allow any considerable hope of setting things upon a primitive basis, a bishop, supported on the one hand by secular law, and interfered with on the other much more than he is supported by it, works, as it were, in chains, and must be content to confine himself to such personal labours, excessive indeed from the magnitude of dioceses, as the system which we have inherited from former ages allows him. But there is no reason why a colonial bishop, freed as he has been by recent judicial decisions from the embarrassments of his brethren at home, should not be as Cyprian, should not speak as Cyprian, should not act as Cyprian. Surely the noble language of the African martyr may well and wisely be the language of such a man, sent to take the oversight of a great colony, with few, or possibly no other bishops near him, each supported by his body of scattered clergy, and thrown back by his very isolation and freedom upon first principles. 'From the very beginning of my episcopate I resolved to do nothing without the counsel of my presbyters and deacons, and without the consent of my lay-people,... to whom also themselves respect is to be paid for their faith and fear, that we may be able to settle everything by the sacredness of united counsel [x].' I will not venture to speak of the details of such things, nor to do more than allude to the success which has attended such efforts in one important colonial province; but I will venture to affirm that unless a colonial bishop so supports himself and his clergy by the real, proportionate aid and consent of the lay members of his flock—men often of very large intelligence and experience, of knowledge and practice in life, and sometimes of sound and deep theological reading, any way baptized and Spirit-bearing members of the Church, and, as such, partakers in their degree in the single source of all spiritual power—he deprives himself of one of the best hopes of lasting and wide influence, of free and powerful and united action, and endangers the loss of a great amount of sympathy and practical help which he cannot spare or supply otherwise, and which may very possibly and very naturally turn to opposition and dismemberment. For there is a very strong and a very fatal reaction in these things.

But however completely any actual participation by lay-people in consultations of council or synod has disappeared in the later ages of the Church, it has never been wholly forgotten that their subsequent acquiescence and approval is requisite to give to the decrees of councils their final and complete authority. Take for example the language of Abp. Laud in the

[x] Vide Note DD.

conference with Fisher the Jesuit.[y] He holds that all the power that any council can have it derives wholly from the catholic and universal body of the Church, and of the clergy in the Church whose representative it is. And, debating the question whether the representing body hath all the power, strength, and privilege that the represented hath, he concludes that the representing body may err, while the represented may still, in virtue of those members who know the truth, continue to hold it inviolate. In like manner, urging that the whole Catholic Church militant possesses an absolute freedom from all liability of error in the prime foundations of faith, he maintains that this power is not communicable to any council which represents it. In support of these views he quotes the Chancellor Gerson, who, at the Council of Constance, urged over and over again that the power of the Church resided in the universal Church, of which the decrees of a general council, provided it represented it faithfully, formed its one and authorized expression; so that those things only are to be held necessary to be believed for salvation which councils teach with the universal consent of the entire Church given implicitly or explicitly, actually or by interpretation. He also quotes Ockam, the 'Locke,' as he has been well called, 'of the middle ages, in his common sense philosophy and in

[y] Vide Note EE.

the singleminded worship of truth[z],' who, speaking of the possibility of errors in a general council, says that when they occurred they would be got rid of by means of the multitude of wiser and better men not present at the council, to whom also the multitude of simple Christians would more readily attach themselves. To this may be added the words of Cardinal Cambray at Constance: 'Many earlier councils, considered general, have, as we read, committed errors. For, according to certain great doctors, a general council may err, not only in fact, but also in law, and what is more, in the faith. For this privilege of inability to err in the faith belongs only to the universal Church.'

And what again is this but the language of St. Basil? 'Where spiritual men,' he says, 'take the lead in councils, and the Lord's people follow them in harmonious accordance of mind, who will doubt that such counsel has taken place by the communication of our Lord Jesus Christ, who poured forth His blood for the Churches[a]?'

But how widely different is all this from the completed Roman theory of which I just now quoted the most recent expression!

This majestic consent, this absolutely universal adhesion, it is which gives to the three great creeds of the universal Church, and to the decrees of the four

---

[z] Milman, Hist. of Lat. Christianity, viii. 157.
[a] Vide Note FF.

first great councils, their full, final, and irresistible authority. The want of this universal consent weakens in various degrees the decisions of smaller and less weighty bodies—of divided national, provincial, or diocesan synods. All these have their own respective and proportionate weight, as part of a great system. As in the case of subordinate courts of law, their judgments are binding as far as regards the matters which come under their cognizance, until appeal to a higher court overrules their authority; so in the case of the lower and lesser assemblies of the Church, the power is complete and sufficient to rule the immediate cases on which they pronounce, and within the sphere to which the authority belongs, but all is subordinate to the higher and more final authority of the universal Church. The whole system of ordered and organized councils testifies to the great and sacred principle that in the whole Church, which is the body of Christ, in all its members collectively, in the due proportion of their separate parts and offices, dwells the ultimate authority which Christ has left behind Him upon the earth for recognising and conserving His truth, and administering it to His people within the Church, and to the world outside of it.

And I cannot but think that the causes which have operated to exclude the lay-people from the direct participation which, in their degree, they might seem to have the right of claiming in the consultations of the Church, have operated also in a most baneful way to diminish their sense of responsibility in respect of Church truth, and of Church work in these later ages, and of their own position in regard to both. While they have been ineffectual in excluding them from *indirect* power—a power working with great and often very injurious effect even in the most sacred things— they have put them into a position which is at once more or less antagonistic to the clergy, and which has seemed to set them free from the responsibility which is really and inalienably theirs. And this, if it be so, is not only a heavy loss, but a terrible evil. It is a loss of sympathy, of union, and of strength, greater than can be measured. It has been productive of division, opposition, even of hostility more than can be told. Above all, it has led men to forget that though they may not have been entrusted with the specially organic offices of the body of Christ, yet they too in their respective places, are members of that sacred body, and that they are by that membership bound to contribute, according to the grace given to them, to every action of that holy corporate life through which their own personal life in Christ has been received, and in which it must be maintained. My present observations bear particularly on the office of spreading and upholding the *truth*. Who can venture to set a limit to the powers of the lay-people if, studying the inherited truth of God with honest and faithful hearts, they helped in their place and degree, and not beyond it—in parish, in diocese, in synod, in parliament, in respect of education at home, in respect of spreading the Gospel abroad—to uphold, to vindicate, and in their lives and conversations to illustrate and offer a practical commentary upon that sacred truth which as a possession and as a trust is not less theirs than the preaching of it belongs especially to the ordained clergy? And none, I suppose, can doubt that responsibility is in all cases co-extensive with power, and that of every talent which God has given, He will demand the exercise.

LECTURE V.

HOLY BAPTISM.

And Jesus came and spake unto them, saying, All power is given unto Me in heaven and in earth. Go ye therefore, and teach all nations, baptizing them in the name of the Father, and of the Son, and of the Holy Ghost: teaching them to observe all things whatsoever I have commanded you: and, lo, I am with you alway, even unto the end of the world.—St. Matthew xxviii. 18-20.

IN obedience to this parting command of their holy Lord and Saviour, the very first action of the Spirit-bearing Church, and that begun within, we may believe, little more than an hour after the actual descent of the informing Spirit on the morning of the great Pentecost, was to baptize. Three thousand people were added to the Church that day.

It was the first act in time, as it was the first in importance. For baptism, the sacrament of the diffusion or enlargement of the Church the body of Christ, is the assured beginning of the Divine life in each several man, the seal of the covenant of grace to his soul, the assurance that he is made to be a son of the covenanted love of God, and an heir of the kingdom of heaven, being made a member of the body of Christ, a branch of the living Vine which is Christ, a spiritual stone of the sacred temple of the Holy Ghost, wherein Christ dwelleth.

However, I have not to speak so much, at least for the present, of the nature of the sacred gift as it is received by the soul of a grown man in his own explicit faith, or by the soul of an infant in the implicit faith of others, as of the methods by which, and the authority under which this sacred gift is administered.

The New Testament gives us considerable information on these points.

Assuming, as we may perhaps not unreasonably do, that the apostles alone baptized on the day of Pentecost itself, what was the case in the other instances of baptism recorded in the Acts of the Apostles?

The first cases mentioned are those of the men and women of Samaria, of Simon Magus, and of the Ethiopian eunuch baptized by Philip the deacon, as recorded in the eighth chapter [a]. It seems to me to be an observable fact that in all these early and signal cases, the administrator should have been a deacon; for though no doubt the deacons were from the first ' not ministers of meats and drinks only, but servants of the Church

[a] Acts viii. 12, 13, 38.

of God ᵇ,' yet were they never regarded as sharers of sacerdotal power or authority.

The next case is that of Saul the persecutor, struck down near the gate of Damascus by the Divine light, and voice of Christ, and baptized by 'a certain disciple, a devout man according to the law, having a good report of all the Jews that dwelt there ᶜ.' Was Ananias a priest? none can tell. His name never occurs again in history or Epistle. And yet he was personally chosen for the high and singular honour of baptizing the only apostle whose baptism is recorded in the sacred history, the great Apostle of the Gentiles. It has been well observed that there is a great significancy in the obscurity of the person selected for this great duty. For it shows how truly, I might say how jealously, the Lord, though ordaining the use of outward means and doing His own great work through human agents, yet guards His ordinance against the danger of being thought to owe anything whatever to the greatness or holiness of the human agent by whom the visible office which yet He makes indispensable, is discharged.

The next case is that of Cornelius and his friends at Cæsarea, where again I observe that St. Peter did not

---

ᵇ Δεῖ δὲ καὶ τοὺς διακόνους, ὄντας μυστηρίων Ἰησοῦ Χριστοῦ κατὰ πάντα τρόπον πᾶσιν ἀρέσκειν· οὐ γὰρ βρωμάτων καὶ ποτῶν εἰσὶν διάκονοι, ἀλλ' ἐκκλησίας Θεοῦ ὑπηρέται· δέον οὖν αὐτοὺς φυλάσσεσθαι τὰ ἐγκλήματα ὡς πῦρ. S. Ignatius ad Trall. § 2.

ᶜ Acts ix. 18, xxii. 16.

baptize with his own hands, but commanded certain others [d]—no doubt those brethren of the circumcision from Joppa which believed—to be the actual administrators of the sacrament.

Of the various instances of baptism recorded more or less incidentally in the narrative of St. Paul's different journeys, there is not much to say, except that the Apostle's language in the First Epistle to the Corinthians [e] forms a suggestive commentary upon them, where he thanks God that with his own hand he only baptized Crispus and Gaius and the household of Stephanas among all the converts at Corinth, lest any should say that he had baptized in his own name, or in any way allowed his own authority or influence to be supposed to contribute to the gift which duly administered by man, is wholly and entirely the gift of God. We may, I suppose, conclude that the Apostle's practice in other Churches was like his conduct at Corinth, and for like reasons.

Of the practice in the Church in the ages immediately subsequent to that of the apostles, we may say in general, that it was agreed that the supreme human authority for administering holy baptism was that of the bishop, the successor of the apostles, and that from him priests first, and afterwards deacons, received commission to baptize; yet that the commission of deacons was not, in the first ages, either so universal or so

[d] Acts x. 48. [e] 1 Cor. i. 14.

universally recognized either as that of priests, or as it afterwards became [f].

But though this was the undoubted practice, there is sufficient evidence to show that the early Church did not regard the power of baptizing in the bishop, and by his commission, as a matter of necessary doctrine, but as one of ecclesiastical order and propriety, according to the words of Tertullian: 'The right of giving baptism belongs to the chief priest, that is, the bishop; then to the priests and deacons, yet not without the authority of the bishop, on account of the honour of the Church; for when that is safe, peace is safe [g].'

That laymen were not authorized to baptize is quite clear, for there are express prohibitions of such practice to be found. But, on the other hand, besides that express prohibitions are some evidence of a claim actual or possible, it is also clear that the ground of such prohibition lay not in the doctrine, but in the ecclesiastical discipline of the Church. This is plain from the sequel of the just-quoted passage of Tertullian, 'for otherwise,' he says, 'laymen also have the right of baptizing. For what is equally received may equally be given. Likewise baptism, equally regarded as of God, can be administered by all; but how much more is the discipline of modesty incumbent on laymen, since these things belong to their superiors, not to usurp the duty

[f] Bingham's Scholastical History of Lay Baptism, Pt. i. ch. i. § 4, 5.
[g] Vide Note GG.

of the episcopal office reserved to bishops.' Add to this the decree of the Council of Eliberis, in the year 305, that 'when persons are upon distant voyages, or if a church is not near, any faithful man who has his own baptism entire, and is not twice married, may baptize a catechumen in extremity of sickness; so that, if he survive, he bring him to the bishop, that by the imposition of hands he may be completed [h].' It was the well-known subsequent usage of the Church to admit, not indeed the propriety (except in extreme necessity) but the validity of lay baptism. Thus the point, which alone at the present moment I desire to urge, becomes clear—namely, that while, as a matter of ecclesiastical order and discipline, the authorized administration of holy baptism proceeding from episcopal authority was delegated to priests, and by degrees universally to deacons, it was yet acknowledged as a matter of Christian doctrine that the Holy Spirit so dwelt in all the members of the body of Christ, that spiritual life could be imparted, however irregularly, and (except in cases of extreme necessity) unjustifiably, by means of any, and that baptism so given, needed only the recognition and completion of the Church by means of episcopal imposition of hands, in order to be in all respects as regards the recipients, entire and perfect.

There is no need to say more upon this part of the subject. It is plain that the usage of the Church

[h] Vide Note HH.

restricted the ordinary administration of baptism to the ordained clergy, yet not so absolutely as to forbid altogether its being administered by lay people in cases of extreme necessity, nor, of course, to disallow of its validity when so administered.

Passing over then the intermediate times as throwing no special light in addition to that of the earlier days upon the subject on which we are engaged, let me invite you, brethren, to consider for a short time the actual scene of the public baptism of an infant in the Church of England, such as we are all happily familiar with, in order to come to a just view, not indeed of the nature of the gift bestowed upon the child baptized, but of the human action not without which we understand that sacred gift to be given.

I will venture then to say that there meet at the scene of such holy baptism, the two parents (to speak, I trust, with no irreverent boldness) of the divine birth of the Holy Ghost in the infant's soul.

First, there is assuredly the sacred presence of God;—specifically of God the Son, of Him who was designated and empowered by the Holy Ghost at Jordan to be the Baptizer with the Holy Ghost, the Father of the new birth of the soul.

But Christ the great High Priest, invisibly present and doing His own divine spiritual work invisibly, acts visibly through His visible representatives, and His great representative upon earth is the priestly Church,—

and she, representing her Lord, performs the visible and outward acts to which is attached, by the mercy of God, the communication of the Divine Fatherhood.

And the priestly Church herself is, in the actual scene which we have before us, represented by the duly ordained priest or deacon, as the case may be, who has been empowered by rightfully descended authority and commission to be the personal administrator of the water and the words, which by the Lord's institution visibly convey, as means and pledge, the death unto sin and the new birth unto righteousness.

The ordained clergyman therefore being the personal representative in the present case of the Church, which in point of priestliness is one with her Lord, is to be regarded as the human channel, as far as man may be said to be so, of the Divine Fatherhood of the new birth.

Now at this point I desire to make a special observation.

We know from St. John's Gospel[1] that the Baptist at the time of the baptism of our Lord Jesus Christ in Jordan, received, from the sight of the dove which descended from heaven and lighted upon the head of the Lord after He rose from the water, some very special and particular information respecting Him.

What then was this information? It could not have been information as to *who* the Lord was, as a matter

[1] St. John i. 33.

of acquaintance and knowledge; for not only was He his cousin in the flesh, but also we know from St. Matthew's Gospel that he had recognised Him when he first saw Him coming to his baptism.

Nor does it seem to have been information respecting His greatness and office; for the mother of the Baptist had known this before He was born, and the Baptist himself, confessing that he himself had need to be baptized of the Lord, would fain have shrunk from the seeming presumption of baptizing one so immeasurably his superior.

What then did the Baptist learn from the dove, which he did not know already?

Let me answer in the words of St. Augustine: 'The Holy Spirit saith not He is the Lord: He saith not He is Christ: He saith not He is God: He saith not He is Jesus: He saith not, He is He which was born of the Virgin Mary, later than thou, yet before thee: He saith not this, for John knew this already. But what then did he not know? That the Lord Himself intended to keep and reserve to Himself, whether present on the earth, or absent in heaven in His body, and present in His majesty that so great power of baptism :—that He purposed to reserve to Himself the power of baptism, lest Paul should say "my baptism" or Peter should say "my baptism." See then, observe the expressions of the apostles. No apostle ever said "my baptism." Though the Gospel was the same

Gospel of them all, yet you do find that they said "my Gospel;" but you never find that they said "my baptism [k].".'

This was then the information which the Baptist received from the descent of the dove:—that his holy Cousin, the Man marked from His mother's womb as the Son of the Highest, to whom the Lord God should give the throne of His father David to reign over the house of Jacob for ever, so that of His kingdom there should be no end,—was to be the Baptizer in all the world with the Holy Ghost, was to keep in His own hands, however He might see fit to delegate to men the ordinary ministration of the outward part of holy baptism, the gift of the Holy Ghost thereby conveyed. He and He only, by the special prerogative of the Holy Spirit, should absolutely retain, as with a sacred jealousy, the great inward gift as His own. He and He only in all the world should baptize with the Holy Ghost.

Brethren, when I read the long controversy between the African and Roman Churches on the subject of schismatical baptism, issuing after much debate and difference in the decrees of the Councils of Arles and Nicæa, and the establishment (gradual indeed, but at last universal) of the doctrine that whensoever and by whomsoever the water and the sacred baptismal words are administered to a person before unbaptized, there the gift of the new birth of the Spirit is in such sort

[k] Vide Note II.

given that the sacrament, though needing the recognition and confirmation of the Church, may not on any account be iterated as if the former administration had been a nullity,—I feel very forcibly reminded of the words of the holy Baptist, and the witness of the dove. Christ alone baptizeth with the Holy Ghost; and jealously, as it were, and absolutely, He retains this sacred power to Himself, and gives the gift where He will. No doubt for ordinary administration He entrusted it to His Church when He bade His apostles go teach and baptize all nations into the name of the Father, and of the Son, and of the Holy Ghost. And no doubt the apostles, for order and honour's sake—to adopt the expressions already quoted from Tertullian—entrusted the administration of it to their ordained successors, but the Lord's prerogative is not limited, nor the freeness of His divine gift bounded by the orderly methods of His own institution: and while we do not doubt but earnestly believe that whosoever is by the orderly ministration of the clergy duly washed with water in the name of the Father, and of the Son, and of the Holy Ghost, is partaker of the divine and inward birth which Christ giveth, we must hold our peace, like the apostles and brethren in Judea on a not dissimilar occasion [1], and glorify God, saying then doth Christ exercise His own prerogative beyond our ordinary means, and attacheth His own sacred gift of the birth

[1] Acts xi. 18.

of the Holy Ghost, even to ministrations which are not ours.

But to return to the point from which I digressed. There meet then at the ordinary scene of baptism, first, the Father of the new birth, Christ, represented by the priestly Church, herself represented on each separate occasion by her own duly ordained and commissioned minister; and secondly, the bearing mother. And here again the mother, the Church, appears by her representatives, who are in this case the sponsors.

That which the mother brings is, first, faith. The infant, incapable by age of coming in faith of his own, comes in borrowed faith. But from whom is his faith borrowed? Is it from his natural parents? Yes, no doubt, in part, if they be good and faithful. But what if they be evil and unfaithful? Is it then from his sponsors? Yes, again, if they be good and faithful. But no man can say for certain that they are so; and God forbid that the spiritual life of the poor child should be thought to be dependent on so frail and uncertain a support as their faith! Nay, it is upon the faith of the Church of Christ, whom the sponsors on the special occasion and for the special purpose represent. Hear again St. Augustine on this point [m]: 'Little children are presented to receive spiritual grace not so much by those in whose hands they are carried, though it is done by them also if they be themselves good and faithful, as

[m] Vide Note JJ.

by the whole society of good and faithful people. For they are rightly understood to be presented by all those who approve of their being presented, by whose holy and undivided love they are assisted towards the partaking of the Holy Spirit. So the whole Church, the mother, who is in all the saints, doeth this thing. The whole Church beareth all, the whole Church beareth each.' Hear again the words of St. Bernard to the same effect [n] : 'Let no man say to me that he hath not faith to whom his mother lendeth hers, wrapping it up for him in a sacrament till he become able to perceive it unwrapped up and clear by his own proper understanding and assent. What? Is the cloak so short that it cannot cover them both? Great is the faith of the Church. Is it less than that of the Canaanitish woman which we certainly know to have been sufficient both for her daughter and herself? For she heard the words, "O woman, great is thy faith; be it unto thee even as thou hast asked." Is it less than the faith of those who, letting down the paralytic through the tiles, obtained for him at once health of the soul and of the body? For you read that "when He saw their faith, He said to the sick of the palsy, Be of good cheer, my son, thy sins are forgiven thee;" and again a little after, "take up thy bed and walk." He who believeth these things will readily be persuaded that the Church is right in presuming not only the safety of such infants as are

[n] Vide Note KK.

baptized in her faith, but also the crown of martyrdom for infants slain for Christ.'

I would here call your attention, brethren, for a few minutes to the introductory portion of the Office for the Publick Baptism of Infants in the First Book of Edward the Sixth, as throwing light upon the subject of which I am speaking, and elucidating in some degree part of our present Service.

You may remember that in that Office the godfathers and godmothers, and the people with the children, are ordered to be ready at the church door; and there the introductory part of the Service is to be performed, that is to say, down to that place where the officiating priest desires the people faithfully and devoutly to give thanks to God, and say the prayer which the Lord Himself taught, and in declaration of their faith to recite the articles contained in the Creed. Then when they have said the Creed openly, the priest is directed to add also the prayer (which we still retain, though its significancy is now somewhat concealed), in which we thank God that He has called us to the knowledge of His grace, and faith in Him.

Now all this portion of the Service belongs to what in earlier times was the Office for the Admission of Catechumens, which was used as much for infants as for adults.

St. Augustine teaches us[o]—and we find the same doc-

[o] Vide Note LL.

trine in St. Cyril of Jerusalem—that it is when persons are admitted catechumens that they are to be regarded as conceived in the womb of the holy Church, their spiritual mother. The cross marked upon their forehead, the salt of the sacrifice put into their mouths, the diligent teaching and catechizing,—all this, he tells us, should be looked upon as the support of the child while yet in his mother's womb, and unborn.

When then the due time comes for the spiritual birth, the catechumen being now, in his own faith if he is an adult, or in that of the Church if he is an infant, sufficiently fitted to receive it, he is brought by the sponsorial company to the church door,—and then, as I said, and not till then, the priest, after various prayers and exhortations, having heard them jointly say the Lord's Prayer and the Creed, and thanking God for their common faith so testified, takes the oldest child by the hand, and leads him, the others following, to the font for the actual celebration of the sacrament.

It was a significant practice, which we find ordered in Pope Gregory's Sacramentary p, that such children as were old enough to stand, should set their foot upon their sponsor's foot, to indicate that they came for the present in the strength of borrowed faith, and rested upon it.

Observe now how all this arrangement of baptism, a little lost sight of in the construction of our present Ser-

p Vide Note MM.

vice, throws light upon what I have said of the parentage of the new birth. The clergyman, representing the fatherhood, meets the sponsorial company with the children at the church door, and having ascertained their purpose, before giving them admission instructs them, and requires them to say openly the Lord's Prayer and the Creed. This done, he has ascertained that they are duly qualified to act as representatives of the Church the mother, and then he proceeds to the font to begin the actual administration. It seems to me like an instinct of a half-forgotten meaning that has led in very recent times to the practice, now become very prevalent, of repeating this thanksgiving after the minister. I know not whether it is a revived practice, but I can find no trace of it. It seems to show that the people have a kind of sense that it is not the godfathers and godmothers only, but they too in whose presence the child is baptized, and in them the whole Church of Christ, in whose faith the child is admitted by the Lord to receive the blessing which is exclusively His, the baptism with the Holy Ghost.

2. But secondly the mother brings the promise of breeding the children up in the faith and fear of God, so as to enable them, by all the means which God has put into her power, to lead the rest of their lives according to that blessed beginning. She undertakes that nothing shall be wanting to them of all the graces of which she is the authorized and empowered channel, whereby they may

grow in the faith and obedience of Christ, and realize at the last that immortal inheritance, of which the right and title have in the sacrament of baptism been effectually conveyed to them. It is true that she delegates to three at least of her faithful people the express and special duty of attending to this spiritual growth, and taking all the requisite means for promoting it in the case of each single child. But she by no means discharges herself of the obligation, which (for fear lest that which is the duty of all should run the risk of being neglected by not being specially assigned to any) she puts into the hands of the sponsors. On the contrary, in the exhortation which she addresses to them, she puts into words her own obligation, and her own acknowledgment of it, while she enjoins them to fulfil it. It is commonly said that the sponsors stand for the child in baptism. And it is very true. They lend him feet to walk, and lips to utter, and an intelligent and faithful heart to undertake what he is still too young to undertake for himself. But it is not less true, though less often said and remembered, that they stand for the Church, and take upon themselves personally that which the Church has already undertaken by bringing them to baptism, and presenting them to God to receive the spiritual blessing.

And here I would fain make one or two observations, brethren, of the nature of corollaries from what I have said :—first, that while *three* is the number of sponsors now fixed by the Church, that number is to be regarded as a *minimum*. There is no reason whatever why there should not be more than three. On the contrary, if more will enter into the same solemn contract,—a contract, be it observed, sacredly made with the Church as well as with the infant, it cannot be otherwise than good and well; provided always that the increase of the number do not operate to dilute the obligation, and so to neutralize in any degree the very benefit which the institution of special sponsors was designed to produce. And secondly, though the sponsors be of course personally charged with the undertaking of which I speak, yet is the Church at large by no means wholly discharged from the obligation of it. Therefore the supply of Church schools, and the support of them, and in like manner the supply and support of churches, and of all the outward means necessary for the maintenance and growth of the spiritual life given in Holy Baptism, is not to be regarded as a matter of Christian bounty or benevolence on the part of Christian people at large, but as a distinct obligation which may not be disowned,— an obligation as binding in its nature upon them as the breeding of children with food and raiment and all things necessary to make them good citizens is obligatory upon the natural parents. The spiritual mother can no more discharge herself of all that is necessary for the spiritual growth of him, whom, by bearing she has undertaken to breed up for his Spiritual Father, than the natural parents can discharge themselves of the corresponding obligation in respect of the natural breeding of their own naturally born child. I venture to think that our appeals to our people for the means of building and supporting churches and schools, and all other things necessary for such spiritual growth on the part of those whom we have baptized, would come with greater weight, because with more perfect truth and justice, if, instead of appealing only to compassionate feeling and sympathy, we urged the *debt*, the obligation, the binding undertaking by which we, in common with the whole Church, had bound ourselves in taking infants to be baptized, and asking for them that seed of immortal life which absolutely requires human tendence, constant, affectionate, and faithful, in order to keep it alive, nay, to prevent its becoming rather an aggravation of sin and evil, than a help towards God and Heaven.

And this observation seems to suggest a further question, how far it is proper in heathen countries to administer holy baptism to infants, as it were, broad-cast, without some adequate undertaking on the part of the Church, the universal mother, to breed the baptized child n the faith and fear of God. I am not speaking merely of the absence of sponsors. They, even in a Christian land, are sometimes dispensed with, as in the case of serious and imminently dangerous sickness; for then the Church dispenses with her delegates under the pressure of circumstances, and is to be understood to appear in person, until the circumstances of the case admit, if the child recovers, of the due delegation being completed. If the child dies, the faith of the Church herself, without delegation, is that in which the due maternal parentage of the child is sufficiently assured. But in a heathen country the case is materially different. There it is undoubtedly necessary that something equivalent to a distinct undertaking on the part of the Church should accompany the due administration of the sacrament. The children are themselves devoid of that inchoate right to baptism which may be argued from St. Paul's words in the seventh chapter of the First Epistle to the Corinthians respecting children of one Christian parent. I confess that when I read of single missionaries baptizing infants in such lands, without adequate provision being made for the continuance of the mission itself, or for the breeding up of the children in the faith and fear of Christ, I feel considerable doubt not only of the wisdom, but of the rightfulness also of the proceeding. And herein is one special topic of comfort in the establishment of colonial and missionary bishoprics. When a bishop is in charge, having assurance of succession, and the Church in all its organization is planted in any territory, then with his sanction and authority the single missionary need have no doubt or hesitation. He may baptize freely. But the bishop, that is the Church, and that again is all the body of

Christian people, must surely understand that in giving such sanction and authority they have undertaken the full weight of the mother's duty—that they are responsible to God, the Father of the new birth, for all the careful and tender breeding which the child needs—that they have in fact undertaken, as a debt and obligation which they cannot in conscience decline or repudiate, to bring those children up to the estate of Christian men, and to do all that is in their power to keep the seed of spiritual life, so given, strong and growing in their hearts.

Thus, brethren, it has been my object to show how the whole Spirit-bearing Church, the body of Christ, is engaged in the administration of the sacrament of Holy Baptism, and therein of the first and chief imparting, through human means and channels, of the Divine and spiritual life: represented, in so far forth as she is one with Christ, the Father of the new birth, by the ordained minister; represented again, as she is the spiritual mother of Christians in whose faith the children are received, and to whose responsible parental care they are entrusted, by the sponsorial company, three at least, who bring them to the font, and there receive her own trust, delegated to them. And this essential and necessary presence of the Church fully exemplified in the ordinary scene of one of our common parochial baptisms, is to be understood in all the less perfect and more exceptional cases of baptism which various accidental circumstances may cause to be less fully and accurately performed. If the sponsors are absent, as in the case of private baptism in extreme necessity, the Church is still virtually present, and the deficiency is to be supplied as soon as the opportunity occurs for supplying it. If the Church herself is absent, as in the case in which the matter and the words of baptism have been used by one who is not of her body, though the fatherhood may not be doubted, yet till the mother's recognition, and with her recognition her assumption of the responsibility which it involves, we may not believe that the entire work, as God has instituted it, has been fully done, or that the new birth, in all its blessed completeness, has really been given.

None, I trust, will so far misunderstand my meaning as to suppose that in arguing that the work of Holy Baptism is the work of the whole Church, I intend in the slightest degree to lose sight of the different offices of different men in the Church, or to encourage the smallest usurpation by any upon the peculiar duties and privileges of others. Nothing can be farther from my thought or meaning. But I have wished to show in this instance, as I hope to do in others also, that the real work is the work not of separate officials, but of the entire body; that, while each retains his own place, and exerts himself to the utmost of his Christian powers in his own sphere without intruding upon the sphere of others, the whole strength and spiritual vigour of the whole body tells upon every separate act of spiritual power and office that is duly exercised. And I trust that it will be perceived that as the whole strength and spiritual vigour of the whole spirit-bearing body is necessary in order to give the full Divine efficacy to every such act, so the responsibility lies, similarly, although not equally in degree, upon every member of that body. The responsibility is not less wide than the power; and if the power is, as I believe it to be, the power of all, the responsibility also undoubtedly is the responsibility of all.

I will not attempt to speculate in any degree upon the nature of the change which takes place in the soul of man in baptism. Suffice it for the present to say the whole language of Holy Scripture respecting it represents it as one different, not in degree only, but in kind, from the various occasional aids and helps of the Holy Spirit, given to other men at other times, and given to the same man preparatory to baptism itself. Whatever may be the real meaning of being born of water and of the Holy Spirit, the expression must mean something not less definite, nor less real, and infinitely more important than the natural birth to natural life. Yet, as actual realities, they are parallel one to the other. The one, to adopt the words of St. Augustine[q], is of the earth, the other is of heaven; the one is of the flesh, the other is of the spirit; the one is of mortality, the other of

[q] Vide Note NN.

eternity; the one is of man and woman, the other is of God and the Church. And as the earth is to the heaven, as the flesh is to the blessed Spirit, as mortality is to eternity, and as the union of man and woman is to the mystical union that is betwixt Christ and His Church, so is the natural birth compared with the heavenly birth which is wrought of God in the sacrament of Holy Baptism. The natural birth makes us children of Adam, earthy, as of the earth. The spiritual birth makes us to bear the likeness of another Father, which is the Lord from heaven. Each is alike real, each can alike be given once, and only once. 'As the birth of the womb cannot be repeated,' says the same St. Augustine, 'so cannot baptism.' Once born, we are alive, or dead. Once reborn, we are saved in Christ, or we are lost for ever. The spark may be feeble, may be latent, may give neither light that man can see nor warmth that he can feel. But so long as it is not totally and absolutely extinct—and it is not mere ignorance that extinguishes it, but deliberate, wilful, and continual impenitence in sin—so long the breath of the Holy Spirit may relume that which the Holy Spirit first gave, which is indeed the Holy Spirit Himself in the newly born soul.

Given then, according to the now wellnigh universal practice of the Church, in early infancy, the new birth conferred in Holy Baptism is the first spark and germ of Divine life, of everlasting union with Christ, of life in the Holy Spirit, of reconcilement with God, of assured immortality in bliss both of body and soul. But it is the beginning only. It is the principle, the seed, the spark. Sufficient no doubt for the salvation of the infant, if as an infant he dies with his soul unstained by the further commission of actual sins of his own. But the same measure of regeneration or sanctification which sufficeth children or infants dying before they come to the use of reason, will no more suffice such as attain to years of discretion, as Dr. Thomas Jackson well says[r], than their childish apparel or clothes will continue to suffice them when they grow to be men.

And the Church of Christ which obediently and faithfully took her part along with her Lord in the regeneration or new birth of her infants, charges herself with their breeding up in the days when the gradually opening mind, imperceptibly in its beginnings, doth also gradually open the avenues of sin, and disclosing the needs of the naturally corrupted soul, requires the daily strengthening of that sacred principle of life which is now by the gift of God divinely bound up with it.

The Christian mother when she teaches her baptized infant to lisp his first words of prayer at her knee, and fills his early thoughts with the holy food of good hymns, and, so far and so soon as he is capable of receiving them, the sacred words of Christ, is not only following the tender instinct of maternal love made more tender by her own earnest faith, but is also doing in

[r] Vide Note OO.

her place the work that belongs especially and personally to her as one of the members of the body of Christ. The child she teaches is much more to her than the child of her own sanctified love and the offspring of her own womb. He is an heir of heaven lent by God to her Christian love. He is a greater than Moses given by the King of kings to his own natural mother to nurse for Him, and to breed him up with the earliest measures of Christian love and habit for His sake.

The Christian father, when, as his child grows older, the growing powers of mind, and the increasing strength and range of temptation require stronger discipline and maturer food—what again is his place, but that of one entrusted by God and the Church of God with the further training of a growing member of the body of Christ, who, for his Lord's sake who has bought him, and whose he is, must be bent to love the ways of holiness and devotion in which he is to walk when he is grown? The lesson of obedience, the lesson of diligence, the lesson of love, the lesson of ordered temper, the lesson of modesty, the lesson of unselfishness—all these, the natural lessons of sweet youth, are put into the parents' hands to teach—lessons of the Church, and lessons of God—in the early days of home, when God and the Church have given back their regenerated little one to those whose natural love, heightened and sanctified by their own participation in the graces of the Holy Spirit of God, supplies the true method, and the most effective channel by which the infant life may begin to be matured towards the more robust strength of Christian youth.

And if any part of the parental office be delegated to other teachers, to tutors or schoolmasters, still the essential view of their position is that they are ministers in their place and office of the Church of God, taking their due part in that which she has undertaken to do by all the best means in her power.

And so, gradually, not forgetting the special office of the sponsors to take care that their godchild be taught, so soon as he is able to learn, the articles of the Christian Faith, the great formula of Christian prayer, and the summary of Christian morals, the Creed, the Lord's Prayer and the Ten Commandments, he is to be trained up in preparation for that day when by the wise care of the Church, modifying in some degree her ancient practice in order to meet the wellnigh universal prevalence of infant baptism, he is old enough to come in his own intelligent faith, with his own earnest prayer, and with his own firm and resolved promise of obedience to receive the seal of the gift of the Holy Ghost in apostolic confirmation.

And then, once more, by means of her sacredly empowered organs, the Church completes, in a manner fitting their maturer age, the work in which she took her sacred part in their first unconscious childhood. Not indeed as though that work were imperfectly done, or only half done at the first. For we do not doubt that the gift, the great gift, the spark, the true germ of the life of the Spirit, was effectually imparted at the font, and that it has grown continually under the gentle influences which suited infancy in the carefully bred child since that time. All that was the milk of the babes, learning to know[s] the Father, which is the special learning, according to the beloved apostle, of the children. But we know that in the first days of the Church it was held requisite for those who were baptized that they should receive the sacred seal from the apostles' hands as the baptized men of Samaria received it from those of Peter and John.

No doubt our confirmation so far differs from that of the apostolic age that we do not look for the extraordinary gifts which the confirmed of that time enjoyed. But neither do we believe that the imparting of these extraordinary gifts constituted the sole, or the most important part of the blessing which the imposition of apostolic hands conveyed to the baptized in the first days. That, we doubt not, was as temporary as the extraordinary gifts themselves were temporary; nor would such temporary blessing have been sufficient to account for the position assigned to laying on of hands in the Epistle to the Hebrews[t], as one of the doctrines of the 'foundation' of Christian teaching. But when this, in the Providence of God was withdrawn, there

[s] 1 St. John ii. 13.   [t] Heb. vi. 2.

remained still the rich effusion of the blessed ordinary gifts, now greatly needed by the young man who is to be strong in the Lord to overcome[u] the wicked one,—those blessed sevenfold gifts[x], the Spirit of Divine wisdom and understanding, the Spirit of mutual counsel and communicated strength, the Spirit of the inward knowledge of God and true godliness,—and in them and above them all, the Spirit of God's most holy fear, keeping wisdom and understanding, keeping counsel and strength, keeping knowledge itself and true godliness, holy, humble, self-distrusting, and reverent in the sight and in the presence of the most holy Lord God. 'None expects now,' says St. Augustine[y], 'that they on whom the hands are laid for the receiving of the Holy Ghost, should at once begin to speak with tongues. But invisibly and secretly we understand that the love of God is breathed into their hearts through the bond of peace, so that they may be able to say, the love of God is poured forth in our hearts through the Holy Ghost that is given to us.'

No doubt, brethren, none expects in these later days the visible effects of the gift of the Holy Spirit in apostolic confirmation; but do I pass the bounds of reasonable exposition in venturing to suggest that as the special extraordinary gifts of the first age have

---

[u] 1 St. John ii. 13, 14.
[x] Isaiah xi. 2. Cf. the Collect in the Confirmation Service.
[y] Vide Note PP.

their corresponding ordinary graces still;—as the supernatural gift of tongues now merges in the natural aptitude and laborious acquisition of languages; as the extraordinary gifts of healing in the patiently won skill of medicine, the supernatural gift of interpretation in the careful study of Holy Scripture and the doctors of the Church, and the Divine gift of prophecy in the studiously acquired skill of preaching, so we may hope that God's children coming to apostolic confirmation may look for special grace upon their special Christian calling, and the missionary amid the heathen islands, the physician, the preacher,—yes, and all others who design to devote themselves in Christ to this or that life of Christian usefulness in the Church, may be strengthened for their express work by the express gift which is not less real and less divine, though it be invisible, than it was in the days when its effect was immediately exhibited to the eyes and ears of the wondering people.

With confirmation, the infant life is matured into the manly life. The early measures of Christian training are to be supposed to have done their work. The child in Christ has been taught to know the Father. Henceforward, he who was a child in the Church is become a man. The fulness of the grace of Christ is his. He is included among the invited guests of the holy altar. Thenceforward he must go on his way in the strength of the meat indeed and the drink indeed which Christ has given for the strength and refreshment of His people's souls; to be strong, to have the word of God abiding in him, to overcome the wicked one, to do the Lord's battle in the Spirit's strength, and to reach the Lord's crown through whatever labours and whatever length of years the Lord may appoint for him.

LECTURE VI.

THE HOLY COMMUNION.

For we being many are one bread, and one body: for we are all partakers of that one bread.—1 Corinthians x. 17.

THE sacrament of Holy Baptism, which was the subject of the last Lecture, completed in apostolic confirmation, diffuses and spreads widely the gift of spiritual life where it was not before. Whether given to a converted heathen, or to the newly-born child of Christian parents, alike it adds another to the Christian name, and as it thus continually widens and enlarges that name, spreading it over larger multitudes, extending it into new regions, and bestowing it upon new nations of mankind, it might possibly seem to tend to enfeeble and relax the union between those who belong to it. A family consisting of many millions, designed to include all nations, of every age and colour and degree of civilization, living on from generation to generation under every various change and phase of circumstance and history, might seem to be destined, by its mere magnitude and duration, to fall inevitably into danger of disunion, unless some further provision were made for its continued cohesion and unity, both laterally, so to speak, and from age to age.

We believe that precise provision to be among the many blessings which we derive from the other of the two great sacraments of the Gospel, the Holy Communion of the body and blood of Christ. If the sacrament of Baptism may be called the sacrament of diffusion, the Holy Communion is the sacrament of unity; the binding, uniting rite, which, while it testifies to spiritual union, also produces it; which, while it sanctifies the separate souls of the faithful communicants, sanctifies them also in the union of their sacred Christian brotherhood; which feeds the individuals through the general body, and feeds the general body again through the sanctification of individuals. Hence it is, says St. Augustine [a], 'that the apostle Paul, setting before us this bread saith, we being many are one bread and one body. O sacrament of holiness! O sign of unity! O bond of love! He who desires to live, has where to live, has whence to live. Let him approach, let him believe, let him be incorporated that he may be made alive. Let him not shrink from the framework of the members, let him not be a corrupt member to be cut off, nor a distorted one to be ashamed of; let him be a fair one, a fitting one, a sound one; let him cling to the body, let him have life in Him

[a] Vide Note QQ.

who is God of God, let him now labour on earth that he may afterwards reign in heaven.'

Thus it is that the altar of Holy Communion is the perpetual centre of the unity of the Church. Not localized in Rome, not virtually inherent in a single bishop,—in parish, in diocese, in province, the altar of Holy Communion is set up in all the Church as the centre to all the Christian people within that parish, diocese, or province, to which they must seek as to the central source of continued blessing, personal and general, the true ubiquitous centre of that unity of the entire body from which their own personal graces first began, and upon which they must, in great measure, still depend.

For the Holy Eucharist is essentially one. Wherever it is duly celebrated in all the earth; however frequent, however wide asunder in point of time the single celebrations may be, yet in all places and in all times, it is essentially the same act [b]. 'Be ye earnest therefore,' says St. Ignatius, 'to use one Eucharist. For there is one flesh of our Lord Jesus Christ, and one cup for the union of His blood [c].' 'It is no other sacrifice, but the same sacrifice,' says St. Chrysostom, 'that we always offer, or rather memorial of the sacrifice that we perform [d].' It is one both in itself, as being wherever it is offered the same offering of Christ's sacramental body and blood, as being sanctified by one

[b] Lyra Innocentium, Continual Services, p. 317.
[c] St. Ignatius ad Philadelph. Δ. Jacobson, p. 422.
[d] St. Chrysostom, xvii. Hom. in Ep. ad Hebraeos.

and the same Spirit, and as the offerers are one, all being in their various degree and position, in their various ages and countries, members of the one body of their Lord. At all times and in all places it is the one Church, which by the one Spirit, offers to God the one sacred commemoration of the one most holy sacrifice.

Thus, as I said, the sacrament of the Holy Communion stands contrasted with that of Holy Baptism. Baptism diffuses life, Holy Communion knits it, and keeps it together. Baptism might conceivably be followed by the division of the possessors of life. For though the life too be in its origin one, and one in its holy being, as it is the effluence and energy of the one Spirit, yet exercised and managed, so to speak, by the multitudes who separately possess it, it might possibly be found compatible with all sorts of exterior disunion and discord. But those who might thus be disunited Holy Communion continually reunites by the holiest and most sacred of bonds. Baptism constantly adds members to the extremities, as it were, of the existing body; Holy Communion makes the one life-blood to flow throughout it, full of strength and Divine force, supporting and refreshing the life that is in it all, penetrating to its furthest and minutest portions, so that the whole body by joints and bands having the Divine nourishment ministered, and knit together, increaseth with the increase of God [c]. Briefly, Baptism

[c] Col. ii. 19; Eph. iv. 16.

is the sacrament of diffusion; the Holy Eucharist is the sacrament of perpetual re-union in and with Christ.

That Divine nourishment is the body and blood of Christ. It is hardly possible, brethren, in these days of division and disputation on all the most sacred articles of the faith to pass by, quite without notice, the extreme diversity of opinion of Churches and doctors on this most sacred, and in its general terms unquestioned doctrine; but it suits little with my purpose to dwell upon such diversities at any length. I will therefore only say that the ancient doctrine of the Church, and, as I read it, the unquestionable doctrine of the Church of England, is that the spiritual presence of the body and blood of our Lord in the Holy Communion is true[f] and real. I do not see how we can consent, as with Hooker and Waterland, to limit authoritatively that presence to the heart of the receiver; for the words of the institution (and these are cases in which we are rigidly and absolutely bound to the exact words of the revelation)—the words, I say, of the Lord in the institution—seem to forbid such a gloss.

I said that this is a case in which we are rigidly and absolutely bound to the exact words of the revelation.

[f] I have omitted the word 'objective,' which in the first edition stood in this place, on the ground whether the grace of the Holy Eucharist come to our souls by and through the elements or no, alike it is objective, as coming to us from without ourselves, and having existence independently of our own thought. Everybody holds the Presence to be 'objective' except the merest Zuinglian.

Let it be observed in confirmation of this statement that not only the three Evangelists, narrating as historians the events of that sacred evening, give uniform testimony as to the holy words [g] of the Lord in the institution, but that in the revelation made to St. Paul (a revelation plainly, in that instance, made in words) the holy words of Christ are the same. Thus reported, and thus specially revealed, the holy words must be understood to convey exactly, neither more nor less, that which they say; and that which they say on this sacred mystery is precisely, neither more nor less, that which God has told, and that which man knows.

If then we are asked, as the question is not unfrequently asked among us, How then do we distinguish the doctrine of such real and true presence from the Lutheran tenet of consubstantiation? It seems to be a just and sufficient answer to say that consubstantiation, like transubstantiation, is a *theory* of the *manner* of the presence, whereas the Church only knows the presence as a fact, respecting the manner and mode and extent of which she is not informed. The body and blood of Christ are present, not corporeally (for that we know from our Lord's words in the conclusion of the discourse recorded in the sixth of St. John [h]) but spiritually, in and with the elements. We know no

---

[g] τοῦτό ἐστι τὸ σῶμά μου. St. Luke xxii. 19; St. Mark xiv. 22; St. Matt. xxvi. 26. τοῦτό μου ἐστὶ τὸ σῶμα. 1 Cor. xi. 24.

[h] St. John vi. 63.

more. We need not suppose that they are further present than in reference to the use for which they are appointed, that is, that men should be partakers of them to the strengthening and refreshing of their souls, and that the Church, the body of Christ, should thereby be maintained in its Divine unity and holiness; but whether the change is of this particular sort or of that, at what moment it takes place, and all such other unrevealed particulars relating to it, we know not, and consider it presumptuous in our uninformed state to speculate.

No doubt some of the ancients, as for example St. Chrysostom in the treatise on the Priesthood, use very strong and remarkable language on this part of the subject. I venture to think that as we should not have scrupled to use similar language if we had lived before the Roman theory of transubstantiation had been elaborated into all its train of evil and superstitious consequences, so would he in all probability have guarded his expressions had he been writing in later days, when that philosophical theory had been invented and made to take the place of the simple doctrine of the real presence of the body and blood of Christ in the sacred elements.

Under the outward and visible form of bread and wine we believe that the body and blood of our Lord and Saviour Jesus Christ are given, taken, and received; and we believe that that divine food, according to the sacred teaching of our own Liturgy in this respect, imparts to every one of those who receive it with true penitent heart and lively faith, these nine inestimable blessings:—the spiritual eating of the flesh of Christ, and drinking of His blood; the dwelling in Christ, and Christ in him; the being one with Christ and Christ with him; the cleansing of his body by the body of Christ; the washing of his soul by the blood of Christ; the assurance of the favour and goodness of God towards him; the assurance of his being still a member incorporate in the mystical body of Christ; the assurance of his continued heirship, through hope, of the everlasting kingdom; the preservation of his body and soul to everlasting life [i].

So to the single souls of penitent and faithful receivers; so wonderfully, so divinely, with such unspeakable comfort, support and strength. But not to the single souls of such receivers only, nor for the independent and merely personal growth of the spiritual life within them only, do we believe that divine food to be effectual; but that to the whole of the sacred mystical body of which they are severally members, strength, and holiness, and unity, and every sort of blessing is therein ministered.

Shall I ask whether the feast which they there celebrate is or is not a sacrifice? Brethren, bear with me while I venture to say that I am not very careful, so far as I can judge, to answer the question. Indeed it appears to me to be little more than a question of

[i] Vide Note RR.

words, which bears upon no important issue. The feast is what it is; and whether that is or is not what constitutes a sacrifice must depend altogether upon the precise meaning attached to the word 'sacrifice,' and the definition given to it. There surely are good and innocent senses in which it may well and rightly be so called,—there surely is a sense, the highest,—that in which the actual offering of the Lord's body and blood upon the altar of the Cross was once offered, the only full, perfect, and sufficient sacrifice, oblation, and satisfaction for the sins of the whole world,—in which we may not dare so to call it. It is perhaps conceivable that in the eyes of Him who from His seat in eternity looks upon the things of time, as the Lamb was once slain from the foundation of the world[j], so the great sacrifice and all its sacred commemorations, its types faithfully celebrated before, its commemorations faithfully celebrated after, may be wholly and absolutely one, the one work of Christ in Himself and His people. I know not; but we whose stand-point is in the things of time, cannot speak so. We could not, without the express word of Holy Writ, have spoken of the Lamb slain from the foundation of the world. To us there is before and after. To us our blessed Lord came, and died, and rose, and ascended at definite dates in this series of things. We must not confound time and eternity, nor our doings with the Lord's doings. It

[j] Rev. xiii. 8.

may sound humble, but I believe it is really presumptuous to do so. I know not why we should not rest content to speak in the language of St. Chrysostom, which I have already quoted, and to call the holy feast which we celebrate our Θυσία, or Ἀνάμνησις τῆς Θυσίας, —our sacrifice, or recollection of the sacrifice.

This great act—sacrifice if you will—this communion of the spiritual body and blood of our Saviour Jesus Christ, this inter-communion of the whole body of Christ militant on earth and resting in Paradise,—is necessarily, whensoever it is celebrated, the act of the whole body, even though in each several instance a few only are the actual partakers in it.

In order to constitute its complete character according to the divine pattern of its institution, it absolutely requires two things. First, there must be the consecration of the elements by the priest, the organ of the priestly Church, empowered by sacred ordinance to do that solemn and indispensable portion of the joint act which none else may presume to exercise or intrude upon. For it is no common nor ordinary work which he has to do. It is no light thing that by the acts that he organically does, and the words which he organically utters, the spiritual presence of the Lord is so brought down upon the elements of bread and wine as that to the faithful they become verily and indeed, however invisibly and mysteriously, the body and blood of Christ. Through him, in this his great priestly work, the whole spiritual life and force which is in the priestly Church, operates as in its highest function. It is only through the sacred gift that is in him by the laying on of apostolic hands, with the laying on of the hands of the presbytery, that he may venture or presume to do it. This is assuredly the first thing. While the Church, in respect of Holy Baptism, has recognized the fact that though for purposes of honour and order it is right to confine the ordinary and authorized administration of the sacrament to the clergy, yet the gift is not so exclusively in their hands as not to be imparted in any degree by lay people in her communion, or even, if the sacred words and the water are used, by the hands of those who are outside of her communion altogether, there has never been a question of the absolute confinement of the power of consecrating the bread and wine to their mysterious efficacy of becoming to the faithful and to the Church of the faithful the body and blood of the Lord, to the ordained clergy. When I say there has never been a question on this point, I must be understood to mean among Church writers, and in the Church—from St. Ignatius to St. Bernard, from St. Bernard to the days in which the tyranny of perfected sacerdotalism produced its unhappy, but not unnatural effect in the disowning of all divine descent of special priesthood in the Church together. It is needless to quote passages. It is the absolutely universal doctrine of Church writers of every age that to the priesthood alone belongs the power of consecrating the elements to become to the faithful the body and blood of Christ. They have been made by personal authorization and empowerment, the only capable organs for this purpose of the priestliness which, as I have repeatedly said, inheres ultimately in the whole priestly Church, which is priestly as being the body of the One and only Priest, our Lord Jesus Christ.

And the other part of the sacred act is not less essential. The Church in its people must be there to receive, in repentance, in faith, and in charity, what by her priest she consecrates and offers. Their part is as necessary to constitute and complete the sacrament as his. It is of the very essence of the rite that it is a κοινωνία, a communion. 'The cup of blessing which we bless, is it not the communion of the blood of Christ? The bread which we break, is it not the communion of the body of Christ [k]?' The sacrificial portion, if I may so call it, of the sacrament has no being nor existence without the other portion, the communion. The communion is null and void of all its special spiritual blessing without the sacrifice. They are not two things. They are one thing only. The rite may not be practically divided or split up into two parts as though some men did exclusively perform the one part and some the other. All, in their separate places and degrees, do all. The people, rendering the sacrifice of praise and thanks-

[k] 1 Cor. x. 16.

VI.] *communicating in faith.* 171

giving, offering, as priests themselves[1], their spirits, souls, and bodies, as a rational, holy, and lively sacrifice to God; partaking in the grace, made more and more to be helpful as channels of the diffused Spirit; responding to the words of the consecrating priest; supporting and confirming them by their audibly expressed assent; in their hands and in their mouths receiving the sacred elements; in faith discerning the Lord's broken and life-giving body,—all these are necessary to the completeness of the great joint act which the Church of God, not the priest alone, performeth. The priest, himself a penitent, himself one communicant among many, saying[m] to himself and for himself the words of confession, absolution and comfort which he says to and for his brethren—the mouthpiece, if I may so speak, and organ of the Church, that is, of his brethren and of himself, in the special and exalted act of consecration,— in all these together in their several positions and duties the Holy Church doeth, hath done, and shall continue to do this great thing, obeyeth her Lord by doing it in sacred remembrance of Him,—declareth, publisheth, proclaimeth to heaven and earth, to angels and to men, the saving sacrifice of the Lord's death until He come again in judgment[n].

Any person who will read the ancient order of consecration as it is described in the Apostolical Consti-

---

[1] Vide Note SS.   [m] Vide Note TT.
[n] τὸν θάνατον τοῦ Κυρίου καταγγέλλετε. 1 Cor. xi. 26.

tutions (it is extracted at length in the fifth book of Bingham's Antiquities) will, I think, see that what I have said agrees very completely with the doctrine and practice of the primitive Church. 'Let the deacons bring the gifts (the elements) to the bishop to the altar. Then let the chief priest having, along with the presbyters, prayed secretly to himself, being clad in a bright vestment, and standing at the altar, after making the trophy of the Cross with his hand on his forehead, say, " The grace of Almighty God, and the love of our Lord Jesus Christ, and the communion of the Holy Ghost, be with you all." And let the people answer with one voice, " And with thy spirit." Then let the chief priest say, " Lift up your hearts," and all repeat, " We lift them up unto the Lord." And the chief priest, " Let us thank the Lord;" and let the people answer, " It is meet and right so to do."' The same is the case with the ancient Liturgies of St. Mark and St. James [o]. Not only is there the repeated interchange of mutual prayer between the consecrating priest and the people, 'The Lord be with you'—' And with thy spirit' (it occurs nine times in the Liturgy of St. Mark, and nine times in that of St. James), but also the 'Amen' of the people is repeatedly interposed in the midst of the solemn words of consecration. So in the Liturgy of St. James, the priest prays, 'Send down the same most Holy Ghost, Lord, upon us, and upon these

[o] Vide Note UU.

holy and proposed gifts; that, coming upon them with His holy and good and glorious presence, He may hallow and make this bread the holy body of Thy Christ.' And the people answer, 'Amen.' 'And this cup the precious blood of Thy Christ.' And the people answer, 'Amen [p].' Now, brethren, I beg that you will listen to the way in which St. Chrysostom comments upon this, and other such like cases, lest I should be thought to strain the inferences unduly which I desire to draw from them. 'Great,' he says, 'is the power of the congregation, that is, of the Churches. Consider how great is the power of the congregation. The prayer of the Church released Peter from his chains, and opened the mouth of Paul. Their suffrage decorates in no trifling degree those who aspire to spiritual authorities. For this cause he that is about to ordain invites their prayers at that time, and they join their suffrages, and utter the cries which we who are initiated know. For it is not right to publish everything in the presence of the uninitiated. Sometimes there is no difference between the priest and the man who is beneath the priest, as for instance when we enjoy the tremendous mysteries; for we are alike thought worthy of the same blessings. Not, as in the ancient covenant, the priest ate some things and the people others, and it was not permitted to the people to partake of what the priest partook. But it is not so now. But one and the same body is

[p] Vide Note VV.

offered to all, and one and the same cup. Again, in the most tremendous myteries the priest prayeth for the people, and the people prayeth for the priest. For these words " And with thy spirit," are nothing else than this. Again, the giving of thanks is common to both. For the priest does not even give thanks alone, but the whole people does so also. For he first receives their answer, and when they have agreed that it is meet and right so to do, then he begins the thanksgiving. And why dost thou wonder if the people sometimes join their voice with the priest? Do they not utter those sacred hymns along with the very Cherubim, and the heavenly powers? Now all this I have said, that each several one of the people too may be sober; in order that we may learn that we are all one single body, differing from one another only so far as some members differ from other members; and that we may not throw all upon the priests, but that we ourselves also may have care for the whole Church, as for our common body. For this both brings greater safety, and helps you to greater progress in virtue q.' It seems plain from these words that while St. Chrysostom assigned to the consecrating priest his own special office and duty, not to be infringed upon or usurped by others, he regarded the communicating people too as adding an indispensable element, in their presence and their prayers, to the holy and mysterious rite of sacred com-

q Vide Note WW.

munion, and urged upon them the high responsibility which such share in the holy office necessarily involved. To the same general effect with these words of St. Chrysostom, but with still more remarkably distinct expression, is a passage in a homily by an ancient abbot, a disciple and friend of St. Bernard, printed in his works : 'Dearest brethren,' he says, 'such ought we to be who consecrate the body of Christ, *when we sacrifice, eating it after consecration.*' Observe these words. 'When we offer to you the same body for the health of your body and soul. Such also ought ye to be, when ye receive the holy sacrament from our hands, knowing that he who receives the body of Christ unworthily, and drinks His blood unworthily, eats and drinks judgment to himself. Nor indeed ought we to believe that the above-mentioned virtues are necessary to the priest only, as though he alone consecrates and sacrifices the body of Christ. He doth not sacrifice alone; he doth not consecrate alone. But the whole congregation of the faithful which standeth by consecrateth along with Him, sacrificeth along with Him. Nor doth the carpenter alone build the house; but one brings laths, another timber, another beams and other things to the work. The bystanders therefore are bound to contribute somewhat of their own as the priest also doth, firm faith, pure prayers, pious devotion [r].'

It may no doubt be said with truth, that passages

[r] Vide Note XX.

like this are rarely to be found in the writings of the ancients. They are more generally occupied in dwelling upon the awful sanctity of the holy feast itself, and of the wonderful loftiness of the power transmitted to the clergy of being the voice and organ of the holy Church[s], of holding the keys of the sacrament, of holding a dignity higher than that of angels, inasmuch as in their hands the bread and wine are spiritually changed into the most holy body and blood of the Only-begotten Son of God,—than of that which it is my more especial object to illustrate, the part namely which the faithful people take in the same office. But as I have already observed in respect of another part of my subject, even single and occasional passages are sufficient to testify to the existence and recognition of a doctrine which none deny, which excites no opposition, but which for one reason or another does not happen to come often to the surface. And I would add that in the more ancient form of the canon of the Mass[t] itself, in the Commemoration of the Living stood the words, 'Remember all those who stand round, who offer unto Thee this sacrifice of praise, for themselves, and all theirs.' Indeed these words stand there still, though they now run thus—'*For whom we offer;*' or, '*Who offer unto Thee.*'

Thus the Church, the bride of Christ, continually performs this her most solemn act of union with her Redeemer. Thus she offers in all the world, and to the

[s] Vide Note YY. [t] Vide Note ZZ.

end of time will continue to offer, the remembrance, the memorial of Him who is her life, and who therein giveth Himself to be the food as well of her corporate being as of that of each one of her separate members. Thus she publisheth, and will continue to publish, to men and angels, the glorious fact and divine efficacy of her Lord's death until His coming again—meeting in all her faithful people at the single altar of her common worship, offering herself an united sacrifice [u], and binding herself together in all her faithful living and all her faithful dead, by the same sacred act which unites her in such close and mystical union with her Lord. But she does it, not by her priests only, though to them appertains inalienably and incommunicably the lofty right and office of uttering the words which consecrate to their sacred and mystical efficacy the elements of bread and wine which she offers. No: she does it by the joint and duly proportioned agency, by the obedient and faithful co-operation of all her members, the people uttering the great 'Amen' which ratifies and completes even the sacred words of the consecrating priest, and partaking in the holy bread and wine which become, in the spirit, not in the flesh, the very body and blood of the Lord by this their joint act of commemoration and faithful devotion and sacrifice. Pardon me, brethren, if I seem to dwell perhaps with somewhat needless repetition upon these statements. For they seem to me to be not less

[u] Vide Note AAA.

important than they are, as I think, true to the holy doctrine of the primitive Church, before it began to be disfigured by false philosophy in respect of the manner of the divine presence in the Holy Eucharist, and by the gradual usurpation of a strong sacerdotalism which naturally if not necessarily culminates in such a system as that of Rome, upon the originally common though duly proportioned and subordinated rights of all the members of the Spirit-bearing body of Christ.

You well know with what uniform and consentient agreement the fathers of the English Reformation disallowed, as a thing never known of nor permitted amongst the fathers of the primitive Church, the practice of private Masses, which had grown up into a vast mass of corruption and superstition in the preceding ages [v]: and yet, if the sacrifice is complete and entire by the single action of the sacrificing priest, I know not how private Masses should be otherwise than things good and holy, and of precious efficacy towards the Christian benefit, and spiritual rejoicing of all the faithful members of the body of Christ. No well-instructed Christian denies, I imagine, that such is the efficacy of the duly celebrated feast of the Holy Communion. How then should we be able to doubt that if the single action of the priest sufficed to perform the sacrifice, it were good for the Church of quick and dead that Masses by the hundred or by the thousand should be perpetually

[v] Bingham, bk. xv. ch. 4.

celebrated by every ordained priest, though he were alone, consecrating and offering from morning till night, and from night till morning? If the single action of the priest did really offer continually, entirely, undoubtedly, the blessed sacrifice of the Lord's body and blood, renewing, continuing, repeating it as often as it was done, how could we doubt that the holy work ought to be going on without intermission and always, as much, as often, and as fast as it could possibly be done? Will any one rejoin upon me that it is hardly a less difficulty to suppose that the same benefits ensue upon the repeated administration of the Holy Communion, if three at least, according to the rubric of the Church of England, communicate with the priest, than if he celebrates alone? I answer confidently that the more times such Holy Communion is *duly* celebrated the better; the better for the communicating individuals, the better for the Church;—yes, the better for the whole body of Christ's Church, whether still militant in the flesh upon the earth, or already passed away from earth to its rest in the Paradise of God. 'Duly celebrated,' I say; and by 'duly,' I mean with sufficient care and thoughtfulness of preparation, as directed by St. Paul, on the part of the receivers, and with all the deliberate and faithful reverence on the part of priest and people which so solemn and holy a thing demands. To celebrate without such sacred preparation and reverence, whether the celebration be rare or frequent, is surely to incur the fearful risk of unworthy receiving, and thus to transform good into evil, and the greatest of blessings into a curse and a judgment. And if the reception or celebration be very frequent there is of course the more danger of such preparation and reverence being omitted. But of due, reverent, and real celebrations—celebrations in which priest and people alike in their several position and duty join to render to God, in repentance, faith, and charity, in all reverence and thankfulness, this most sacred act of Christian worship, which unites them more closely than anything else that is conceivable with their dear Redeemer, and, in His sacred body, with one another,—of such reverent, due, and real celebrations, I say confidently, and I do not think that any well-instructed Christian will gainsay it, there cannot possibly be too many. How many, is no doubt a matter of Church discretion and order; but the limit is to be set not with reference to any possible excess of frequency, but with reference to the danger of imperfect reverence and preparation.

The observations which I have made upon the primitive doctrine of Holy Communion, as excluding the Roman practice of private Masses, appear to me to tell with not less force against the recently introduced usage in some churches of the Anglican communion, of persons of adult age, and confirmed, who are therefore capable of communicating, remaining in the Church during the time of the celebration, and witnessing without partaking of the sacrament. Is it supposed that this is a primitive practice? Is it not certain that St. Chrysostom speaks of it in the severest terms when adopted, apparently as a new thing, among the careless and imperfectly instructed Churchmen of Constantinople in his own days? And if other denunciations of it are seldom found in the writings of other ancient fathers, is not the true explanation of the absence of such denunciations to be found in the fact that such an usage was absolutely unknown and unthought of in the early Church? And does it not militate directly against the very fundamental idea of the commemorative sacrifice as the great and solemn offering on the part of the whole Church that men should thus, not refrain only, but exhibit, in a sort of presumption of will-worship, the fact of their determination to refrain from communion? Is it not in fact a part of the natural result,—of the logical consequence of the Romish doctrine, which regards the entire sacrifice as completed by the sacrificing priest singly and alone, and ignores the necessary though subordinate part which the Church in her faithful people contributes to the joint act? The only possible place which a faithful lay Christian, or, I would add, a priest not celebrating, can rightly have when the Holy Eucharist is celebrated, is the place of a communicant. If there be reasons and causes personal to himself why he should not on the particular occasion communicate, the same reasonable causes require his absence from the celebration. 'I say not these things,' says St. Chrysostom, 'in order that ye should partake anyhow (ἁπλῶς), but that ye should make yourselves worthy. Art thou not worthy of the sacrifice, nor of the participation? Then neither art thou worthy of the prayers. Thou hearest the crier, who standeth and saith, Depart all ye who are in penance. All that do not partake are in penance. If thou art one of those who are in penance, thou must not partake; for whosoever doth not partake is one of those who are in penance. Consider,' he goes on to say, 'consider, I beseech you. The King's table is spread, angels are ministering at the table, the King Himself is present; and dost thou stand gaping by? He speaketh these words to all who shamelessly and boldly stand by. For every one who refuseth to partake of the mysteries doth stand shamelessly and boldly by. Tell me, if any man invited to a feast should wash his hands, and sit down, and be ready for the board, and then refuse to partake, does he not insult the giver of the invitation? Were it not better that such an one should not be present at all? In such a way thou didst present thyself. Thou didst sing the hymn; amid all the rest thou didst acknowledge thyself to be one of the worthy, by not having withdrawn along with the unworthy. How is it then that thou didst remain, and yet partakest not of the table[x]?' It is indeed very possible that there is this great difference between the conduct

[x] Vide Note BBB.

of those whom St. Chrysostom refers to, and of those who do the like in the present day, that while in the former case it may have been merely a fashion of carelessness and neglect, it is in the latter the effect of theory, and intended as reverence. But I do not see that the argument is the less applicable to the one case than to the other, even if this be so, while the theory exemplified in the modern practice is precisely that against which it is my particular purpose to object.

Such then I believe to be the position which the holy sacrament of the Lord's Supper holds in the system of the rites of the Church, and such, speaking generally and in the way of a sketch, is its efficacy in respect of the administration of the Holy Spirit in the body of Christ. The usage of the modern Church, dissociating apostolic confirmation from the now wellnigh universal practice of infant baptism, and requiring therefore from the persons confirmed, now of age to make their own profession, the personal vow of repentance and faith, has correspondingly postponed the reception of Holy Communion to the same age. It is well. Not intending to utter a syllable in disparagement of the ancient practice of infant communion, we may say that, as now ordered, personal self-examination, personal confession, explicit personal faith, express Christian charity and love, go to the altar now with every worthy receiver.

It is the greatest act of personal devotion—the devotion of ourselves in body, soul, and spirit to God. We do therein actually offer and present, according to the good words of our Liturgy, ourselves, our souls and bodies, to be a reasonable—that is, an intelligent—holy, and lively sacrifice to Him. We withhold nothing. Sins past have been confessed. Whether by the action of our separate and real priestliness, or, if our souls have needed it, by the intervention of God's ordained priest, we have received the assurance of their being forgiven. The little gift we severally give, while it is the firstfruits of much else to be Christianly given, and the pledge that all we have shall be Christianly spent, is the special token before God that no brother hath aught against us, that we are in reconcilement, in love and charity with all men. We render ourselves up— every time we communicate we render ourselves up again—to do the will of God in all our lives wholly, unhesitatingly, unreservedly.

It is the greatest act of faith. To worship, to pray, to praise God, to confess sin, to ask for pardon and help, all these, good and holy and necessary as they are, are but the natural expressions of a pious soul, conscious of weakness and sin, and of the presence and goodness of God. But he who, bowing himself down in faith at the altar of God, partakes of the consecrated bread and wine as spiritually and divinely, and to his soul, the body and blood of his Redeemer and Lord, what mystery is there of Christian revelation and belief that he does not therein and thereby acknowledge and proclaim? The mercy and love of the Father, the condescension of the eternal Son, His incarnation, the shedding of His blood upon the cross as a ransom for many, His resurrection-triumph over Satan and the grave, His ascension into heaven, His mission of the other Paraclete, His return in judgment, His mysterious presence in the Church, the dispensation of the Holy Spirit, His sanctifying grace in the body of Christ, and in every faithful member of that body;—he, I say, who in faith bows himself down to eat of that bread and drink of that cup as verily and indeed the body and blood of Christ to the strengthening and refreshing of his soul, doth as it were visibly and really set his seal to the holy creed of God in all its life-giving particulars.

And it is the greatest of prayers. While other prayers have their own times of occasion, and their own topics of petition, this great prayer supports, strengthens, gives spiritual fervency and sacred effect to them all. In it the Christian soul has drawn most near, has, so to say, touched most close the ascended Lord, and all the offices of more ordinary worship and service are the holier and the more effectual for that mysterious contact.

It is, no doubt, the most precious and efficacious of all the means whereby the grace of the Holy Spirit is imparted to each separate Christian soul planted into the body of Christ by holy baptism, for except we eat the flesh of the Son of Man, and drink His blood, we have no life in us. And this is the aspect of it with which we are most familiar in practical and parochial teaching, and in books of devotion. But this, great as it is, and vital, is but one side of its sacred meaning and power. The other side is not less true and real; and I will venture to say not less important, though less frequently urged and insisted upon in sermons and devotional writings. I mean the witness that it gives, and the sacred bond that it furnishes to that mystical union of believers in the body of Christ, which Christ Himself in the last solemn prayer recorded before the Crucifixion so earnestly prayed for, which has the promise of so great and peculiar blessing, and which is made by Himself to be the witness to the world of His own Divine mission[y]. In these days of division and separation, when not only national churches are disjoined from one another, but every parish in our own Christian country is so divided against itself in matters of religion that Dissent numbers wellnigh as many, if not in some cases quite as many, adherents as the true and apostolical Church of God in the land, it seems to be a matter of the most primary and pressing importance to press upon men's minds this aspect of the holy and mysterious efficacy of the blessed communion. It has been, I think, the weakness and deficiency of the Church of England in the revival of

[y] St. John xvii. 21.

earnestness which ensued, more or less, upon the preaching of Wesley and Whitfield, that it has preached religion chiefly in that subjective manner, if I may so term it, which they and their followers adopted. To preach the Gospel was to present the atonement of Christ to the fervid faith of sinners. To preach spiritually was to refer everything that could conceivably be good or acceptable to God absolutely to the workings of God in the soul. To preach faith was to discountenance the preaching of repentance and holiness as such, to keep out of sight, or at least in a very secondary position, external means and helps of grace, and to teach men that they must be saved by abandoning, and utterly disclaiming all idea of being or becoming good, really good, themselves. Now a scheme of doctrine like this, though indeed it contains a great deal that is most true and precious in its own place, if it be balanced and strengthened with other truth, and is faulty rather in its omissions than in its actual statements, has this obvious and melancholy tendency in it, that it directly operates to scatter the one Church of God, and to break up the precious unity of the body of Christ into a multitude of independent believers, following their own ways, selecting their own teachers and tenets, and seeking heaven by the light of their own eyes and in the security of their own personal convictions. If this be the true and entire preaching of the Gospel, I do not know what I have to say to the Dissenter who deserts his parish church, and goes to the meeting-house. He feels himself to be edified by what he hears there. He hears what he considers to be the Gospel. He is convinced that he has been at a definite time and with distinct consciousness converted by the Holy Spirit, and having been so perceptibly converted is saved for ever. He tells me that he has faith in Christ, and that he prays. I know that he is often a man of exemplary life and apparent piety. How can I urge him to leave his chapel, and to come to church? I confess that upon the principles which seem to me to have pervaded a good deal of the preaching of the Church of England, I feel very powerless to answer such a question satisfactorily. I cannot put it upon State authority, even if State authority did not break down under me. Church authority he wholly declines to recognize, and without his recognition of it, it were idle to talk of it.

I know of no essential bond of Divine unity so great, so holy, so binding as that which is provided for all the faithful members of the body of Christ in the Holy Communion. In that one altar where the Church by her joint and holy offering, remembers and publishes the sacred death of her Lord until He cometh again, there, and from thence the Church is one. Meeting at that one altar set up by the authority of the Church in ancient days, and ministered at by men who have received the divinely descended power to consecrate the elements of bread and wine to become to the faithful the body and blood of Christ, the members of the Church, separately and severally priests of God as members of the one Priest, renew and confirm their own separate and individual priesthood, testify to the oneness of the Priesthood which they all share, drink afresh of the fountain of their common life, go back refreshed and strengthened to exercise before God upon themselves, and in the various ways in which it is given to them to exercise it upon others, the office of their own personal priesthood, maintain and publish to heaven and earth the unity of the body by partaking, in repentance, faith and charity, in that which alone keeps the body alive and holy before God, the sacred communion with Christ, and with each other.

Herein is, assuredly, the true remedy for that thin religionism which has been widely prevalent among us, and which, while holding more or less firmly the main articles of the Creed, threatens to make religion little more than a personal sentiment, ignoring almost wholly the Divine institution of the Church of God, the body of His Christ.

God forbid that I should doubt that there may be,—nay, that their *is*, a deep, secret unity in Christ, which it is not given to us either to fathom, or to limit—that souls of men rendering themselves up to God in Christ, in sincere faith and devotion, even though they be disjoined and separate in respect of outward communion, may yet, in the unseen unity of the Holy Spirit belong to the sacred body of their Lord, and inherit, in Him, the kingdom which He has purchased for them by His most precious sacrifice. No doubt it may be so; and amidst all the rents and schisms of our divided Christendom— yes, and the lesser divisions which set house against house, and man against man even in our own country— it is the one topic of comfort which we store in our heart of hearts to cheer us in the miserable strife of tongues, never, alas! so keen, or liable to be so bitter as when engaged upon the holiest and most divine subjects. But it is the very characteristic of the divine scheme of Christ's religion that the deep, inward, spiritual agencies, those which alone are really and in themselves efficacious in the regeneration, the growth, and the salvation of the souls of men, have their outward and appointed signs and tokens, whereby we are bidden to win, and whereby alone we may be assured that we do win, the secret and invisible graces in which we live before God. The regenerating Spirit may no doubt seize, if He will, upon the hitherto unregenerate spirit of a man, and give him without human aid or interference the sacred new birth which brings salvation,—yet, unless we have risen, and been baptized, and washed away our sins in the consecrated elemental water, we may not presume that that mysterious change has passed upon our souls, even as we must not doubt the fact that it has done so when that outward rite has been duly done. And even so is the case with the other sacrament of the Gospel. There may be, as I said, a deep invisible unity, wherein the souls of men, divided on earth even to the utmost extent of persecution on the one hand, and suffering on the other, may yet (so that in their hearts they cling to God in Christ) be bound together in the Spirit; yes, and fed mysteriously with the sacred spiritual body and blood of the Redeemer which is the food of Divine life : yet none may presume upon such a doctrine, comforting though it be, nor venture to assure himself that he is himself a sharer in that secret bond, so as to be a member incorporate in the mystical body of Christ, which is the blessed company of all faithful people, unless he derive that assurance from the use of those outward means to which Christ has given the mysterious power of conveying it, and which he has made the pledge to our souls that it is conveyed.

LECTURE VII.

ORDINATION AND ABSOLUTION.

Then Peter said unto Him, Lord, speakest Thou this parable unto us, or even to all? And the Lord said, Who then is that faithful and wise steward, whom his lord shall make ruler over his household, to give them their portion of meat in due season?—St. Luke xii. 41, 42.

THERE is one question which has not as yet been expressly discussed in these Lectures, but which underlies all that has been said, and which must be no longer deferred, although the discussion of it must necessarily be very short and summary. The question is this: How far are we to understand the various things which our Lord spoke, sometimes to His disciples, and sometimes more expressly to His apostles, as said to the Church in general, though addressed to them representatively, or as said to them personally, and so to their personal successors in the specially apostolic position and the authority which belongs to it? In short, I desire to ask in general very much the same question which was asked by St. Peter in the text respecting the parable of the servants waiting for their Lord when He should return from the wedding. Spake He all these gracious words unto the apostles only, and so to the bishops and clergy, or spake He them even to all?

I need hardly say, after what I have urged in the previous Lectures, that I adopt the latter of these alternatives, and believe (and indeed the whole force of the view I have taken depends in great measure upon that conclusion) that when the Lord speaks to the disciples, or the Twelve, He generally, if not always, speaks to them as representing the Church. In a certain way no doubt He speaks to them personally as the appointed and empowered representatives of the Church, but not in such sense personally as to exclude at any time, or in any instance, the idea of a real and true representation.

But it seems necessary not to assume this conclusion silently, but to face the question directly, however short and incomplete must necessarily be the consideration which I can give to it.

And I would say that so far as my reading of ancient writers enables me to speak, I find a singular absence of uniformity of language in them respecting it; and that, not only in one writer as compared with another, but in the same writer in different parts of his own writings. At one time words seem to be interpreted of the apostles and their special successors only, while at another there is plain acknowledgment that the whole body of the Church is not to be excluded from the application. In truth, so far as I know, the precise question which I have asked does not seem in general to present itself in the express and distinct shape in which I feel it necessary for the purpose of my argument to regard it. In like manner we have been for many years in the habit of reminding one another that the Church embraces the lay-people as well as the clergy, and of complaining of the injurious expression of 'going into the Church' when used for 'taking Holy Orders;' yet, so far as I know, none has pressed the truth which underlies this just complaint to its full consequences, nor given a connected view of the Church, the body, in its relations to the clergy, the empowered organs of the authority and powers of the body.

When we open St. Matthew's Gospel the question presents itself to us at once. The Lord begins to preach[a], in the same language as the Baptist, 'Repent, for the kingdom of heaven is at hand.' He calls the two sons of Jonas (who had already believed) to leave their fishing, and to follow Him. He also calls the two sons of Zebedee; and so far as the narrative of St. Matthew goes, He calls no more at that time. Great multitudes follow Him from a very wide circuit of country. Seeing the multitudes He goeth apart into a mountain, and His disciples came unto Him[b]. He

[a] St. Matt. iv. 17, 18, 21, 25.   [b] St. Matt. v. 1.

opens His mouth, and teaches them in the Sermon on the Mount. This discourse then is expressly addressed to 'the disciples,' of whom we already know from St. Matthew the names of four only. We do not, I presume, doubt that whether the number of those who actually heard this discourse with their ears were few or many, yet that it was spoken in anticipation of the days in which the Church should be fully founded, and spoken with reference to the whole Church. Who were to be the salt of the earth? the apostles? Yes; primarily, no doubt, the apostles; yet surely not exclusively. The clergy? Yes, chiefly, no doubt; to the extent that they keep the pureness of doctrine and life which help to keep truth and holiness alive among the people. Which is the city set on an hill? Is it the governors and teachers of the Church, or is it the Church herself, the city of God, the new Jerusalem which the glory of God doth lighten, and the Lamb is the light thereof? In like manner the Christian interpretation of the commandments, the rule and reward of almsgiving, fasting, and prayer, and the more scattered precepts of the seventh chapter, are undoubtedly the inheritance of the whole Church of Christ, even though it be possible that they may have been actually uttered in the hearing of a comparatively small audience.

That which I have said of the Sermon on the Mount applies with equal force to a very large proportion of our Lord's discourses, respecting which, whether they were spoken to few or to many, none have ever doubted that they belong in their ultimate application to all.

But there are some discourses which appear to be of a more directly personal kind, such as those of the sixteenth of St. Matthew, in which the Lord speaking to St. Peter promised to him the keys of the kingdom of heaven, and the power to bind and to loose [c], and of the eighteenth of the same Gospel, where the same words, at least so far as regards the power of binding and loosing, are repeated respecting the Church [d]. How far then are we, as a matter of interpretation, to explain the former of these discourses as applying to St. Peter only, or the latter of them as applying only to the Twelve? On the first of these questions I might refer to passage after passage from the works of St. Augustine in which he explains the words of our Lord to St. Peter, as said, not to himself personally, but to the Church represented in his person. Such is the following: 'For the sake of that character of the Church which he alone' (because the confession was uttered by him alone) 'was then bearing he earned to hear the words, "to thee will I give the keys of the kingdom of heaven [e]." For it was no single man that received these keys, but the unity of the Church received them. Herein therefore is the excellence of Peter declared,

[c] St. Matt. xvi. 16.   [d] Ibid. xviii. 18.
[e] Vide Note CCC.

that he bore the figure of the universality and unity of the Church, when it was said to him, "I deliver to thee that which indeed was delivered to all." For that ye may know that the Church received the keys of the kingdom of heaven, listen to what the Lord said in another place to all His apostles: "Receive ye the Holy Spirit," and immediately after, "Whose soever sins ye remit, they shall be remitted to him, and whose soever sins ye shall retain, they shall be retained." This belongs to the keys of which it was said, "Whatsoever thou shalt bind on earth shall be bound in heaven: and whatsoever thou shalt loose on earth shall be loosed in heaven." But this then He said to Peter. But that thou mayest know that Peter then was bearing the character of the universal Church, listen to what is said to himself, and what to all faithful saints, "If thy brother trespass against thee, rebuke him: and if he repent, forgive him. And if he trespass against thee seven times in a day, and seven times in a day turn again to thee, saying, I repent, thou shalt forgive him." It is the dove that binds, the dove that looses. It is the building on the rock that binds and that looses.'

'It is enquired,' says Cornelius à Lapide, commenting on this great passage of the eighteenth of St. Matthew, 'what the word "Church" here signifies. St. Jerome, St. Anselm, and St. Gregory understand by it the assembly and multitude of the faithful, as though Christ intended that such a man should be convicted in their presence, in order to be brought to shame, and so amended. Zuinglius and the Innovators greedily adopt this, in order to sanction the democratic and popular government of the Church, and to flatter the people. But St. Chrysostom, Theophylact, Euthymius and others understand throughout by the word "Church," the pastors and prelates of the Church, who either separately, or in synod and council represent the Church, as the magistrate represents the republic, and the king the kingdom.' I do not know why the views sanctioned on either side by such great names should be held to be inconsistent with each other. It is surely possible that the real power may be the power of the whole body, the Church of God at large, and yet that the organs for its use and administration may be those who by a Divine descent of ordination have been empowered for that precise office and duty. To such extent is this principle of the representative application in our Lord's words acknowledged in ancient writers, even in such passages as seem to have the most obviously *personal* character, that St. Augustine [f] interprets the predictions which the Lord addressed to St. Peter and St. John in the twenty-first of St. John's Gospel as by no means exclusively applicable to themselves, but as designed to belong to the Church at large in its two aspects of activity and contemplation.

[f] Vide Note DDD.

If then, returning to the question as at first proposed, we ask whether words like these are to be understood as spoken to the apostles and their ordained successors only, or even unto all the Church, I venture to reply in terms borrowed in the way of paraphrase from those in which the Lord replied to St. Peter in the text. The words are spoken unto all: but they also are spoken unto you. You are stewards amid and over the household: servants among many fellow-servants, having the special duty of giving them their meat in due season: trusted with special offices for the transmission of Divine grace for your own support and theirs in spiritual life, and encouraged by the promise of especial and higher reward if at His coming He find you so doing:—but yet not so separate or disjoined from them as to be otherwise than members in the very same body, needing for yourselves the very same food which they need, penitents yourselves as well as priests, just as they too are, in their own place and degree, priests as well as penitents.

Of the official powers which in the name of the Church at large the apostles exercised in their life-time, there is one which they left, so far as the sacred history and the early Christian writers give us information, absolutely and altogether in the hands of their proper successors, the bishops: I mean ordination by imposition of hands. It is possible that the imposition of hands in confirmation may have been practically confined to the bishops, according to the passage which I have already quoted from St. Jerome, as a matter of honour and precedency rather than of principle and necessity. But the imposition of hands which consecrates bishops to their high office, and that which confers the Christian priesthood, have been regarded at all times as the inalienable office and honour of the episcopate.

With respect to the consecration of bishops it is sufficient to quote the second Canon of the fourth Council of Carthage: 'When a bishop is ordained, let two bishops place and hold the book of the Gospels over his head; and whilst one offers over him the prayer of blessing, let all the other bishops who are present touch his head with their hands [g].'

As to the ordination of priests, St. Paul exhorting Timothy reminds him of the gift that is in him by the laying on of his hands [h], and with the laying on of the hands of the presbytery, and therein gives the formula, so to speak, of apostolic ordination for all times, which has ever been dutifully followed. The practice cannot be more plainly shewn than in the next canon of the same council just referred to. 'When a priest is ordained, while the bishop blesses him and holds his hands upon his head, let all the priests also who are present hold their hands upon his head, near to the hand of the bishop.'

What then was the action, or was there any, of the

[g] Vide Note EEE.   [h] 2 Tim. i. 6; 1 Tim. iv. 14.

rest of the Church, in respect of this great rite of ordination? Granted that the ordaining authority rested altogether with the bishops, not however without the concurring aid of the presbyters, did the lay-people contribute any part or portion towards this most important act?

It cannot be denied that they had a very real share first in the selection of the persons who were to receive ordination, whether as bishops or priests. No doubt St. Paul is not recorded to have been assisted by any popular choice in appointing Timothy to Ephesus or Titus to Crete; but even in the Acts of the Apostles the general principle of specific consent on the part of the multitude of the Church is sufficiently clear from the story of the selection of St. Matthias and of the seven deacons. No doubt again St. Clement[j] of Rome, in the very age of the apostles, says of them that 'preaching throughout the countries and the cities, they constituted those who were the first-fruits thereof, having proved them by the Spirit, to be bishops and deacons of those who believe.' Yet the same writer, not many lines after, speaks of those who were so ordained as having been appointed by them, or by other men of great mark in succession to them, along with 'the joint acclamation of the whole Church.' But it will suffice on this point to quote the words of Cyprian[k]: 'The lay-people who obey the Lord's precepts, and fear

[j] Vide Note FFF.   [k] Vide Note GGG.

the Lord, ought to separate themselves from a sinner who is set over them, and not mingle in the sacrifices of a sacrilegious priest, inasmuch as they chiefly have the power either of choosing those who are worthy, or refusing those who are unworthy. Which very thing we see descends from divine authority, namely, that the priest be chosen in the presence of the laity under the eyes of all, and be approved as fit by the public judgment and testimony:—Which thing is observed, according to the divine rules in the Acts of the Apostles, when Peter speaks to the multitude about ordaining one into the place of Judas the apostle. Peter rose, it says, in the midst of the disciples, but the multitude was collected together. Nor only in the ordinations of bishops and priests do we remark that the apostles observed this practice, but in those of deacons also, respecting which it is written in their Acts: "the twelve called together the whole multitude of the disciples, and spake unto them." Wherefore that order which is observed among us and in almost all provinces, from the divine tradition and the apostolic practice, is to be diligently observed and maintained, namely, that for the proper celebration of ordinations, the neighbouring bishops of the same province come together to that multitude over which a bishop is to be ordained, and that a bishop be chosen in the presence of that multitude which knows the life of each individual most perfectly, and has thoroughly seen the actions of each from his daily behaviour.' It is quite clear that in the primitive ages the voice of the lay-people in the choice, and their 'acclamation' and assent in the ordination of clergy, whether bishops or priests, were by no means disregarded. Their testimony and their approbation were distinctly asked for, not silently assumed and taken for granted. Thus they had a real and substantial weight—a weight so real as to give them a real share in the responsibility of the choice. It would seem to be alike a corruption of the primitive practice to confine such choice absolutely to the clergy, whether bishop or pope, or to let it fall altogether into the hands of a lay-government. Both are of the nature of usurpations,—but the second has been a reaction from the first.

To the bishops then, as the personal successors of the apostles, belonged the right of laying hands, together with the laying on of the hands of the presbytery, upon persons to be ordained to the holy office and function of the priesthood. While the whole body took its own part in the choice of fit persons for ordination, and was called upon for the acclamatory 'Amen,' and the whole clerisy joined, subordinately, in the actual ceremony, the ordaining hands were those of the bishops, and of the bishops only. Nothing, as it seems to me, can shew more plainly the corporate character combined with the divinely descended administration of the powers of the Spirit-bearing Church than the whole of the primitive practice in this most important matter of ordination.

That we have lost, lost unspeakably, by losing the full sympathy, assistance, co-operation, and consequent joint-responsibility of the lay-people in respect of ordination, is, alas! only too clear. I will not now speak of the subject of their aid in selection, further than to allude to the immense accession of strength and influence which could not fail to be imparted to all church work, if the spiritual men whose duty it was to take the lead in such work were themselves deliberately chosen by careful, earnest, prayerful selection on the part of all those[1], clergy and laymen, whom they were to be called to govern, and if thus the action of the whole Church in its Spirit-bearing strength might be made to tell upon the choice of fit men as pastors for the charge of the separate portions of the flock. But who can think of the large amount of earnestness and piety, of energetic zeal for God, which has gradually broken away from the outward unity of the Church in this country, bringing division, opposition, unkindness, and extreme danger of mistaken teaching of all kinds, without reflecting sadly upon the narrowness which has surely on our side helped to make the breach and to keep it open; and without most earnest prayer that God will of His great mercy give us all such heavenly wisdom and charity as may teach us how to gather again into the one fold those who love the Lord in sincerity; to avail ourselves of many real gifts in men who are now separated from us,

[1] Vide Note HHII.

and so to enable us to speak with that one heart and one voice to the world by which the world is to know and accept the divine mission of the Redeemer?

No doubt it does not belong to my special subject to dwell upon such thoughts now; but I cannot refrain from expressing my own belief that as by the gradual elimination of the lay share and the lay responsibility in the various actions of the body of Christ, the evil we so deeply lament has been in part caused, so by the restoration of ancient practice under the great primitive principle, that melancholy evil might in some degree be remedied. That the special priestly powers descend by due imposition of hands from the apostles, and may not be invaded without sacrilege, we hold fast as one of the chief pillars of the constitution of the Church of Christ; but saving this, there is immense scope, as there is boundless need, for the action of earnest men, if with wise and charitable and loving hearts, with large united counsel, we would address ourselves to the task of winning them to an orderly share in the great work which we all have in common.

There is one other important branch of the subject which it is necessary to touch upon, however briefly and lightly, before we leave the general topic of the administration of the collective powers of the spirit-bearing body of Christ. I mean Absolution.

The origin of this power, so far as it can in any degree or in any sense be exercised by man, is of course to be sought in the gift of Christ bestowed upon the apostles by the Lord on the day of the resurrection, as recorded in the twentieth chapter of St. John's Gospel, when 'He breathed on them, and said, Receive ye the Holy Ghost: whose soever sins ye remit, they are remitted unto them; and whose soever sins ye retain, they are retained[m].' This power so given, the Lord had promised twice before: once, as written in the sixteenth chapter of St. Matthew, when in answer to the great confession of St. Peter He had said, 'Thou art Peter, and upon this rock I will build my Church; and the gates of hell shall not prevail against it. And I will give unto thee the keys of the kingdom of heaven: and whatsoever thou shalt bind on earth shall be bound in heaven, and whatsoever thou shalt loose on earth shall be loosed in heaven[n].' At which time we understand Him to have spoken to St. Peter as the representative of the Twelve; and again, in the eighteenth chapter of St. Matthew[o], when giving direction as to what His followers should do when brother sinned against brother, He repeated the same words respecting the Church in general which he had already spoken to St. Peter, and in him to the Twelve.

Let it be observed here what a close parallelism there is between the double promise and the double fulfilment. As the Lord gave the same promise first to the Twelve

---

[m] St. John xx. 22.   [n] St. Matt. xvi. 18, 19.
[o] Ibid. xviii. 18.

represented by St. Peter, and then to the Church in general, so when the Holy Spirit was given was the actual gift as double as the promise had been before. First to the Twelve, the breath of the Lord Himself gave it as recorded in the twentieth chapter of St. John; and then again on the great day of Pentecost, the actual descent of the Holy Spirit gave it to the Twelve as representing the whole body of believers.

From this observation we seem to find a clue to the somewhat difficult question which has perplexed interpreters of Holy Scripture of all times; the relation, I mean, which the gift of the resurrection-day bears to the gift of the day of Pentecost. For while it seems difficult on the one hand to suppose that words so plain as those used by our Lord in the twentieth chapter of St. John imparted no real gift, 'insomuch that,' as Hooker says, 'it were absurd to imagine that our Saviour did both to the ear, and also to the very eye express a real donation, and yet they at that time receive nothing,' yet on the other hand it is very difficult to distinguish as separate gifts the power to remit and retain sins of the resurrection-day, and the power to baptize for the remission of sins which was undoubtedly given at Pentecost; besides that we believe that all other methods whereby sins are forgiven spring and issue from the covenanted remission, promised, upon the due use of the means of obtaining it, in holy baptism. And to this again is to be added the general force of the statement that the Holy Ghost was not given till Jesus was glorified in the Ascension [p], and that He might not send the other Paraclete before He Himself was gone away in the flesh. From the consideration of this difficulty several of the ancients, as Theophylact, Euthymius, Aquinas, conclude that the apostles did not actually receive the Holy Ghost upon that former occasion, but were made capable of receiving it. But may not the interpretation which I have indicated give sufficient explanation of the difficulty? The gift on the resurrection-day designated, for all time, the personal administrators of that power from on high which was to be actually given to the whole Spirit-bearing body at Pentecost. The gift on the resurrection-day marked, empowered, and distinguished for perpetual succession those who were to be the organs and representatives of the whole Church in regard to these high powers, when the Holy Spirit who conveyeth the powers should be actually given. There is no need to suppose that the distinction lies in the powers, as though some were given at one time and some at another, and so it were necessary to find some difference between them. The two givings, like the two promises in St. Matthew's Gospel, were really givings of the same gift; but the one marked and empowered, and by an antepast of grace sanctified the organs or channels, through the agency of which the actual powers which the other gave should be,

[p] St. John vii. 39; xvi. 7.

in orderly communication, administered to mankind [q]. If I may borrow an illustration from the narrative of the miracle of the giving of sight to the blind man as recorded in the eighth chapter of St. Mark, it is as though on the former occasion the eye, not without a certain amount of visual power, had been created as an organ, and on the latter the body were put in full possession of its mighty collective life, and the brain won the divine skill of transforming all that organic power into real and perfect sight.

What then do we understand to be the continuing power which these sacred words bestowed upon the apostles first, and still bestow upon those who by due ordination succeed to their place? If it be true, as I have suggested, that they designated and empowered, in the first instance, the personal organs of that plenary authority which, fifty days later, was poured in its fulness upon the whole Church, what do we believe to be the still living effect which they have upon those whom the apostles by imposition of their hands put into their own place before they died, and those who still by the perpetual succession of the same rite, hold the same proportionate position in the body of Christ?

There can be no doubt that all covenanted remission of sins given in any way through the agency of man in the Church of Christ, has its root and beginning, to the receiver, in holy baptism. This I presume is the mean-

[q] Acts i. 8.

ing of the clause in the Nicene Creed, 'I believe one baptism for the remission of sins.' The efficacy of repentance, the effect of absolution, the pardon involved in the growth of grace in general, and in the communion of the body and blood of Christ in particular, and if there be any other means whereby sins are forgiven, all have their origin in the great gift of holy baptism, which is the imparting of present, and the covenant of all future forgiveness.

It might have been thought that the gift of the twentieth chapter of St. John would have confined the whole subject of the remission of sins, so far, I mean, as human agency might be employed in it, absolutely to the apostles, and their personal successors; that so baptism, with all its covenanted consequences, and all the subsequent methods, should have been given into their hands exclusively to administer to the people. And no doubt the theory of the relation borne by the clergy to the body of Christ would have been more systematically perfect if this had been the case. But as has been shewn in a former Lecture, the prerogative of God's mercy infringes upon the strictness of the theory, and it has been ascertained to be His will that the use of elemental water with the sacred words, by whomsoever administered, suffice to bring into the fold and flock of God any soul of man, at least to such extent as that the germ of spiritual life, though not the fulness of spiritual living, should be given thereby. We thankfully acknowledge the gracious truth. But with this exception the general theory remains complete. Even in baptism the general order of the Church confines the usual and orderly administration of the Sacrament to the clergy, while to the bishops alone is given the power of completing by laying on of hands the irregular and imperfect gift when given by lay or other unauthorized agency. But all the other methods of divine forgiveness, subsequent to that of baptism, in so far forth as they are conveyed through human agency to those who are by baptism made capable of receiving them, are, without exception, delivered to the clergy, bishops and priests, under the original charter of the words of the Lord, sealed by His most holy breath, to be conveyed to His people.

Putting aside then, until the next Lecture, the whole subject of self-examination and repentance, that is to say the privileges of the Personal Priesthood, whereby every baptized man has his own separate right of access to the Father through Christ, we may observe in general that the ministry of absolution is correlative to the ministry of discipline, that loosing answers to binding, and that sin either public and notorious so as to offend the congregation, or so weighty and grievous, though secret, as to burthen and distress the conscience beyond its own unassisted power of obtaining peace, requires the aid of the collective powers of the Spirit-bearing Church in order to give it that correction first, and after due repentance that assured peace and restoration to the favour of God which such sin had greatly endangered. These collective powers it is the special privilege of the priesthood to administer, and I own myself at a loss to understand how any person who believes in the continual presence, even to the end of the world, of Christ with His Church, and by consequence, the perpetual maintenance of the powers with which He originally endowed the Church, can doubt the fact that it is so.

This is the meaning of that precept of St. James, 'Confess your faults one to another, and pray one for another, that ye may be healed [r].' For in the body of Christ in general there is a power of healing different from that which is in each separate member of that body, and able to supplement and fill up its deficiencies. This is at least part—the chief part—of the meaning of that πόδας νίψασθαι [s], that washing of one another's feet, which even they require who have been wholly bathed in the bath of baptism. 'For whereas,' says St. Augustine, 'as long as we live in the midst of human things the earth is necessarily trodden: so our very human affections, without which we cannot live in this mortal state, are as feet. But if we thus confess our sins, He who washed His disciples' feet forgiveth us our sins, down to the feet wherewith we walk upon the earth [t].'

Inherent then in the whole body, as one of the main

---

[r] St. James v. 16.   [s] St. John xiii. 10.
[t] Vide Note III.

incidents of its collective priestliness, and administered by those who hold by due succession under the sacred breath of Christ as breathed upon the twelve, this great power is plainly twofold, according to the words of the Lord who gave it. The power of binding or of retaining sins, and the power of loosing or remitting them.

In respect of the former of these kinds of power, besides that the words of Christ in the eighteenth chapter of St. Matthew promise it distinctly to the Church in general, and not to a separate class within the Church, the single case of discipline recorded with particulars in the New Testament—I mean the case of the incestuous sin spoken of in the two Epistles to the Corinthians[u]—seems to shew beyond question where such power resided, and in what manner it was to be exercised. 'For I verily,' says St. Paul, 'being absent in body, but present in spirit, have judged already, as though I were present, concerning him that hath so done this deed, in the name of our Lord Jesus Christ, ye being gathered together, and my spirit, with the power of our Lord Jesus Christ, to deliver such an one unto Satan for the destruction of the flesh, that the spirit may be saved in the day of the Lord.' See here the authority of excommunication. The power of the Lord Jesus Christ, the authority of the apostle, the assembly of the Corinthian Church. It was a

[u] 1 Cor. v. 3-5 ; 2 Cor. ii. 5.

public scandal, a case in which the Church of Corinth should have mourned, that he that did this deed might be removed from among them. And again, when the Corinthians obeyed the apostle, and the offender was excommunicated, St. Paul repeats in other terms a like statement of the authority under which the act of forgiveness or absolution was done: 'sufficient to such a man is this punishment which was inflicted by the more part of you[x].' 'To whom ye forgive anything, I forgive also, for indeed what I have forgiven, if I have forgiven anything for your sakes forgave I it in the person of Christ.' See here again the course of authority: the person of Christ in whom alone is the real spring and source of power, the enjoining apostle, the punishment inflicted and the comfort given,—not apparently unanimously, but by the greater part of the Christians of Corinth.

In like manner the power of loosing or remitting sins, ultimately residing, under Christ, in the Church, and entrusted to those for administration who are authorized by divine descent of ordination to exercise it, is given to help to peace and recovery of grace those who, by public sentence or by the secret consciousness of sin, feel the face of God averted from their souls, and crave the aid which He has mercifully given for their restoration.

In the ordinary offices of public prayer, where many

[x] Ἱκανὸν τῷ τοιούτῳ ἡ ἐπιτιμία ἡ ὑπὸ τῶν πλειόνων. 2 Cor. ii. 6.

Christians unite their voices in general confession, each articulating, so to speak, the general tones and language of the confession-prayer with his own personal conscience of sin and sorrow, the voice of priestly absolution continually falls as an unfailing and gentle dew from heaven, freshening the hearts that are laying their griefs before the Lord, while it adds to the comfort of their personal priestliness the further assurance of pardon, wherewith the collective priestliness of the whole Church of God is authorized to support, uphold, and strengthen their peace.

Moreover, inasmuch as the sacrament of the Lord's Supper is, as has already been explained, the sacrament of the complete restoration of the separate members of the body, operating to the perfect re-union of the whole body, it follows that in that sacrament, in the preparation for it beforehand, and in the actual administration of it, the most special and characteristic exercise of that power is to be found. Those who are in notorious sin, whereby the congregation is offended, are to be repelled from communion, and not re-admitted to it until restored by due absolution upon repentance; and those who are in such distress of mind from the burthen of secret sin as to feel themselves unfit to communicate, and really, though without the knowledge of others, outside for the present of the pale of God's people, are by the ministry of God's Holy Word to receive from the priest the benefit of absolution, together with ghostly counsel and advice, to the quieting of their conscience, and avoiding of all scruple and doubtfulness. So before: and in the actual scene of Holy Communion again, but with stronger and clearer voice now than in the daily prayers, the accents of the priestly Church uttered through her priestly organ, assure with authoritative comfort those who turn to God with hearty repentance and true faith, of God's unfailing promise of the forgiveness of their sins.

And, in the time of heavy and dangerous sickness—in the time when death seems to be impending, when the conscience is likely to be burthened with weighty matters lightly regarded, perhaps hardly remembered at all in the days of health and strength, when bodily and mental powers are enfeebled, and the heart is tempted to sink down and despair under the prospect of appearing immediately in the presence of the most holy God with all its sins upon it,—is the blessed comfort of the solemn confession to God in the presence of His priest, and the tender administration of God's Holy Word and promise, crowned by the audible words of authorized and express absolution, not to be refused to the afflicted and dying sinner, humbly and heartily desiring it. O let no shrinking from the honest and faithful use of the divinely descended powers that come to the Church and to her priest from the holy words and breath of Christ,—let no base fears of worldly objection or scorn lead a priest of God to grudge to his dying brother the clear, outspoken, ringing words of holy absolution, which the Church has put into his mouth, which the sad sinner humbly and heartily craves, which his faithful full confession has earned! Do not mock the dying patient by reminding him that he too is a physician. Do not cheat the broken-hearted penitent by telling him that he is a priest himself. God has provided an express comfort for him in his extremity of distress. God has given to you, and to none but you, the very anodyne for his poor soul's pain. You are cruel, you are faithless, you are untrue to your holy calling and duty, if, out of fear of man, you shrink from using it.

Nor let it be supposed that in this last case the priest is claiming to exercise any other powers than those which he exercises in the more ordinary cases of the absolutions in the Daily Service, and in the Communion Office. No doubt the words in which he is directed in the Prayer-book to pronounce the sentence of forgiveness are different—perceptibly and markedly different—in the three cases. But the difference arises not from any difference in his own power, but from the difference in the circumstances under which the same identical power is exercised. In the Daily Service he is speaking to a mixed congregation, consisting of he knows not whom. To them, as having just united their voices with his own in confession to the throne of the heavenly grace, he, standing up in the power of his holy office while they kneel, pronounces the sentence of God's assured absolution and remission of sins to such as 'truly repent and unfeignedly believe His holy Gospel.' In the Communion Office, where none are (or ought to be) present and taking part, except such as ought to have given their names at least some time the day before, and by their presence profess to repent truly and earnestly of their sins, to be in love and charity with their neighbours, and to intend to lead a new life of holiness and obedience, the priest's words of absolution take a stronger tone. Speaking with the authority which God has given to him, he addresses them expressly to the people present. That which in the former case had sounded only like a general statement of forgiveness on God's part to the penitent and faithful, is now not put any longer in the mere form of a statement, but in that of a conveyance directed expressly to the persons actually present in the Church. In the Visitation Service, where the penitent is one only, and he very sick, and probably with death in prospect, where he feels his conscience troubled with weighty matters, where he has made special confession of his sins to Almighty God in the priest's hearing, so that the priest verily and with good ground believes that he has poured out the secrets of his heart in full and unreserved sorrow for his sins, there,—on his own humble and hearty desire, the priest is bidden to speak without further reservation the sentence of absolution, free and full, which the divine succession that dates from the sacred breath and the holy words of Christ Himself, to which I have so often referred, empower him to pronounce. But all the three absolutions of the Prayer-book are to be understood as throwing mutual light upon each other. As, on the one hand, the power claimed and exercised in the last and most strongly worded of them is not less truly present in the second and in the first, so that both in the Communion Office and the daily prayers the more general methods of statement by the priest of God's forgiveness wheresoever repentance and faith are present, do actually convey to any who have made their confession in such real repentance and true faith the actual and undoubted sentence of delegated absolution not less certainly nor less strongly than the stronger form of the Visitation Service, so, on the other hand, the strong form of the Visitation Service is to be interpreted by the sober and general statements of the other absolutions; and the priest's words are not to be understood further than as the more clear and unreserved expression of that delegated authority whereby he is empowered to carry home to the trembling and anxious soul of the single penitent to whom he speaks, the blessed truth that God in whom alone resides any conceivable power to forgive the sins of His creatures, doth truly pardon and absolve him, as 'He pardoneth and absolveth all them that truly repent and unfeignedly believe His holy Gospel.'

But while we desire to vindicate, as an undoubted power of the priesthood, the divinely descended authority of pronouncing the sentence of sacred absolution upon true repentance, it is never to be forgotten that it is in the very essential nature of that power to be remedial, helpful, and, if I may so call it, supplemental. The first and foremost doctrine of the Gospel on the subject of the forgiveness of sins is surely this,—that as it is certainly given freely and fully in holy baptism to all such as receive that sacrament in true repentance and faith, so after baptism it is no less freely and fully promised to all those who continually turn in like repentance and faith back again to God. This we must lay down with the most unreserved and unhesitating confidence as one of the very first principles of the divine doctrine of the Gospel. 'For if we confess our sins, God is faithful and just to forgive us our sins, and to cleanse us from all unrighteousness.' But it is of the great and tender mercy of God also that, knowing the frailty of man and his liability to heavy and continual sin, and knowing too the weakness of his heart, and the self-distrusting feebleness of the conscience, very often as little able to support itself as a broken reed when really awakened to the full sense of its guilt and danger, He has added to this gracious scheme of restoration what I have called the remedial and supplementary institution whereby the collective priestliness of the universal body may operate to support and supply the otherwise failing and imperfect strength of the single guilty and desponding Christian. But it is of the utmost importance to keep in mind this its remedial and supplementary character. It is not to be in any degree a substitute for conscience.

It is not to be in any degree a substitute for personal strength, for self-direction, for personal communion with God in prayer, for living in the conscious sight and presence of the Holy Spirit, who face to face with the soul, and deeply penetrating its most inward and profound secrets, searcheth, and is ready and willing to strengthen and sanctify it, if it will be strengthened and sanctified, with a power which needs no help nor aid nor addition of any conceivable kind.

And I cannot doubt that the practice of continual confession to a priest, and the craving for continual absolution at his hands—much more the habit of seeking constant 'direction,' as it is called, of conscience from him, has a distinctly enfeebling effect upon the personal strength with which a Christian ought to learn to walk before God, and to order his own steps according to His law. It is with things spiritual as it is with things natural in this respect. To lean unduly upon helps, to depend for guidance upon other men further than is absolutely necessary, is to betray the personal powers which God designed that we should cultivate, and to lose the precious lessons which such cultivation is intended to teach us. Add to which that the same practice has a dangerous tendency to weaken the sense of the Holy Spirit's presence in the heart, and the awful consciousness of the searching and unerring scrutiny with which He sees and knows and balances with the most exact and unfailing rightfulness, the very truth of man's secret being, the reality of his repentance, the depth of his devotion, the real nature and heinousness of his sin. For man cannot look into the heart of man; nor can man convey to man in words, except in the roughest and most imperfect way, the actual reality, the full true reality of the consciousness that is within him. Words are too strong sometimes, sometimes too weak, always inadequate; they leave untold great tracts of consciousness, and the more they are multiplied in the attempt to tell them, are apt to leave them untold all the more. The impressions which words convey are uncertain, fallacious—now too weak, now too strong, now mistaken, always uncertain. But He with whom we have to do, the Word of God, and His Spirit, is living, and powerful, 'and sharper than any two-edged sword, piercing even to the dividing asunder of soul and spirit, and of the joints and marrow, and is a discerner of the thoughts and intents of the heart y.' He needeth no words. He maketh no mistakes. Everything is utterly manifest in His sight. To Him the heart may learn (and happy is the heart that so learns!) to open its grief with the certainty of the tenderest sympathy, with the certainty of the divinest appreciation, with the fulness of outpouring and confidence that belongs to those who know that when their heart condemns them, God, and God only, is greater than their heart, and knoweth all things z.

y Heb. iv. 12.   z 1 St. John iii. 20.

This in caution; in what I believe to be wise and necessary caution. To the baptized the offices of the personal priesthood in the way of repentance and forgiveness come first, those of the collective priesthood are secondary and subsidiary. It is a fault in theory, as it is dangerous in practice, to elevate them, or to run the risk of elevating them, into the first place. No doubt it is a question of degree. The line has to be drawn somewhere. It is in the Christian faithfulness—the brave Christian faithfulness of the penitent, and the Christian wisdom of the priest—to draw it with a very grave reserve, a reserve doubly necessary in a case where disuse, and much past corruption, and the obvious liability of various kinds of danger, and I will add, the scantiness of special and particular directions from authority, embarrass the exercise of a real, and in its own place, a most precious and sacred power.

And thus, brethren, I have endeavoured to trace the operation of the two great principles which I have laid down through the main ordinances of the Gospel, desiring to show that in them all, while the ultimate spiritual power and authority, so far as it is entrusted to man at all, resides in the universal Church, the body of Christ, the administration of it is put into the hands of a special priesthood, representative and organic, empowered by divine descent of ordination to exercise the various priestly functions upon themselves and their brethren. I have spoken very shortly upon each point, from the necessity of the case: and plainly; for if I may not speak plainly, I must not speak at all. If the principles that I have laid down are sound and true, they certainly are not unimportant. To your candid and thoughtful consideration I commend them.

It only now remains to speak of the personal priesthood of every single Christian—that blessed and sacred right of access, whereby each baptized member of the body of Christ is free to approach his merciful Father which is in heaven, in the strength of the Holy Spirit, and with the sacred assurance of the Divine love and favour won for him by the blood of Christ.

LECTURE VIII.

THE PERSONAL PRIESTHOOD.

For by one Spirit we are all baptized into one body, whether we be Jews or Gentiles, whether we be bond or free; and have been all made to drink into one Spirit.—1 Cor. xii. 13.

THUS far I have spoken of the exterior administration of the Holy Spirit of God to the souls of men, through the operation of the Church, the body of Christ. There is no occasion to recapitulate at present the view which I have taken, which must be abundantly familiar to those who have heard the preceding Lectures. I believe that view to be sound and true; and though I cannot pretend to find it either laid down as a thesis, or stated in its completeness by ancient writers, yet I venture to think that in all its main and essential particulars, it will be found to pervade the writers of the ancient fathers, and to be present as a basis of doctrine in the sober theology of the chief writers of the Church of England. I also believe the view which I have taken to be one capable of leading to results by no means few or unimportant, if it should be adopted in its breadth and fulness. For it seems to recognise the justice and the place in the Christian scheme of a great number of points held with much force as characteristic by various Christian bodies, while it rejects such as, though held with equal force by those bodies, have been regarded by other Christians as their characteristic errors; and that, not in the way of an eclectic or arbitrary piecing of heterogeneous materials, but in the way of consistent and clear consequence from an intelligent, and, I hope, not unfounded theory. With the Roman Catholics it acknowledges the peculiar powers of the priesthood, and claims for them exclusively the administrative functions which are derived from the long descent of the Holy Spirit, ever since the breath and words of Christ first imparted it to the Twelve on the resurrection day. With the school of the late Dr. Arnold, it altogether admits and insists upon the personal priesthood of every baptized member of the body of Christ, and, by consequence, his unimpeded access, in all the offices of personal devotion, to the grace and favour of God for Christ's sake. But it adds to both that which both greatly need, the full confession of the other part of the great twofold truth, which each in its turn has lost, holding that the inherent priestliness of the whole body helps, in a way that cannot be dispensed with, the official priestliness of the organic priesthood, and that the organic priesthood, in various departments of its exercise, is requisite, as to produce, so also to maintain and keep up in its full strength and under its deep occasional needs, the priestliness of each single member of the entire body. With the whole Church of God of ancient, and, I may add, of modern times, it acknowledges the absolute authority of Holy Scripture, down to the smallest details of what is written; but it lays itself open to no critical attacks as to the methods, or degrees, or limits of Divine inspiration in the sacred writers, being content to believe that in an historical religion, the continuity of which extends over wellnigh four thousand years, and of which every part and portion is essentially necessary to all the rest, it is a sound as well as an inevitable conclusion, that God has given to each age the specific duty of determining those points which it alone has the means of determining, and that thus every single part of the whole connected scheme or fabric becomes a real evidence and a satisfactory proof of all the rest. So, having received the books of Holy Writ as a sacred inheritance from those ages which alone had the duty, because they alone had the means, of forming a judgment upon their authority, we may on this view decline to examine and re-examine for ever questions which have been settled, and respecting which the greater part of the evidence which once existed, has in the course of things, that is, in the providence of God, perished.

I also venture to think that, if both sides of the great twofold truth which it has been my wish to put forward were fully realized in their respective and united strength, they might be found to help in throwing light upon many questions of no slight importance and difficulty which are now pressing upon the Church. For example, the extremely urgent question of winning back into the full communion and brotherhood of the Church the Wesleyan body,—men who by no professed difference of doctrine, nor, apparently, by any insuperable difference in respect of discipline,—with great gifts of earnestness and influence, have slid away from us, against their founder's earnest desire and repeatedly expressed warning,—might seem to be not wholly incapable of solution, if we took deeply into our hearts the mighty scope for every sort of various action in the Church, which the full doctrine of the general priestliness of all the members of the body of Christ brings prominently into view. In like manner, the whole subject of non-established Churches, as in the colonies,—a subject daily growing in importance, and imperatively requiring some well-considered and deeply-digested method of uniform settlement, is never seen in so true a light as when both parts of the twofold truth which I have insisted upon, are fairly and fully recognised. The isolation and quasi-despotic action of the single bishop, or of several bishops together, very feeble as it can hardly fail to be, if he or they be regarded as the only holders of sacred spiritual authority, is at once changed into an infinitely greater, because truer and more truly founded power, if it be backed and supported by the full momentum of the priestly Church or Churches over which they rule. Even the more difficult and complicated questions which arise in respect of Churches established by law, gain a reflex light from the practical exhibition of principles in such Churches as are by the condition of the circumstances so placed as to be able to act them freely and fully out.

We have now to consider, in conclusion, the personal priesthood, so to call it, of every single Christian man, whereby (putting out of sight for the present the graces which are continually ministered to him by the agencies of others) he, singly and alone, in the dignity of his own real and personal priestliness, has direct and unimpeded access to God, now become his loving Father in Christ.

It is necessary at this point to consider with some attention what information is given to us in Holy Scripture respecting the origin and beginning of the work of God in its secret dealings with the heart of man, in order that we may trace in some degree the distinct threads, if I may so speak, of Divine grace—that of the inward and personal, and secret operations of the Holy Spirit in the soul on the one hand, and that which belongs to exterior and appointed methods of sacramental and covenanted efficacy on the other. Both, according to the Divine scheme of religion, are necessary to the full Christian perfection of each member of the body of

Christ. But they are not identical, and they must not be confounded. Neither can be spared in the examination of the true history of the Christian soul, without the risk of serious evil arising from the omission.

'Whence is it,' asks St. Basil the Great, in that most precious Treatise on the Holy Spirit, 'that we are Christians? Through faith, every one would answer. And how is it that we are saved? No doubt, by having been born again through the grace of baptism. For from what other source can it be?' 'Faith and baptism, the two means of salvation, are of like nature with one another, and not to be divided. For faith is perfected by baptism, and baptism is founded upon faith, and each is effected by the same Divine names. For as we believe in the Father, and the Son, and the Holy Ghost, so also are we baptized into the Name of the Father, and the Son, and the Holy Ghost. The confession going before leadeth the way to salvation, and baptism following after setteth the seal to our assent [a].'

Weighty words these, and capable, if they be carefully considered, of furnishing a clue to lead us through the intricacy of the subject on which we speak.

For what is this precedent faith, which thus going before leadeth the way unto salvation, upon which baptism following after thus setteth the seal? It is surely a personal, secret, inward growth, begun when first the soul of man, touched inwardly by the illuminating and

[a] Vide Note KKK.

sanctifying grace of the Holy Ghost, turns [b] itself, and is turned towards the acceptance and love of Divine truth, and culminating in that fulness of assured conviction which is ready to receive the impression of the seal of God in the outwardly administered sacrament of Holy Baptism.

No doubt the whole world is in such sort full of the operation of the Holy Spirit of God, that all that is in any degree good or holy, or tending to goodness or holiness in created things, is derived from that single source. We do not doubt that the holy angels themselves depend for all their stability, their order, their foreknowledge, their powers of acceptable duty and praise, upon His gift. In the power and by the gift of the Holy Spirit, our first father, like the rest of the visible creation, was made very good. And all that remained of good after the Fall among his descendants, whether in the favoured race of Abraham the friend of God, or in the heathen nations, came in like manner from the free overflowing mercy of God in the Holy Spirit.

All this in general: but this would not have brought men to God in Christ, nor have sufficed to begin the

---

[b] 'O wondrous chain! where aye entwine
   Our human wills, a tender thread,
   With the strong will Divine!
   We run as we are led.'
   Miscellaneous Poems by the Rev. John Keble.

actual movement of their hearts in the direction of faith, properly so called, without some intervention of express human teaching. (For 'how shall they believe in Him of whom they have not heard? and how shall they hear without a preacher?') So wonderfully even in its inmost operations the work of God is blended with the work of men, and needs its joint action.

When then, in the merciful providence of God, the due preacher is sent with the message of the Gospel—that message which, revealing the depth and enormity of human sin by the greatness of the sacrifice required for its forgiveness, reveals also the infinite love of Him who is at once the Priest and the Victim, the Mediator and the Judge—why is it that that message falls upon various hearts with so very different power, and receives so different welcome? Why is it that one heart, recognising its own sinfulness and inability of help, clings with the warmest, most intense and earnest clinging to the tidings of the crucified Lord, while others, commonly the most, either scorn it, or at least give it little heed, and pass it by?

No doubt, as in other and more general ways, the uncovenanted overflowings of the Holy Spirit have never altogether deserted the fallen race of man, so it has been also in this more especial and definite instance. As it was by the Holy Spirit that the voice of the preacher was sent to cry aloud in the wilderness of ignorance and sin, so was it also by the unseen operation of that same Holy Spirit that the hearts of men turned and opened themselves, like the heart of Lydia the seller of purple of Thyatira, to believe and welcome the blessed words of the Gospel[c]. Not necessarily at once, not necessarily with any outward observation, not necessarily with any direct or visible connexion with the preacher's words, the Holy Spirit of the Most High God doth sow in the hearts of men that secret seed of Divine faith, which, not yet assured of increase, nor of the means of increase, and liable to be overpowered by all sorts of alien and poisonous growths, feeble, insecure, perhaps temporary only, is yet the beginning of that personal faith, that sacred confession of and from the heart, which, according to the words of St. Basil, leadeth the way unto salvation.

I speak for the present of adult baptism only, as exhibiting the theory of Divine grace in its simplest and most intelligible form; and so speaking, I venture to say that there must be in each single soul of man a secret, original, separate springing of Divine grace, constituting the first beginning of that personal faith, which, as it first leads the way to salvation, so lives on, with whatever increase and addition and help and assurance to be afterwards given, and forms the necessary basis of the personal priesthood of each single Christian, and, as it were, the ground and capacity of life in his soul.

[c] Acts xvi. 14.

So, I say, in respect to the simpler and more readily intelligible case of adult baptism: but how stands the case in respect to persons baptized in infancy, when vicarious faith is for the time accepted in place of personal faith, and the outwardly administered grace begins before the child is old enough to be capable of any personal or conscious turning to God in Christ? For vicarious faith is not the same thing as personal faith, nor equivalent to personal faith, except in the case of infants dying in infancy; and personal, conscious, and willing faith is, at least in all other cases, that which leadeth the way to salvation.

No doubt the Holy Spirit of grace, imparted through the outward administration of water and the holy words, is so surely present with every baptized child, as to enable him, in proportion to his growth of mind, to listen and take in, with that loving childish heart, which is of itself of the nature of Divine and Christian faith, the early measures of sacred doctrine taught by his mother's lips: and many, no doubt, there are in every Christian country in whom the two threads, as I have called them, of Divine grace have been so undistinguishably blent and interwoven in all their lives, that there has never been a time, since the blessed birth of the font, when, frail and uncertain and tottering as they have felt their faith and obedience to be, they have been otherwise than growing under the joint and sacred influence of inwardly cultivated and outwardly accepted grace. But this, though the due, and I firmly believe, by no means an unusual, or other than an usual case, is very far indeed from being an universal one; and, alas! we know only too well that there are multitudes in whom, though vicarious faith has been allowed to admit them to the holy sacramental and outwardly administered gifts of Divine grace, yet, so far as man can judge, there has not sprung up, under the action of the inwardly operating Spirit of God, that personal and sacred faith, that conscious willing faith which leadeth unto salvation, which assimilates the blessed exterior gifts of grace, and which is absolutely necessary to form the basis of the high position of personal priesthood in Christ. They need a true, real, inward conversion of the soul. They need a real personal beginning of active, however secret and invisible, vitality in the soul by the action of the Holy Spirit. They need a real personal beginning, conscious and willing, of that spiritual virtue of holy faith within them which leadeth the way unto salvation. I do not know whether I have succeeded in making my meaning clear; and this is a point on which I would fain not be misunderstood. I mean to distinguish three separate cases :—the first, the simplest, where in the conversion of persons of mature age, the faith that leads the way to salvation springs in the heart first, secretly, divinely, and is after a time so far matured as to receive the seal of holy baptism; the second, the happiest, where vicarious faith is accepted for an infant child, and the indispensable personal faith grows up, regularly and sweetly strengthening, under the perpetual dew of the graces which descend upon it through all the exterior ministrations of Christ's Church; the third, the most anxious, where vicarious faith has been equally accepted for the child in unconscious infancy, but the signs of personal faith, the indications of the working of the Holy Spirit in the heart, the marks of the activity of the new nature bestowed by the new birth are, alas! not to be recognised. To such as these the conversion of the soul—a real, inward, secret turning of the soul to God in Christ (I do not speak of the fictitious conversions, the foolish excitements which afflict our poor country parishes, scattering away all sober reverence, engendering all kinds of presumption and conceit)— a real, inward, secret turning of the soul to God in Christ, the secret work of the Holy Spirit, is absolutely needful.

For the outwardly administered gift has been given, and it has been received. The spark and germ of divine life is there: of that life which can only be begun once, and which, if once extinct, absolutely extinct, knows no means [d] of restoration. No doubt it may be latent long, and to human eyes completely latent, and yet by no means lost. It may give no visible indication whatever of its presence for many

[d] Heb. vi. 4-8.

years, and yet not really have expired; dormant indeed, yet real still, awaiting the hope of revival in the springing up of real faith and repentance. 'Now,' says St. Basil (meaning by the word 'now' this present life), 'even though the Holy Spirit is not wholly mingled with the unworthy, yet doth He appear to be present in a certain manner with those who have been once sealed, awaiting their salvation by means of repentance. But then'—that is, when the next world is come, and the unworthy have not repented—'He will be altogether cut away from the soul that has profaned His grace [e].'

And therefore I hail the preaching of conversion as a great need of these unspiritual times; not such a preaching as should in any degree depreciate the blessed gift of Holy Baptism, God forbid! nor such as should lead any one to doubt the exceeding happiness of such as from the blessing of Christian homes, and early imbibing of the rich gifts which belong to the infant child of God, have never known the dreariness of feeling exiled, the dry heart which cannot pray, the feeling of scornful doubt and unbelief: but such a preaching of conversion as might by the blessing of God be not unhelpful towards wakening up the beginnings of that personal faith and repentance—that conscious and willing faith and repentance—which, alike in the baptized and those who are not yet baptized, leadeth the way unto salvation. For how shall the corporate blessings

[e] Vide Note LLL.

of the Church of God produce their effect upon a heart which, though duly baptized in vicarious faith, has never learned by its own faith and repentance to digest and, as it were, assimilate them? Is it not plain that every blessing of Holy Communion, the blessing of joint prayer, the blessing of priestly absolution—every blessing that flows down upon the single member from the vitality of the whole body—must depend for its effect upon the existence of an inward liveliness of faith in that single member? As the sap will not flow from the healthiest tree into a branch which by decay has become incapable of receiving it, so will not the choicest graces which are imparted to the separate members of the life-giving body, reach the soul which is not by its own proper faith and intended holiness in a fit condition to receive and entertain them. As again, a branch grafted into another tree, cannot convey the rich sap which is to make it swell into bud and flower, and enable it to ripen fruit, unless it have a certain amount of original life, as well as a capacity of receiving further and borrowed life within itself, so neither can the member, grafted into the body of our Lord Jesus Christ, taste and convey the graces of the body, unless he have such personal life of faith in himself as shall enable him to receive and assimilate those graces. His own faith must needs discern the Lord's body in Holy Communion, or else to him, for any blessing to be derived from it, it is not the Lord's body. His own faith must give sincerity and filial sorrow to his confession, fervency and real outpouring of heart to his prayers, reality and strength to his repentance, or else the voice of the united prayers of the Church is to him but as the tinkling of cymbals, and the utterances of priestly absolution but as drops which, while they sink deeply and with divine power into the rich and good soil of a neighbour's heart, run off from his as from the hard rock without the slightest benefit or fertilizing effect.

But besides such personal sincerity and faith as will enable a Christian man to receive and entertain the graces which flow richly down upon him from the body of Christ, through its authorized channels, and by the agency of its appointed organs, he also possesses a distinct priesthood of his own, which, while it forms part of that great and universal priesthood of which I have already often spoken, is for himself his full and sufficient right of admission and access to the presence and mercy of God in Christ.

In the power of this priesthood he may cultivate a true and perfect faith—faith of his own, faith which is acceptable to the Father for Christ's sake. I speak of faith now in the sense of that deep and self-abandoning reliance in which a man trusts himself, in body and soul, and in all that he loves, in his present interests and future hopes, altogether and perfectly to God. In the solitude of his own soul, where none may approach save the Holy Omnipresent Spirit of God, who seeth and knoweth every movement and wish and winding of his thought, he may by the unfailing help of that Holy Spirit learn to anchor himself in trust unfeigned and complete upon the love and mercy of God in Christ. He may learn to find a divine power in his faith, of strength sufficient to support him under any degree of earthly trouble or sorrow, giving him cheerfulness, calmness, and a lofty sense of the Divine presence in the utmost decay of outward fortune, in the severest and most afflicting dispensations of pain and sickness, even lasting on to the very last spark of consciousness, and the very gates of the grave. It is his own. It is the gift of God to the separate soul of His child in Christ. He possesses it alone. It is a treasure greater than anything else upon the earth. It is heaven in anticipation. It maketh the great and glorious things that are hoped for to be substantial to his soul, and evident though they are not seen.

In the sight and power of his own personal priesthood he has a right to the Holy Scriptures. They are undoubtedly, inalienably his. They are his to study, to read, to mark, to learn, and to digest them inwardly; so that from their light he may have a lantern for his path, and be ready at all times to render unto any that shall ask him a reason for the faith that is in him; and from the comfort and patient continuance in them he may constantly embrace and hold fast in his soul the blessed hope of everlasting life. It is a cruel injustice, and a miserable overthrow of the fundamental principles of the doctrine of the Church of God, the Spirit-bearing body of Christ, which would withhold,—which has withheld, and, alas! would still withhold—the life-giving word of God in Holy Scripture from the possession and study of any part or portion of the people of God. If any be ignorant, so as to be in danger of perverting or misusing the great gift of the open Bible, he is to be taught, that so his love may abound ever more and more in knowledge and all perception, that so he may discern the things that are more excellent, and thereby become sincere and without offence in the day of Christ. But to withhold from him the open Bible, the very written charter of his inheritance, is to deprive him of the very means—at least of one of the very greatest of the means—whereby he is to learn to do the good service in the Church of God which is due from every baptized member of the body. They are his to ponder, to learn by heart, to know with the fullest intimacy, to hide within his heart that he may have them at call to help him that he may not sin[f]; to have them in his house, to teach them to his children, to repeat them when he lieth down to rest, to repeat them when he lieth sleepless on his bed, when he waketh from his sleep, when he walketh by the way, when he sitteth down, and when he riseth up. They are sacredly, inalienably, for ever his; his as assuredly as the very air which he breathes, which is

[f] Ps. cxix. 11; Deut. xi. 18-21.

hardly more essential to his natural life than they are to his spiritual.

And together with the Holy Scripture, the divine rule of faith is his: for he has inherited it by the very right and title of his new birth—I mean the sacred doctrine of the Father, the Son, and the Holy Ghost[g], the holy triple Name of God into which he was baptized, that good Name that was called over him at the font, that sacred Name which is the sum of creeds.

His it is to believe, to hold fast, to study with all the helps of various knowledge that he can command; to understand more and more profoundly; to keep undefiled from the various tendencies of corruption that may assail it,—from injurious gloss, from unauthorized addition or subtraction threatening its clear and dogmatic purity and completeness, whencesoever they may come. It is not indeed his special calling, if he be a layman, to preach, or to be a public teacher of it. But his clear and well-trained Christian understanding is the due support of the teaching clergy, a support which they can ill spare: and for his own heart's food, and for the benefit of his children, and of those who in various ways come under his influence, his own sound and well-grounded faith in the objective and dogmatic truth of God, with which he and all the other members of the Spirit-bearing body are entrusted[h], is of a value which

---

[g] St. Matt. xxviii. 19; St. James ii. 7.
[h] Rom. iii. 2.

cannot be exaggerated, while the absence of it is a heavy and dangerous loss.

In the power of his own personal priesthood he may go before God in repentance and hearty confession of sin; laying his conscience bare before God, and weeping over sins—which no man knows, it may be, nor necessarily need know—whether they be sins of secret thought by which he has dishonoured God in the deep of his inner soul, or sins of word, or overt sins of deed and act, in the only presence of his loving and merciful Father which is in heaven. And in so doing he may entirely assure himself, that as certainly as his Father knoweth already all the details and aggravations of those sins, before he utters them in word, or mourns over them in heart, so certainly He loveth to see His son in Christ prostrate himself, with all the burthen of his soul, in filial confession at his feet. He has a right in Christ to the absolute assurance of forgiveness, in so far as he knows and feels, and does not deceive himself in knowing and feeling, that his repentance is real, and his confession earnest and true. He doth not need that any man should necessarily come between God and his own priestly soul, in order to win, or in any way to obtain for him the pardon and the peace which are promised to faithful confession; 'For if we confess our sins, He is faithful and just to forgive us our sins, and to cleanse us from all unrighteousness [i].'

[i] 1 St. John i. 9.

In the power of his own personal priesthood he may enter into his closet, and when he has shut to the door, he may fall on his knees and pray to his Father which is in secret, and his Father which seeth in secret will surely not fail to give him for Christ's sake such answer to his prayers as will be best for him to receive [k]. The promise is absolutely without exception, as it is without reservation or stint: 'Ask and ye shall have, seek and ye shall find, knock and it shall be opened unto you. For every one that asketh receiveth, and he that seeketh findeth, and to him that knocketh it shall be opened [l].' He doth not indeed of necessity receive the precise boon which he may have asked, for it may be for his greater good that such particular requests may be refused; but as long as he asks as his Lord asked, with the perpetual reservation, 'Nevertheless, not as I will, but as Thou wilt [m],' so long he may be sure that he will be as certainly heard as his Lord was heard, who knew that the Father heareth Him always [n], and whose prayer, though literally unfulfilled, was yet heard in that He feared [o]. In this priestly power of prayer (and prayer is one of the chiefly characteristic offices of priesthood) the child may pray at his mother's knee, the boy in the midst of the very real and very critical temptations of school-life, the young man in the searching trials which beset both body and mind in the days of the freshness of the powers of both, the man

[k] St. Matt. vi. 6.   [l] Ibid. vii. 7-12.   [m] Ibid. xxvi. 39.
[n] St. John xi. 42.   [o] Heb. v. 7.

in the secrecy of his chamber, in the midst of the stern realities of his life, the old man with grey hairs and feeble limbs, and with the daily nearing prospect of the grave before his eyes—one and all admitted with the freest, most loving and welcome access to the Father, who regardeth them all with good will and favour for His own dear Son's sake, one and all accepted in the beloved.

And as he may pray for himself, so may he make authorized and effective intercessions for others. 'Pray for one another that ye may be healed. The effectual fervent prayer of a righteous man,' whether that righteous man be clerical or lay, 'availeth much;' or, as we may render the forcible words of St. James more closely, 'very strong is the praying of a righteous man in its working [p].' It is a real and great power, a very energetic and active power, though science knows not of it, nor so-called philosophers believe in its existence. The father, praying for his family in all the various trials of their lives; the Christian mother for her boys and girls as they grow old enough to encounter the inevitable onset of all kinds of temptation; children, dutiful and loving Christian children for their parents and for each other; all in their various relations of life beseeching the grace and blessing of God for those with whom they are connected, whether as above them and with some responsibility of government over them, or as below them and

[p] πολὺ ἰσχύει δέησις δικαίου ἐνεργουμένη. St. James v. 16.

bound to render them obedience and duty ; friends mutually asking the prayers of friends, and paying back the kindly intercession by like earnest prayers of their own ; Christian men and women faithfully asking for the guiding grace of God upon the governors of the state in which they live, and upon all that bear rule and office and stewardship in the Church ;—there is a wonderful power, a mighty unseen network of holy intercessory prayer, a vast invisible force of incalculable strength at work in all this, which affects in infinitely various ways the well-being of men and women in their inward and in their outward lives, which touches the fortunes of nations more deeply and really than the triumphs of successful generals or the crafty wisdom of statesmen, which brings down the rich and varied blessing of God in ways which no thought can trace nor imagination limit, upon the complicated and wonderfully interwoven system of things that surrounds us, and of which we form our part.

All this, and much more than can be specified, is his, because of his personal priestliness ; and the secret origin of all this heavenly power, the real and only source of it, is in the undoubted presence of the almighty Spirit of God in his separate soul, as he is a member of the Spirit-bearing body of Christ. The single soul of the Christian man duly planted into the divine body, is a temple of God, or shall I call it, a chamber of the temple of God [q] upon the earth, wherein His sacred presence dwelleth.

[q] Vide Note MMM.

That single soul is, morning, noon and night, in the hours of sleep and of wakefulness, whether conscious of the presence and willing to encounter it, or unconscious of it and desirous to hide away its shame and guilt, face to face with the almighty Spirit of God. As Christ walketh in the midst of His great temple, built up of lively spiritual stones, so is each single stone instinct with that living Spirit, and the Christian man, whosoever and wheresoever he be, and whatsoever he doeth, cannot, if he would, flee from the almighty presence [r]. Not watched from without, but known from within; not occasionally seen and noticed, and sometimes overlooked; nor coerced nor overpowered; nor forced to believe or pray, or repent, but brought near to God,—provided that with conscious willingness of soul he be earnest to be so brought near,—with a wonderful nearness, while in the Holy Spirit, the Father and the Son both love him, and come unto him, and make their abode with him [s].

And the struggles, and the yearnings, and the efforts after good and holiness in that Christian man are indeed the strugglings and the yearnings and the longings of the Holy Spirit that is within him. The faith in his heart, in the strength of which he puts his whole trust and confidence in God in Christ, the devout study and inward digesting of Holy Scripture, the secret sacred meditation upon the holy mysteries of the revelation of

[r] Rom. viii. 9. [s] St. John xiv. 23.

the Name of God, the heart-deep confessions, the true outpoured prayers, whether personal or intercessory, are but the details of that great inward activity and work wherein the conscious and willing spirit of a man, sanctified, lifted, ennobled, glorified, if I may say so, by the indwelling Spirit of the most high God, is continually rising to a nearness and closeness to God which is itself the essence and perfection of the priestly condition. Won for him by the great sacrifice of the cross, brought home to himself through the agency of the organized body of Christ, the Church, yet so won and brought home to him, it is absolutely his. The Spirit of God itself from his heart maketh intercession for him [t] with groanings too profound, too divine, too infinitely various, mingled, subtle, and delicate to be capable of any adequate utterance in human words. And He that searcheth the heart knoweth what is the mind of the Spirit, that He maketh intercession for the saints according to the will of God.

So worketh on the earth that 'other Paraclete [u],' the blessed Spirit, who in the absence of the Lord of the Church in the flesh has been sent down to abide in the Church, to comfort, to instruct, to help and to sanctify the souls of His servants.

And that which thus the Paraclete upon the earth, the Paraclete in the souls of men, suggests, quickens, and keeps alive with a holy and divine activity, the Paraclete in heaven—He who sitteth at the right hand

[t] Rom. viii. 26.   [u] St. John xiv. 16.

of God to make intercession for us [x]—perpetually presents, in His own most holy Name and in the virtue and efficacy of His own most holy sacrifice, before His Father. Each is truly Comforter [y], truly Advocate. But if driven by the poverty of our language to distinguish, and so in some sort to divide, these offices, we may say that the Paraclete-Advocate in heaven, that is, our Lord Jesus Christ, knows no other prayers, nor acknowledges no other yearnings of the soul, nor presents no other petitions before His Father's throne than such as are the utterances of the Paraclete-Comforter upon earth. It is all one work of love, grace, and blessing. It is God's work for man, in man, and in some sort by means of man—a work in which redemption and sanctification and salvation, though, no doubt, taking place in orderly series, and not to be confounded with one another, yet all are blent in one in the eternal counsels of God, and all make one great loving divine work, which restores poor lost man to God, and replaces him in the heaven of his original inheritance.

God forbid that I should be so far misunderstood as to be thought, from anything that I have said to-day, to wish to put out of sight, or in any degree whatever to undervalue, the vast increase and added fulness of blessing which, even in the exercise of all these personal powers, the single Christian receives from the constant flow of the graces of the general body. Those

---

[x] 1 St. John ii. 1.   [y] Vide Note NNN.

who have heard the earlier Lectures of this course will not doubt the wonderful and divine efficacy which I have desired to attribute to the Holy Communion of the body and blood of Christ, which, as Holy Baptism is the first spring and source of the personal priesthood, is the perpetual brook by the wayside[z], the rock that follows the people of God in their wandering through the wilderness of life, the constantly accompanying flow of grace and union with Christ, by which the personal priesthood is supplied, invigorated, and increased. Nor will they doubt that I wish to represent as most helpful and real the divine power of the absolution duly pronounced by the ordained priest, holding authority to declare the Church's peace, by descent from the ordaining breath of Christ, whether uttered in the more general forms that are suitable to the larger gatherings of men in daily prayer, or to the more special cases of Holy Communion, or Visitation of the Sick; nor that I desire to acknowledge the wonderful effect of joint prayers, when two or three being gathered together in the name of Christ, He is assuredly in the midst of them[a], and His presence carries with it the unfailing assurance of the hearing and answering of their prayers.

No: it is in the breadth and fulness of all these things together that the real greatness of the estate of a Christian consists; and it is not until we begin

[z] Ps. cx 7; 1 Cor. x. 4.   [a] St. Matt. xviii. 19, 20.

to see them together in their combination and close mutual relation that we can begin to conceive with any adequate justice the greatness—and with the greatness the immense responsibilities—of the man who is planted by the grace of God into the body of Christ, and therein is made to partake of the wonderful riches of the grace of the Holy Spirit of God so given.

And observe that as we are now regarding them, priest and layman are the same. When a man is in his closet, when he is on his knees before God, his soul open, willingly, consciously, unreservedly opened to his Maker's eyes, all outer differences, of priest or layman, or whatever else they be, have fallen off for the time from him. No exterior differences go with him into the close, immediate presence of the Holy Trinity. Member of Christ—be his outer duties of one rank or office, or of another, man or woman, bond or free, greater than the greatest, as men esteem greatness, or less than the least,—he is only now God's own redeemed child in Christ, in whose heart the Holy Spirit dwells, from whose heart the Holy Spirit cries, with whom the loving Father and the Son make their abode.

On him descends all the dew from heaven won by innumerable prayers—the prayers of dear friends, or of strangers in the flesh who pray for all faithful servants of the Lord in all churches of the world. On him falls with much and well-founded comfort the voice of priestly blessing. On him rest, with much assuring and strengthening power, the continual accents of ministerial absolution, proclaiming and conveying the audible pardon of the most high God for daily repented and confessed sin. For him, as for all the sacred brotherhood of believers, day by day, in some portion or other of the Church on which the sun never sets, the Church goes before God to offer the one commemoration of the one sacrifice, of which he in his place never fails to take his own due and appointed part.

> 'For the dread offering, all day long,
>   All prayer, all duty blends.
> The Eucharist of God's dear Son,
>   Like Him, undying,
> Is mighty, worlds and hearts in one
>   For ever tying [b].'

Brethren, is all this true? Is all that I have been saying, lofty as it sounds, the simple, honest, real truth of God? or is it only heated fancy—talk to be endured by sensible men, though with some impatience, on a Sunday, but *unpractical*; that is to say, when it comes to be reduced to the sobriety of real and actual life, *not true?*

I know that it is very unlike the reality of our common modern life. Put it all into sharp contrast with the smart and glittering literature of our common modern life, with brilliant essay or article in review, gazette, or newspaper, and it jars—I know it jars— utterly and irreconcileably with them. I grant—I

[b] Cf. Lyra Innocentium, Continual Services.

sadly grant—that both cannot be true together. If all *that* be the truth of God; if the real state of Christian men, their duty, their condition, their responsibility, be really such as day after day, and week and month after week and month, we see them represented, then perhaps a Church which shall choose its own doctrines and not be particular about any—a State, ruling the Church in things pertaining to its inner life, while it comprises within itself elements most alien to the body of Christ, and professes merely to be the representative of an 'advanced civilization;' sacraments held unimportant, spiritual realities derided, Church authority regarded as priestcraft, Holy Scripture evacuated of all its sacredness;—all this, and such as this, may be the development of the Christian revelation suited to an age of proud intellectual pretension, the religious inheritance of these later days, these dark days which seem to be coming upon us, these anxious days in which our children are to live.

But if the doctrines which I have endeavoured in some degree to set before you be indeed such as are not imaginary but true, if it be the very truth of God that the Holy Spirit dwells, as a soul dwells in a body, in the mystical framework of the body of Christ, diffusing throughout it powers of life, powers of authority, powers of strong mutual support, powers of unlimited personal holiness and perfection—and at the same time authorizing, empowering, and sanctifying men, organs of the

universal body and representatives of it, to do the
blessed offices of the collective priesthood to the souls
of the single priests—if the estate of Christian men in
the Church of God be really such as I have tried
faithfully to represent it—do we not need, one and all,
to rise to a much loftier and truer, and more soul-
subduing sense of our condition, and of the mighty
responsibilities which that condition involves? One
and all—clergy and laity—clergy much, and laity, I
will say, much more. For it is the very bane of the
imperfect and one-sided form of doctrine to which we
have, I think, been too much accustomed, to sever these
things from one another; and both sides have suffered,
the clergy much, but the laity much more, by the sever-
ance. For the responsibility which indeed belongs to
all alike in their respective places and degrees, is thrown,
as if it were a professional burthen, or privilege, or
interest, or craft, upon the clergy; and so the lay-people
are taught to think themselves free—outside of the
sacred framework of the Spirit-bearing Church, and
therefore outside (except so far as out of their own free
bounty and personal activity they volunteer to do work
not their own) of all the gracious and spiritual labours
of that Spirit-bearing Church—forgetting that according
to the words of the apostle, 'all the body by joints and
bands having nourishment ministered, and knit together,
must increase with the increase of God c.'

^c Col. ii. 19. Cf. Eph. iv. 26.

It has been in the endeavour to set these things upon what seemed to be a sound, because the true basis of Church doctrine, that I have traced the course of the argument of these Lectures. I have thought for many years past that the particular danger of the times was aggravated, in no small degree, by the one-sidedness of the views which religious men take of the constitution and powers of the Church, and that the consequence has been a great and most mischievous releasing, in their own minds and the minds of others, of the lay-people from their due share in these powers, and the very serious responsibility of using them. And I have thought that if it were possible in any degree to suggest to men's minds the deeper and truer doctrine of the collective priesthood of the entire body of Christ, with its diffused responsibility, as compatible with the personal priesthood of each separate member of the body, and in a multitude of ways essential to its being and well-being and helpful and subsidiary to its exercise, such doctrine might, by the blessing of God, tend to check the occasional extravagance of one-sided doctrine on either side, and fall in helpfully to aid the settlement of various important questions, which, as the life of the Church developes itself under new and ever-varying conditions, and in one country after another, are continually arising and pressing for solution upon intelligible and well-established principles.

I believe that I have spoken, I am sure that I have

intended to speak, no otherwise than according to the rule of the primitive truth, and in accordance with the doctrine of the Church of England. In that doctrine—not legally pared down to the barest and nudest letter of the Thirty-nine Articles, not diluted to a saltless savour by the neutralization of everything specific and definite in the long-descended creed of the Church—in that doctrine held in its completeness, in its depth, in its mysterious loftiness, in its Divine richness—held with entire and real devotion and earnestness of body, soul and spirit, the single spirit of each several Christian man and woman acknowledging, and by grace acting up to the deep responsibility of their own real personal priesthood in the midst of the great collective priesthood of the whole body of Christ, I verily believe that the strength of the future Church of England, and I will add, the welfare of England herself as a nation blessed by Almighty God, depends.

NOTES.

NOTES.

NOTE A, p. 5.

'QUOD ergo salvâ cooperatione inseparabilis Deitatis, quædam Pater, quædam Filius, quædam propriè Spiritus Sanctus exsequitur, nostræ redemtionis dispositio, nostræ salutis est ratio. Si enim homo ad imaginem et similitudinem Dei factus in suæ honore naturæ mansisset, nec diabolicâ fraude deceptus à lege sibi positâ per concupiscentiam deviasset, creator mundi creatura non fieret ; neque aut sempiternus temporalitatem subiret, aut æqualis Deo Patri Filius Deus formam servi et similitudinem carnis peccati assumeret. Sed quia invidiâ diaboli mors introivit in orbem terrarum, et aliter solvi captivitas humana non potuit nisi caussam nostram ille susciperet, qui sine majestatis suæ damno et verus homo fieret, et solus peccati contagium non haberet, divisit sibi opus nostræ reparationis misericordia Trinitatis; ut Pater propitiaretur, Filius propitiaret, Spiritus Sanctus igniret. Oportebat enim ut etiam salvandi aliquid pro se agerent, et conversis ad Redemtorem cordibus ab inimici dominatione discederent.'—S. Leo Magnus, *Serm. III. de Pentecoste*, vol. i. p. 310.

NOTE B, p. 25.

Τῶν μὲν οὖν ἄλλων ἑκάστη δυνάμεων ἐν περιγραπτῷ τόπῳ τυγχάνειν πεπίστευται· ὁ γὰρ τῷ Κορνηλίῳ ἐπιστὰς ἄγγελος οὐκ ἦν ἐν ταὐτῷ καὶ παρὰ τῷ Φιλίππῳ, οὐδὲ ὁ ἀπὸ τοῦ θυσιαστηρίου τῷ Ζαχαρίᾳ διαλεγόμενος κατὰ τὸν αὐτὸν καιρὸν καὶ ἐν οὐρανῷ τὴν οἰκείαν στάσιν ἐπλήρου. Τὸ μέντοι Πνεῦμα ὁμοῦ τε ἐν Ἀββακοὺμ ἐνεργεῖν, καὶ ἐν Δανιὴλ ἐπὶ τῆς Βαβυλωνίας πεπίστευται, καὶ ἐν τῷ καταρράκτῃ εἶναι μετὰ Ἱερεμίου, καὶ μετὰ Ἰεζεκιὴλ ἐπὶ τοῦ Χοβάρ.— S. Basil. *De Sp. S.* § 24. vol. iii. p. 64. Cf. S. Hieron. *In Libro Didymi de Spiritu Sancto*, § 6. vol. ii. p. 112.

NOTE C, p. 25.

'Multæ Scripturæ sunt, quæ sine ambiguitate convincant, alterius eum à cunctis conditionibus esse naturæ. Quidam etiam Spiritu Sancto pleni esse dicuntur : nemo autem sive in Scripturis, sive in consuetudine, plenus creaturâ dicitur. Neque enim aut Scriptura sibi hoc vindicat, aut sermo communis, ut dicas plenum esse quempiam angelo, throno, dominatione : soli quippe Divinæ naturæ convenit hic sermo . . . .

'Angeli autem præsentia, sive alicujus alterius excellentis naturæ quæ facta est, non implet mentem atque sensum : quia et ipsa aliunde completur.'—S. Hieron. *De Sp. S.* § 8, p. 115.

NOTE D, p. 27.

Ἡ τοίνυν ὁδὸς τῆς Θεογνωσίας ἐστὶν ἀπὸ τοῦ ἑνὸς Πνεύματος, διὰ τοῦ ἑνὸς Υἱοῦ ἐπὶ τὸν ἕνα Πατέρα. Καὶ ἀνάπαλιν, ἡ φυσικὴ ἀγαθότης, καὶ ὁ κατὰ φύσιν ἁγιασμὸς, καὶ τὸ βασιλικὸν ἀξίωμα ἐκ Πατρὸς, διὰ τοῦ Μονογενοῦς ἐπὶ τὸ Πνεῦμα διήκει. Οὕτω καὶ αἱ ὑποστάσεις ὁμολογοῦνται, καὶ τὸ εὐσεβὲς δόγμα τῆς μοναρχίας οὐ διαπίπτει.— S. Basil. *De Sp. S.* § 18.

NOTE E, p. 28.

Οὐ μὴν ἐπειδὴ πρῶτον ἐνταῦθα τοῦ Πνεύματος ὁ Ἀπόστολος ἐπεμνήσθη, καὶ δεύτερον τοῦ Υἱοῦ, καὶ τρίτον τοῦ Θεοῦ καὶ Πατρὸς, ἤδη χρὴ καθόλου νομίζειν ἀντεστράφθαι τὴν τάξιν. Ἀπὸ γὰρ τῆς ἡμετέρας σχέσεως τὴν ἀρχὴν ἔλαβεν· ἐπειδὴ ὑποδεχόμενοι τὰ δῶρα πρῶτον ἐντυγχάνομεν τῷ διανέμοντι· εἶτα ἐννοοῦμεν τὸν ἀποστείλαντα· εἶτα ἀνάγομεν τὴν ἐνθύμησιν ἐπὶ τὴν πηγὴν καὶ αἰτίαν τῶν ἀγαθῶν.— S. Basil. *De. Sp. S.* § 16.

NOTE F, p. 34.

On the completeness of the Lord's baptism before the descent of the Holy Spirit, and the consequent disjunction of Baptism and Confirmation as separate rites, see Hammond's treatise *De Confirmatione contrà Dallæum*, c. vi. sec. iii. vii.

NOTE G, p. 35.

Most earnestly should I wish to recommend to theological students the work of the late Dean of Canterbury, Dr. Lyall, entitled *Propædia Prophetica*. It is unfortunate that neither the title of the book, nor, I must add, the style in which it is written, is such as to introduce the argument so favourably as might be desired. But the argument itself is of the greatest justice and value. I do not know where else to find the real argumentative weight of the Lord's miracles stated in so forcible, and I will add so original a way. I extract a very striking and characteristic passage :—

'But Hume proceeds to state another case, and one more incredible than that which we have here considered. "Suppose," says he, "that all the historians who treat of England should agree that on the 1st of January, 1600, Queen Elizabeth died ; that before and after her death she was seen by her physicians, and her whole court, as is usual with persons of her rank ; that her successor was acknowledged and proclaimed by the Parliament; and that, after having been interred a month, she again appeared, resumed the throne, and governed England for three years : I must confess that I should be surprised at the concurrence of so many odd circumstances, but should not have the least inclination to believe so miraculous an event. I should not doubt of her pretended death, and of those other public circumstances that followed it : I should only assert it to have been pretended, and that it neither was nor could be real. You would in vain object to me the difficulty and almost impossibility of deceiving the world in an affair of such consequence ; the wisdom and solid justice of that renowned queen ; with the little or no advantage she could gain from so poor an artifice. All this might astonish me, but I still would reply, that the knavery and folly of men are such common phenomena, that I should rather believe the most extraordinary events to arise from their concurrence, than admit of so signal a violation of the laws of nature."

'I incline to think that Hume has rightly expressed what, in the circumstances he has stated, would be the conclusion of most persons of sound understanding. But let us try what would be the effect, if we connect the events which he has stated with a supposed antecedent expectation among mankind.

'And first let us amend the case, as here imagined. Queen Elizabeth is supposed dying in her bed, privately, surrounded by her physicians and court, that is by her friends and dependents. But instead of Queen Elizabeth let us substitute the name of Charles the First, whose head was cut off before thousands of spectators, and whose executioners were his bitter enemies, or at least men who had a direct interest in his death. This alteration of the circumstances of the case will bring it nearer to the one which, not improbably, was in Hume's mind at the time of writing. Moreover, it renders the fact to all appearance more unequivocally miraculous, and therefore, no doubt, more impossible in itself, and more difficult to consider as having really happened.

'The case being thus assumed, let us suppose mankind in general in the year 1648, though otherwise enlightened and highly civilized, yet in the matter of religion to have been immersed in ignorance as dark as that which prevailed throughout the world in the days of Augustus. Suppose, further, that one nation there was very numerous in itself, and individuals of which were to be found in almost all parts of the world, professing a purer form of religion, among whom a rooted opinion was well known to prevail, that in the very generation we are speaking of, a revelation would be made to mankind by God, the effect of which would be to subvert idolatry in the world, and to introduce a new religion in which the worship of the one true God would form the leading feature. Let us suppose, finally, that when the surrounding people had enquired what was to be the sign by which the arrival of this epoch was to be known, they had received for answer that, when the time arrived, mankind would know it by the King of England being put to death by the public executioner, and afterwards rising from the grave and resuming his throne.

'The question now is, whether, if this fact had happened, or (which is nearly the same thing for all the purposes of the argument) if all mankind had believed it to have happened; and if, dating from this belief of mankind, paganism had immediately begun to stagger, and had thence rapidly declined, and the worship of the alone true God had immediately begun to spread itself, by a simultaneous dispersion over all the nations of the world, so as to have become in the course of two or three generations the predominant faith:— the question, I say, is whether, in these circumstances, Hume would think "the knavery and folly of mankind" the most probable explanation of the phenomena? For my part I feel inclined to think that in such a case as is here supposed, the most sceptical reasoner that ever lived would look about him for some very different solution, and whether he found it or not, could at least understand why mankind in general should have been content to receive the facts as marked by the hand of God.'— *Propædia Prophetica*, part ii. chap. i. p. 150.

NOTE H, p. 37.

'Apostolos suos vivæ lucis fonte perfudit, ut ipsi postmodum universum mundum tanquam duodecim solis radii, ac totidem lampades veritatis illuminent, et inebriati novo vino repleant, atque irrigent sitientia corda populorum.'— S. August. *Serm.* 185. *de Tempore*.

NOTE I, p. 40.

'Non ambigamus, quod cum in die Pentecostes discipulos

Domini Spiritus Sanctus implevit, non fuit inchoatio muneris, sed adjectio largitatis; quoniam et Patriarchæ, et Prophetæ, et Sacerdotes, et omnes Sancti, qui prioribus fuere temporibus, ejusdem sunt Spiritus sanctificatione vegetati,' &c.— S. Leo, *Serm. II. de Pentecoste.*

NOTE J, p. 42.

'Ex hoc autem quod hic dicitur intelligitur quod jam Petrus baptizatus fuerat : intelligimus enim ejus discipulos per quos baptizabat, jam fuisse baptizatos, sive baptismo Joannis, sicut nonnulli arbitrantur, sive, quod magis credibile est, baptismo Christi. Neque enim renuit ministerium baptizandi, ut haberet baptizatos servos per quos cæteros baptizaret, qui non defuit humilitatis ministerio quando eis pedes lavit.'—S. August. *Ep. ad Seleucianum.* Cf. *Tractat. in Joh. Evang.* cap. xv. vol. iii. pt. ii. p. 408.

'Sed quidam dicunt, quod baptizati erant solum baptismate Joannis : quod non videtur verum, quia sic non erant loti : nam baptisma Joannis non mundabat interius à culpâ. Et ideo dicendum quod baptizati erant baptismo Christi, secundum Augustinum. Et si objicis quod Christus non baptizabat sed discipuli ejus, ut dicitur suprà iv., dico quod non baptizabat turbas, sed discipulos suos sibi familiares et domesticos baptizavit.'—Thomas Aquinas, *In S. Joann.* cap. xiii.

NOTE K, p. 47.

'Loquitur Dominus ad Petrum : Ego tibi dico, inquit, quia tu es Petrus, et super istam petram ædificabo Ecclesiam meam, et portæ inferorum non vincent eam. Et tibi dabo claves regni cœlorum, et quæ ligaveris super terram erunt ligata et in cœlis : et quæcunque solveris super terram, erunt soluta et in cœlis. Et iterum eidem post Resurrectionem suam dicit, Pasce oves meas. Super unum ædificat Ecclesiam suam. Et quamvis apostolis omnibus parem potestatem tribuat ac dicat, Sicut misit me Pater, et ego mitto vos, accipite Spiritum sanctum : si cui remiseritis peccata, remittentur illi : si cui tenueritis, tenebuntur : tamen ut unitatem manifestaret, unitatis ejusdem originem ab uno incipientem suâ auctoritate disposuit. Hoc erant utique et ceteri Apostoli quod fuit Petrus, pari consortio præditi et honoris et potestatis : sed exordium ab unitate proficiscitur, ut Ecclesia una monstretur.'—S. Cyprianus, *De Unitate Ecclesiæ*, p. 107. Cf. Ep. lxxiii. Cyprianus Jubaiano, p. 201 ; lxxv. Firmilianus Cypriano, p. 225, &c.

Compare also S. August. *De Doctrinâ Christianâ*, § 18 ; *Enchiridion de Fide et Charitate*, 65 ; *De Agone Christiano*, § 30 ; *Sermo* 295. *in Nat. Apost. Petri et Pauli.*

NOTE L, p. 50.

The writers on the Roman Catholic side undoubtedly acknowledge the general principle of representation, at least in terms ; but the *fact* entirely disappears in the way in which the principle is dealt with practically.

'Episcopi sunt Ecclesia repræsentativè, ut nostri loquuntur,' says Bellarmine : 'quilibet enim Episcopus gerit personam suæ ecclesiæ particularis, et proinde omnes Episcopi gerunt personam totius Ecclesiæ.'—*De Concil. Auctoritate*, iii. 14.

Again : ' Dico igitur concilium illud non posse errare quod

absolutè est generale, et Ecclesiam universalem perfectè repræsentat. Ejusmodi autem Concilium non est antequam adest sententia summi Pontificis. Nam Episcopi ceteri repræsentant quidem corpus Ecclesiæ, et quod illi faciunt corpus Ecclesiæ facere censetur. Ac legati Papæ non ita repræsentant caput Ecclesiæ, i. e. ipsum Papam, ut quod ipsi faciunt absolutè censeatur fecisse Papam : alioquin nulla requireretur confirmatio. Sed solum repræsentant Pontificem tanquam vicarii, et internuncii ipsius, qui ad ipsum referre debeant cum oriuntur dubia, et sententiam ejus exspectare et exsequi. Itaque tale Concilium cum non repræsentat absolutè auctoritatem capitis, non nisi imperfectè totam Ecclesiam repræsentat.'—Lib. ii. c. 11.

The idea of representation, thus in terms recognized and in fact annulled by the older Roman Catholic writers, hardly finds any place in the still more thorough-going Ultramontanism of Archbishop Manning. 'The pastoral authority, or the Episcopate, together with the priesthood and the other orders, constitute an organized body, divinely ordained to guard the deposit of the Faith. *The voice of that body*, not as of many individuals, but as a body, *is the voice of the Holy Ghost*. The pastoral ministry as a body cannot err, because the Holy Spirit, who is indissolubly united to the mystical body, is eminently and above all united to the hierarchy, and body of its pastors. *The Episcopate* UNITED TO ITS CENTRE *is, in all ages, divinely sustained and divinely assisted to perpetuate and to enunciate the original revelation.*'

Very faint indeed in statements like these is the remaining recognition (if it can be called any recognition at all) of the 'mystical body' at large.

NOTE M, p. 65.

St. John xvi. 13: τὸ Πνεῦμα τῆς ἀληθείας ὁδηγήσει ὑμᾶς εἰς πᾶσαν τὴν ἀλήθειαν. The Vulgate renders roughly 'docebit vos omnem veritatem.' Maldonat well says, 'Deducere in omnem veritatem non significat quoquo modo veritatem omnem docere, sed ita docere quasi magister discipulum manu ducat viamque illi accommodatè ad ejus ingenium veritatis ostendat: ut non omnia simul, non ordine præpostero, priusque difficiliora, deinde quæ faciliora sunt tradens, sed contrà faciliora prius, mox difficiliora, suo quidque tempore, prout proficit, prout potest capere. Hoc est ὁδηγήσει.' (Cf. Acts viii. 31; Rev. vii. 17; Ps. xxiv. 5, &c.) Certainly the idea contained in the word seems to be that of a guide or teacher; not of one to supersede, or act instead of another, but of one who will point the road, and so lead a willing follower, as I have said in the text:—indicating that the help of the Holy Spirit does not consist in superseding the natural powers of a man, but guiding[a] and leading them, so that they may themselves see and follow the way of divine truth.

The thought of the Πνεῦμα ὁδηγοῦν of the sixteenth chapter seems to connect itself with that of the Lord in the fourteenth chapter, saying ἐγώ εἰμι ἡ ὁδὸς, ἡ ἀλήθεια, καὶ ἡ ζωή—a passage the difficulty of which I have never seen fully explained. It is easy to say eloquent things about it, as very beautiful passages are quoted from St. Ambrose, St. Augustin, and St. Bernard; but the real question remains unsolved, why the Lord adds 'the truth, and the life,' and what these words, so added, signify. The following remarks may help to throw some little light upon them.

[a] On the Divineness of the guidance, see S. Basil. *De. Sp. S.* c. xix.

NOTE M.

The Lord had said, 'Whither I go ye know, and the way[b] ye know.' Thomas replied, 'We know not whither thou goest, and how can we know the way?'

Thus far it seems clear that the Lord speaks of two things only: a point to which He was going, and a way by which that point is to be reached.

The Apostles, it appears, ought to have understood both, but, speaking by the lips of Thomas, they acknowledge that they do not know the first, and therefore cannot know the second.

What then was the first? It is plain from the conclusion of the sixth verse. It is *the Father*.

What then was the second? It is *Christ*. Christ is the Way. 'No man cometh unto the Father but by Me.'

Thus far all is plain; and we may say with Maldonat, 'Si Christus minus fuisset in respondendo liberalis, minus nobis in hujus loci interpretatione laborandum esset.'

Why then does He add to the plain answer, 'I am the Way,' the further words, 'the Truth and the Life'?

It seems to me to be no answer to this question to shew from other passages (e. g. Col. ii. 3; St. John vi. 37; v. 21; xvii. 3) that Christ is indeed both 'the Truth and the Life.'

Is it not possible that these words may be, so to speak, epexegetic of the first words, as though He said, 'Ἐγώ εἰμι ἡ ὁδός, εἰμὶ γὰρ ἡ ἀλήθεια, καὶ ἡ ζωή? *I am the Way*, that is the answer to St. Thomas's question; *the Way to the Father*. For (or, inasmuch as) I am the Truth and the Life. I am the Way to the Father, for planted in Me, and guided therein

---

[b] Let it be observed that the Lord does not mean the way by which He is going Himself, but the way by which they are to go in order that where He is there they may be also (ver. 3).

by My Holy Spirit, My people are led into all truth, and therein have the earnest of life. 'Sanctified through the Truth,' that is, I apprehend, led by the Πνεῦμα ὁδηγοῦν to know and acknowledge all Divine truth, and to act it out in holiness of life and conduct, Christians are in possession of Divine Life. Thus it is that I am the Way to the Father.

I do not understand the Lord to say 'I am three things, the Way, the Truth, and the Life,' as if they were co-ordinate: but rather 'I am the Way,'—so, answering St. Thomas, 'being both the Truth, and the Life.'

NOTE N, p. 76.

The distinction taken in the text as to the right and wrong use of the words 'infallible' and 'infallibility' may seem trifling, and of little real use. But the more I read controversies relating to the Church, and especially such as regard the claim of authority in teaching set up by the Church of Rome, the more I feel convinced that it really is not without some importance, and that good may be done by calling attention to it.

'Infallibility' I suppose to signify such a sure and certain possession of truth as to render the possessor incapable of error; and 'infallible' as an adjective to be applicable to such persons, if there be such, as *cannot* either deceive, or be deceived, *qui neque falli neque fallere possunt.*

Infallibility then is a widely different thing from authority in pronouncing upon truth, or correctness in the decision pronounced.

Infallibility cannot be said of writings, decisions, judgments. If it exists at all, it must be a quality of persons. Infallibility cannot admit of degrees. The possessor of it

NOTE N.

must be capable of being identified as possessing it beforehand (I mean before his writings, decisions, judgments, are delivered), and not recognised afterwards or inferred from the correctness, even if that correctness should be supposed to be uniform and invariable, of those decisions or judgments.

Is 'infallibility' rightly attributed to the Church? Granted that it has the promise of being guided into all truth, granted also that the gates of hell shall not prevail against it (from which it is legitimately argued that it shall never wholly fall into error, but there shall always be witnesses of the truth, keeping it alive in the Church), do these privileges amount to what is rightly called infallibility? I apprehend not, though I confess that we have sometimes been in the habit of expressing ourselves as though it did so.

They constitute a security against universal error. They also constitute an assurance of the general maintenance of truth. But this is widely different from the possession of truth in certain identified persons rendering them incapable of being deceived or of deceiving, so that they may be consulted beforehand with a divine certainty of receiving from them the answer which is the utterance of the Holy Ghost, which alone can constitute any (legitimately so called) infallibility.

The Roman writers tell us broadly, and insist upon it, that the decrees of General Councils are infallible. Now not to urge that Cardinal Bellarmine, who lays this down with the utmost confidence, adds the strange proviso, 'nisi manifestissimè constet intolerabilem errorem committi [c],' I complain that it ought to be proved beforehand, that such

[c] Lib. ii. de Conc. c. 8.

and such persons meeting together under such and such circumstances are necessarily possessed of the Holy Spirit, either all, or the more part of them, in such a high way as that the Council in general is therefore incapable of being deceived, or of deceiving. A thesis which few, I imagine, in the face of the history of Councils, and human nature, would undertake to support. But Archbishop Manning, whose logic does not condescend to take account of fact or history, lays down the same doctrine with equal breadth : 'The decrees of General Councils are undoubtedly the voice of the Holy Ghost, both because they are the organs of the active infallibility of the Church, and because they have the pledge of a special Divine assistance according to the needs of the Church and of the Faith.' *Organs of the active infallibility of the Church ?* I seem to comprehend. Because the Church has the promise of being saved from falling totally into error, so that there shall always be those who shall possess and maintain the truth, therefore the Church may in some sense be said to be infallible. But this is a sort of 'passive' infallibility, a dead infallibility, useless for practical purposes. It must be converted into an '*active*' infallibility which can cope with emergent questions, and settle them without the possibility of error or mistake.

But, in the first place, I deny that it is any infallibility at all, properly so called, even in a passive sense; and secondly, I maintain that it is utterly incapable of being converted into an active infallibility. And thirdly, even if these considerations should be thought insufficient, I demand to have it shewn what the conditions are under which persons meeting together in Council can be proved *beforehand* (and I specially insist upon the word 'beforehand,' as necessary in order to distinguish infallibility as the assured proof

NOTE N. 273

of correctness, from infallibility as the inferred conclusion from correctness) to be so thoroughly, universally, and indubitably filled with the Holy Spirit that their decrees, not yet given, shall be absolutely incapable of error. And this is a demand essential to the satisfying of the case, which I do not think that my old friend the Archbishop will condescend to reply to.

But the Archbishop further lays down 'that the Definitions and Decrees of Pontiffs speaking *ex cathedrâ*, or as the Head of the Church and to the whole Church, whether by Bull, or Apostolic Letters, or Encyclical, or Brief, to many or one person, undoubtedly emanate from a Divine assistance, and are infallible.'

Putting aside the impropriety of attributing the 'infallibility' to the decrees, rather than to the Pope pronouncing the decrees, we seem to have here an approach to what we want. 'The Bishop of Rome, then, is the person who, whenever he speaks as Head of the Church *and to the whole Church, whether to one person or to many*, is so assisted by the Holy Spirit as that he is incapable of deceiving or being deceived [d].'

'The infallibility of the Head of the Church extends to the whole matter of revelation, that is, to the Divine truth and the Divine law, and to all those facts or truths which are in contact with faith and morals. The definitions of the Church include truths of the natural order, and the revelation of supernatural truth is in contact with natural ethics, politics, and philosophy. So again the judgments of Pontiffs in matters which affect the welfare of the whole Church, such as the condemnation of propositions. In all

---

[d] I do not know how to reconcile these two clauses printed in italics.

T

declarations that such propositions are, as the case may be, heretical, or savouring of heresy, or erroneous, or scandalous, or offensive to pious ears or the like, the assistance of the Holy Spirit certainly preserves the Pontiffs from error; and such judgments are infallible, and demand interior assent from all e.'

I thought we were going to find what we were in search of—a person, so possessed of truth, that it was absolutely certain *beforehand*, that in whatever he should say, he was incapable of being deceived or deceiving. But no: even on the highest Roman theory, I find no such person. The Bishop of Rome is not held even by his most ardent followers to be in any such possession of truth. He may be, even according to their own divines, ignorant, perverse, heretical. We, reading history with our eyes open, may add, vicious, sensual, impious, stained with every sort of notorious sin, a man like John XIII, or XVIII, or XXII, like Boniface VIII, or Alexander VI.

He may be all this: but when he speaks '*ex cathedrâ*,' and upon any of the forementioned subjects, *then*, and then only, he is speaking by the Holy Ghost and is infallible.

I find it difficult in the face of this audacious claim,—unheard of for the first thousand years of the Church, and then maintained in defiance of all Christian history, on the strength of the misinterpretation of two or three passages of Holy Scripture,—to remember that I am speaking only on the logical use and abuse of the words 'infallible' and 'infallibility,' and that I must put aside all idea of arguing against the substance of the Roman theory, even to the extent of urging how Pope Honorius I, *ex cathedrâ*, adopted

e Archbishop Manning, pp. 83, 84.

the heresy of the Monothelites ; and how Pope Alexander III, *ex cathedrâ*, condemned Peter Lombard of heresy respecting the human nature of the Lord, while thirty-six years after, Pope Innocent III, equally *ex cathedrâ*, reversed the sentence and condemned his accusers.

Putting aside all this however, and a thousand other instances of usurpation and wrong in matters political, moral, and physical on the part of the Popes, I wish to point out that even this audacious claim is not a claim of *infallibility* in any such sense as to warrant the application of the word *infallible* to the Pope, or to carry any of the consequences which follow readily enough when the application is once assumed and granted.

To be notoriously, obviously, and confessedly a mere fallible man, and under certain circumstances and conditions very difficult to be certainly defined, and in respect to certain subjects equally difficult of definition, to be assured of freedom from error,—this, though a claim utterly baseless and deceptive, does not constitute infallibility in any proper sense of the term. There is no possession of truth, claimed, or to be inferred. If the claim made were well founded, all that it would shew is that in certain utterances, so many and no more, the Bishop of Rome had been made a mouthpiece of the Holy Spirit, and consequently, not that he was infallible, but that these utterances, so many and no more, were divine.

But infallibility is a very convenient word. Once jump to the conclusion that the Pope is infallible, and the conditions and circumstances under which exemption from error is (however falsely) claimed for certain Papal utterances are forgotten, and the convenient phrase remains, to justify, beyond denial on the part of those who have admitted it, innumerable acts of usurpation and aggression with which it really has no sort of connection.

A very convenient word indeed ; and a very comfortable word to those who shelter themselves in Rome. But there is a worm in the gourd, so that its shelter is not worth much to those who will take any account of logic or of the facts of notorious history.

The fact is that we have all been using the words 'infallible' and ' infallibility' in a very loose and inaccurate way, confounding them on the one hand with assured exemption from total error, and the general possession of truth, and on the other with authority in decrees, and truth in doctrines. What I wish to point out is the desirableness of using the words accurately. I apprehend that if only used accurately, they will be very rarely used at all. Certainly the loose and random use of them is altogether in the interest of Rome, which has never been slow in taking advantage of it.

NOTE O, p. 77.

' Ex iis commentatoribus quos habemus, Lucam videtur Marcion elegisse quem cæderet. Porro Lucas non apostolus sed apostolicus, non magister, sed discipulus ; utique magistro minor, certe tanto posterior, quanto posterioris apostoli sectator, Pauli sine dubio : ut si sub ipsius Pauli nomine Evangelium Marcion intulisset, non sufficeret ad fidem singularitas instrumenti, destituta patrocinio antecessorum. Exigeretur enim id quoque Evangelium quod Paulus invenit, cui fidem dedit, cui mox suum congruere gestiit. Si quidem propterea Hierosolymam ascendit ad cognoscendos apostolos et consultandos, ne forte in vacuum cucurrisset, id est, ne non secundum illos credidisset, et non secundum illos evangelizaret.'—Tertull. *Adv. Marcionem*, lib. iv. c. 2.

It is true that Tertullian (alone, so far as I know, of ancient interpreters of this passage of the Epistle to the Galatians) indicates his opinion that St. Paul felt some uncertainty of the soundness of his teaching until his communication with the Apostles at Jerusalem. For the purpose of my argument I have no need of any such idea. On the contrary, I believe St. Paul's personal authority to have been abundantly sufficient to teach without hesitation, misgiving, or need of support. It is enough for me that for the satisfaction of the converts (ἵνα διδάξω τοὺς ταῦτα ὑποπτεύοντας ὅτι οὐκ εἰς κενὸν τρέχω, Chrysost., v. Ellicott and Lightfoot in loco) he found it wise and desirable to ascertain and to be able to declare the uniformity of his teaching with that of the older Apostles. 'Ipse Apostolus Paulus,' says St. Augustine, 'post ascensionem Domini de cœlo vocatus, si non inveniret in carne Apostolos, quibus communicando Evangelium ejusdem societatis esse appareret, Ecclesia illi omnino non crederet.'

NOTE P, p. 78.

The supposition of the text is precisely that of Tertullian in the passage quoted at length in the preceding note, and the conclusion drawn is in effect identical with that which he draws. The 'single document,' even supposing its genuineness absolutely undoubted, would not suffice to rule the faith of the Church, if it were devoid of the support of those that went before it—the preceding Apostles, and their writings. For just as St. Paul, whether for his own satisfaction or that of his converts, went up to Jerusalem μήπως εἰς κενὸν τρέχῃ ἢ ἔδραμε, so for the satisfaction of the Church, his (supposed) writing must be ascertained to be in accordance with the Apostolic faith and writings which the Church already possesses.

NOTE Q, p. 83.

On the Preface to St. Luke's Gospel.

It has been commonly assumed by interpreters of St. Luke's Gospel that in his Preface he attributes the authority of his narrative to 'eye-witnesses and ministers of the word' in such a manner as to disclaim, and exclude altogether, the idea of his having been an eye-witness himself of the events which he records.

This interpretation of the Preface is a very universal one. It has, I suppose, arisen from the supposed contrast of the two clauses ἐπειδήπερ πολλοὶ,—ἔδοξε κἀμοί:—and it seems to be held, somewhat inconsistently as it seems to me, even by writers who at other times attribute the authority of the Evangelist to the dictation of St. Paul, who received his own information from revelation.

I am disposed, however, to doubt this interpretation, for the following reasons:—

1. It seems to put St. Luke into a position considerably lower and less authoritative than that which the Church has always assigned to him. It makes him say, 'Since many men have tried their hand at constructing a narrative, so will I,'—a parallelism which, whatever be the meaning of the words παρηκολουθηκότι ἄνωθεν πᾶσιν ἀκριβῶς, is surely hardly consistent with the position of an inspired Evangelist, whose words the Church of Christ has always accepted as dictated by the Holy Spirit of God.

NOTE Q.

2. If the words παρηκολουθηκότι ἄνωθεν πᾶσιν ἀκριβῶς mean that he has examined, and by diligent search ascertained, the accuracy of the narrative which he delivers (and this, I suppose, must be the meaning of the words on the usual interpretation), he plainly disclaims both the information of St. Paul and the inspiration of the Holy Spirit. He simply puts himself on a level with the other narrators whom he unquestionably means to put into the background, and to allege nothing but his own industry and care in examining authorities as the ground of the superiority of his own narration as compared with theirs.

If however the words of the Preface undoubtedly mean what this interpretation conveys, then, however inconvenient and inconsistent with our preconceived notions the consequences may prove, there is no help for it. The words are undoubted. There is no difference of reading of the least importance in them, and we must put up with any inferences which they legitimately bear.

But I venture to except to this interpretation. It seems to me to proceed upon a somewhat hasty and superficial view of St. Luke's words.

First, I take quite a different view of the *logic* of the passage, as will appear from the following considerations.

Ἡμεῖς I apprehend means the Church.

Τὰ πεπληροφορημένα ἐν ἡμῖν I suppose to mean the events of the life of the Lord, His miracles, and His discourses, as they are most surely believed by the members of the Church.

Καθὼς παρέδοσαν ἡμῖν κ.τ.λ. These words I understand to assign the grounds on which the Church (ἡμεῖς) assuredly believes all these things.

Now all this is preliminary in point of logic to anything

said about unauthorized narrators, or St. Luke's own authority as preferable to theirs. He seems thus far to say, 'We, the Church, are in possession of a large number of facts recorded respecting the life and discourses of our Lord, by those who were during His lifetime upon the earth His companions, who saw His deeds, heard His words, and in various ways ministered unto Him.'

Now then we proceed to the persons who have without adequate authority attempted to narrate these things.

'Many writers have tried their hands to draw up in order consecutive narratives of these things.' But, I suppose we may add, they had not sufficient warrant. They took them at second-hand. They were not eye-witnesses themselves. They merely 'tried their hand' at such narratives, and I fear that you, Theophilus, instructed and catechized as you have been in these things, may derive not confirmation in the truth, but mischief and error from their compilations.

'Therefore I' ($παρηκολουθηκὼς$ &c., whatever these words may mean) 'will teach you better, and in such a way that you may receive confirmatory instruction ($ἵνα\ ἐπιγνῷς$) on the subjects in which you have been already catechized.'

Thus it appears to me that the Evangelist, instead of excluding himself from the class of eye-witnesses in these words, rather puts himself (not indeed directly, but by implication) among them. He seems to say, Eye-witnesses have taught the Church, so I will teach you. Or, to put the same thing in another way: Unauthorized narrators, not eye-witnesses, have darkened the message which eye-witnesses have delivered, so I, better informed than they, will teach you more correctly.

Thus it seems to me that, according to the logic of the passage, St. Luke, regarding Theophilus as one of the Church (ἡμεῖς) who requires accurate instruction in addition to his previous training in the history of the life of the Lord, puts himself by implication into the category of those who can give that accurate and trustworthy information, that is, the eye-witnesses.

Leaving then the logic of the passage, let us now look more closely into the words in which St. Luke confessedly assigns the ground of his own authority, represented as greater and more to be trusted than that of the pseudo-evangelists.

Παρηκολουθηκότι ἄνωθεν πᾶσιν ἀκριβῶς. What is the meaning of παρηκολουθηκότι? The following is the article upon παρακολουθέω from Liddell and Scott's Lexicon, 4th edition :—

'Παρακολουθέω, f. ήσω, *to go beside* or *near, follow close* or *on the heels*, τινί Ar. Eccl. 725, Plat., etc.: *to follow close, dog one's steps*, Dem. 519. 12., 537. 2 ; οὓς σὺ ζῶντας μέν, ὦ κίναδος, κολακεύων παρηκολούθεις Id. 281. 22 : of rules, *to hold good throughout*, π. δι' ὅλης τῆς ἱππικῆς Xen. Eq. 8. 14 : π. χρόνοις *to follow all* the times and dates, *to trace accurately*, Nicom. ap. Ath. 291 B ; so π. τοῖς πράγμασιν ἐξ ἀρχῆς Dem. 285. 22.

'II. metaph. *to follow with one's thoughts*, i. e. *to understand*, τοῖς πράγμασι Dem. 285. 21 ; τοῖς δικαίοις Demad. 178. 32, etc. ; προσέχειν νοῦν καὶ παρ. εὐμαθῶς Aeschin. 16. 9 ; so esp. as Stoical term, usu. absol. ; they also said ἑαυτῷ παρακολουθεῖν ὅτι ... *to understand* that ..., Epict. 2. 26, 3 ; also c. part., Id. 4. 5, 21.'

And it may be taken as a full account of the classical usage of the verb, except that in the passage of Demosthenes *De Coronâ*, there twice referred to under different senses, it seems to me to have more precisely the meaning of having *personally accompanied the events*, than of having followed them in thought and understood them. Let the reader judge. Ἀλλ' ὡς ἔοικεν, ἐκεῖνος ὁ καιρὸς, καὶ ἡ ἡμέρα ἐκείνη οὐ μόνον εὔνουν καὶ πλούσιον ἄνδρα ἐκάλει, ἀλλὰ καὶ παρηκολουθηκότα τοῖς πράγμασιν ἐξ ἀρχῆς, καὶ συλλελογισμένον ὀρθῶς τίνος ἕνεκα ταῦτ' ἔπραττεν ὁ Φίλιππος, καὶ τί βουλόμενος.

However, the more important question is, What is the meaning of the verb in the later or Alexandrian Greek? And in answer to this question I would quote a passage from the fragments of Papias preserved by Eusebius[f]: Εἰ δέ που καὶ παρηκολουθηκώς τις τοῖς πρεσβυτέροις ἔλθοι, — 'if it chanced that some person who had been present with the elders (the Apostles) came;' and another of Eusebius himself, commenting upon their words: Καὶ ὁ νῦν δὲ ἡμῖν δηλούμενος Παπίας τοὺς μὲν τῶν Ἀποστόλων λόγους παρὰ τῶν αὐτοῖς παρηκολουθηκότων ὁμολογεῖ παρειληφέναι. And there is a passage of Josephus[g] which is so very clear and strong to my present purpose that I must quote it at length: Φαῦλοι δέ τινες ἄνθρωποι διαβάλλειν μου τὴν ἱστορίαν ἐπικεχειρήκασιν, ὥσπερ ἐν σχολῇ μειρακίων γύμνασμα προκεῖσθαι νομίζοντες. κατηγορίας παραδόξου καὶ διαβολῆς. δέον ἐκεῖνο γιγνώσκειν ὅτι δεῖ τὸν ἄλλοις παράδοσιν πράξεων ἀληθινῶν ὑπισχνούμενον, αὐτὸν ἐπίστασθαι ταύτας πρότερον ἀκριβῶς, ἢ παρηκολουθηκότα τοῖς γεγονόσιν, ἢ παρὰ τῶν εἰδότων πινθανόμενον. ὅπερ ἐγὼ μάλιστα περὶ ἀμφοτέρας νομίζω πεποιηκέναι τὰς πραγματείας. τὴν μὲν γὰρ ἀρχαιολογίαν,...τοῦ δὲ πυλέμου τὴν ἱστορίαν ἔγραψα, πολλῶν μὲν αὐτουργὸς πράξεων, πλείστων δὲ αὐτόπτης γενόμενος.

Here we have the two sources of knowledge expressly distinguished from one another, personal witness, and derived information; and any person who reads the whole passage contained in the previous chapters will see how definitely the writer means to declare by the words παρηκολουθηκότα τοῖς γεγονόσιν his own personal witness of the events he relates.

[f] *Hist. Eccl.* iii. 39.   [g] *Contra Apionem*, lib. i. c. 10.

When then to all this we add the fact that there is an ancient tradition that St. Luke was one of the Seventy, or, at least, a personal disciple of the Lord, I confess that it appears to me to be a somewhat hasty reading of the Preface which leads interpreters to conclude, with well-nigh one voice, that St. Luke expressly disclaims in it the authority of having seen with his own eyes any of the events which he records.

The only passages which I can find in which it is stated that St. Luke was of the number of the Seventy are the following.

In the dialogue of Adamantius (probably not the same as Origen): E. πόσους ἔσχεν ὁ Χριστὸς ἀποστόλους; A. πρώτους ἀπέστειλεν ιβ´. καὶ μετὰ ταῦτα οβ´ εὐαγγελίσασθαι. Μάρκος οὖν καὶ Λουκᾶς ἐκ τῶν οβ´ ὄντες, Παύλῳ τῷ ἀποστόλῳ εὐαγγελίσαντο.— Pseudo-Origen, *De rectâ in Deum fide.*

I do not find it in Theophylact himself, who on the contrary says, Ἐκ τούτου δῆλον ὅτι οὐκ ἦν ὁ Λουκᾶς ἀπ᾽ ἀρχῆς μαθητής, ἀλλ᾽ ὑστερόχρονος. But in the Synopsis of St. Luke attributed to Dorotheus we read, Λουκᾶς ὁ Θεῖος, Ἀντιοχεὺς μὲν ἦν, ἰατρὸς δέ, καὶ τὴν ἔξω σοφίαν πολύς· οὐ μὴν ἀλλὰ καὶ τὴν Ἑβραικὴν παιδείαν ἐξησκήσατο, τοῖς Ἱεροσολύμοις ἐπιφοιτήσας, ὅτε δὴ καὶ ὁ Κύριος ἡμῶν ἐδίδασκεν· ὥστε φασί τινες ἕνα καὶ αὐτὸν γενέσθαι τῶν ἑβδομήκοντα Ἀποστόλων.—*Opera Theophyl.* vol. i. p. 266.

Ἀπέστειλε δὲ καὶ ἄλλους ἑβδομηκονταδύο κηρύττειν, ἐξ ὧν ἦσαν οἱ ἑπτά, οἱ ἐπὶ τῶν χηρῶν τεταγμένοι· μετὰ τούτους δὲ τοὺς ἑπτά, καὶ Ματθαῖον τὸν πρὸ αὐτῶν, Μάρκον, Λουκᾶν, Βαρνάβαν καὶ Ἀπελλῆν, Ῥοῦφον, Νίγερα καὶ τοὺς λοιποὺς τῶν ἑβδομηκονταδύο.—Epiphanius, lib. i. p. 50.

ἐπείδητερ πολλοὶ ἐπεχείρησαν· ἵνα τινὰς μὲν ἐπιχειρητὰς δείξῃ, φημὶ δὲ τοὺς περὶ Κήρινθον, καὶ Μήρινθον, καὶ τοὺς ἄλλους· εἶτα τί φησι; ἔδοξε κἀμοὶ καθεξῆς παρηκολουθηκότι ἄνωθεν τοῖς αὐτόπταις, καὶ ὑπηρέταις τοῦ λόγου γενομένοις, γράψαι σοὶ, κράτιστε Θεόφιλε.—Ibid. lib. ii. p. 428.

'Primùm quidem Christo adhæsit, et ab eo pietatis semina suscepit. Postea vero Paulo diù conjunctus, maximeque familiaris effectus est, ac discipulus ejus, comesque, itineris, quemadmodum et Marcus Petro cæterorum principi. Dicunt autem quidam, et maximè Origenes, quod Marcus et Lucas ante Dominicam passionem inter septuaginta discipulos connumerati sunt.'—Euthymius, *Ex Præfatione*.

NOTE R, p. 97.

'Nemo tamen istos insignes Apostolos separet. Et in eo quod significabat Petrus, ambo erant; et in eo quod significabat Joannes, ambo futuri erant. Significando sequebatur iste, manebat ille : credendo autem ambo mala præsentia hujus miseriæ tolerabant, ambo futura bona illius beatitudinis expectabant. Nec ipsi soli, sed universa hoc facit sancta Ecclesia sponsa Christi, ab istis tentationibus eruenda, in illâ felicitate servanda. Quas duas vitas Petrus et Johannes figuraverunt singuli singulas ; verum et in hâc temporaliter ambulaverunt ambo per fidem, et illâ in æternum fruentur ambo per speciem. Omnibus igitur sanctis ad Christi corpus inseparabiliter pertinentibus, propter hujus vitæ procellocissimæ gubernaculum, ad liganda et solvenda peccata claves regni cœlorum primus apostolorum Petrus accepit, eisdemque omnibus sanctis propter vitæ illius secretissimæ quietissimum sinum, super pectus Christi Johannes Evangelista discubuit. Quoniam nec iste solus sed universa Ecclesia ligat, solvitque peccata : nec ille in principio Verbum Deum apud Deum, et cetera de Christi divinitate . . . . . de fonte Dominici pectoris solus bibit.'—S. August. *In Joh. Ev.* c. 21. Tr. cxxiv.

NOTE S, p. 101.

Τοῦτο τὸ κήρυγμα παρειληφυῖα, καὶ ταύτην τὴν πίστιν, ὡς προέφαμεν, ἡ Ἐκκλησία, καίπερ ἐν ὅλῳ τῷ κόσμῳ διεσπαρμένη, ἐπιμελῶς φυλάσσει, ὡς ἕνα οἶκον οἰκοῦσα· καὶ ὁμοίως πιστεύει τούτοις, ὡς μίαν ψυχήν, καὶ τὴν αὐτὴν ἔχουσα καρδίαν, καὶ συμφώνως ταῦτα κηρύσσει καὶ διδάσκει, καὶ παραδίδωσιν, ὡς ἐν στόμα κεκτημένη. καὶ γὰρ αἱ κατὰ τὸν κόσμον διάλεκτοι ἀνόμοιαι, ἀλλ' ἡ δύναμις τῆς παραδόσεως μία καὶ ἡ αὐτή, καὶ οὔτε αἱ ἐν Γερμανίαις ἱδρυμέναι Ἐκκλησίαι ἄλλως πεπιστεύκασιν ἢ ἄλλως παραδιδόασιν, οὔτε ἐν ταῖς Ἰβηρίαις, οὔτε ἐν Κελτοῖς, οὔτε κατὰ τὰς ἀνατολάς, οὔτε ἐν Αἰγύπτῳ, οὔτε ἐν Λιβύῃ, οὔτε αἱ κατὰ μέσα τοῦ κόσμου ἱδρυμέναι· ἀλλ' ὥσπερ ὁ ἥλιος, τὸ κτίσμα τοῦ Θεοῦ εἷς καὶ ὁ αὐτός· οὕτω καὶ τὸ κήρυγμα τῆς ἀληθείας πανταχῆ φαίνει, καὶ φωτίζει πάντας ἀνθρώπους τοὺς βουλομένους εἰς ἐπίγνωσιν ἀληθείας ἐλθεῖν.—S. Irenæus, c. *Hæreses*, I. x. p. 49.

NOTE T, p. 102.

This passage is from Bingham's *Antiquities*, Bk. I. c. v. § 5, quoted from Ruffinus, lib. i. c. ix., and Socrates, lib. i. c. xix. xx.

NOTE U, p. 103.

Cf. *Concil. Carthaginense IV*, sive *Statuta Ecclesiæ Antiquæ*, Canon xcviii. : 'Laicus præsentibus clericis, nisi ipsis jubentibus, docere non audeat.' Cf. also Eusebius, lib. vi. cap. xix. : Ἐλθὼν (Ὠριγένης) ἐπὶ Παλαιστίνης, ἐν Καισαρείᾳ τὰς διατριβὰς ἐποιεῖτο· ἔνθα καὶ διαλέγεσθαι, τάς τε θείας ἑρμηνεύειν γραφὰς ἐπὶ τοῦ κοινοῦ τῆς ἐκκλησίας οἱ τῇδε ἐπίσκοποι, καίτοι τῆς τοῦ πρεσβυτερίου χειροτονίας οὐδέπω τετυχηκότα αὐτὸν ἠξίουν. Alexander, Bishop of Jerusalem, and Theoctistus of Cæsarea, defended this against the objection of Demetrius (who urged ὅτι τοῦτο οὐδέ ποτε ἠκούσθη, τὸ παρόντων ἐπισκόπων λαϊκοὺς ὁμιλεῖν) by saying that it was not so: "Ὅπου γοῦν εὑρίσκονται οἱ ἐπιτήδετοι πρὸς τὸ ὠφελεῖν τοὺς ἀδελφοὺς καὶ παρακαλοῦνται τῷ λαῷ ὁμιλεῖν ὑπὸ τῶν ἁγίων ἐπισκόπων; and alleging several instances to the point.

NOTE ON P. 103.

'The list of laymen who have written in support or illustration,' &c.

I should have wished, if it had been in my power, to draw up a tolerably complete list of laymen who by their writings, more or less directly or indirectly theological, have contributed to the illustration and defence of Christian truth. But the task is a much more difficult one than I had anticipated, and I must be content to make such a scattered and imperfect list as from the comparatively small means within my reach I can.

For the early ages we have the lists of St. Jerome and Gennadius. I have assumed that the writers who in these lists are not expressly called bishops or priests, were laymen, as the writers certainly seem to intend to make the distinction accurately. I have however omitted such as I found reason to suppose were really ordained, though their ordination was not expressed, and introduced such as, though certainly ordained, were not ordained till late in life, and after they had become known as writers; such, for instance, as Origen, and Macarius the elder.

As to the monks, they were in the early ages, as a rule, laymen. 'Ainsi,' says Fleury, speaking of the clerical Canons set up by Chrodegang of Metz in the seventh century, 'voilà deux sortes de religieux, les uns clercs, les autres laiques ; car les moines l'étoient pour la plupart :' and even in the ninth century, he says, 'il paroît qu'il y avoit peu de prêtres entre le moines.'—*Hist. Eccl.* Discourse viii. No. 2. p. 9. See also Guizot, *Civilisation en France,* Leçon xiv.

After the lists of St. Jerome and Gennadius, I have felt at a great loss, partly from the long blanks which I cannot supply, and partly, when the age of the Reformation comes, from the multitude of writers, chiefly German, of whom I cannot ascertain with certainty whether they were in Holy Orders or no. I have therefore been content to select a few great names from Italy, Germany, and France, of whom there is no doubt, and to fill the English list somewhat more fully. But here too is a difficulty ; for several of the writers can hardly be said to have written upon theological subjects, though the current of their thoughts and their influence were strongly in the direction of religion. On these grounds I have not scrupled to add the names of Bacon, Selden, Wotton, and others, as of writers who undoubtedly contributed, and several of them in a very high degree, to the advancement and support of religion in their own days.

Hermas—'Cujus Apostolus Paulus ad Romanos scribens meminit, asserunt auctorem esse libri qui appellatur Pastor, et apud quasdam Græciæ Ecclesias jam publicè legitur.'—S. Hieron. *De Vir. Illust.* c. x.

Aristides—'Atheniensis Philosophus eloquentissimus, et sub pristino habitu discipulus Christi, volumen nostri dogmatis rationem continens...Hadriano Principi dedit.' c. xx.

Agrippa—'Vir valdè doctus adversum viginti quatuor Basilidis hæretici volumina fortissimè disseruit.' c. xxi.

Hegesippus—'Vicinus Apostolicorum temporum, et omnes

à passione Domini, usque ad suam ætatem, Ecclesiasticorum actuum texens historias, multaque ad utilitatem legentium pertinentia hinc inde congregans, quinque libros composuit.' c. xxii. Cf. Routh, *Reliq.* i. 189; Euseb. *Hist. Eccl.* iv. 22; Lightfoot, *Ep. to the Gal.* 268, &c.

Justinus (Martyr)—' Philosophus habitu quoque Philosophorum incedens...pro religione Christi plurimum laboravit,' &c. c. xxiii.

Musanus—' Non ignobilis inter eos qui de ecclesiastico dogmate scripserunt.' c. xxxi.

Modestus—' Adversum Marcionem scripsit librum, qui usque hodie perseverat.' c. xxxii.

Pantænus—' Stoicæ sectæ Philosophus... Hujus multi quidem in S. Scripturam extant commentarii.' c. xxxvi. Cf. Routh, i. 337.

Rhodon—' Genere Asianus, a Tatiano Romæ in Scripturis eruditus, edidit plurima.' c. xxxvii. Cf. Routh, i. 346.

Miltiades—' Adversus Montanum, Priscam, Maximillamque scripsit volumen præcipuum.' c. xxxix.

Apollonius—' Vir disertissimus, scripsit adversus Montanum,' &c. c. xl. Cf. Routh, ii. 53. ' Hunc Ephesiorum antistitem fuisse asserit auctor *Prædestinati, De Hæret.* cap. xxvi. nescio quam verè.'

Apollonius (alter)—' Romanæ urbis Senator...insigne volumen composuit.' c. xlii.

Maximus—' Famosam quæstionem insigni volumine ventilavit, unde malum, et quod materia a Deo facta sit.' c. xlvii. Cf. Routh, i. 423.

Candidus—' In Hexaemeron pulcherrimos tractatus edidit.' c. xlviii.

Appion—' In Hexaemeron tractatus fecit.' c. xlix.

Sextus—'Librum de Resurrectione scripsit.' c. l.

Arabianus—'Edidit quædam opuscula ad Christianum dogma pertinentia.' c. li.

Judas—' De 70 apud Danielem hebdomadibus plenissimè disputavit.' c. lii.

Origenes—Ordained, after many writings, in his forty-third year.

Tryphon—'Origenis auditor, ad quem nonnullæ ejus extant Epistolæ in Scripturis, eruditissimus fuit.' c. lvii.

Minucius Felix—'Romæ insignis causidicus scripsit Dialogum Christiani et Ethnici disputantium qui Octavius inscribitur.' c. lviii.

Gaius—'Disputationem adversum Proculum, Montani sectatorem, valdè insignem habuit.' c. lix. Cf. Routh, ii. 2.

Arnobius—'Florentissimè Rhetoricam docuit, scripsitque adversum gentes quæ vulgò extant volumina.' c. lxxix.

Firmianus qui et *Lactantius*—'Arnobii discipulus... ad scribendum se contulit.' c. lxx. (*Divinæ Institutiones, De irâ Dei*, &c.)

Antonius—'Monachus... misit Egyptiacè ad diversa monasteria Apostolici sensus sermonisque Epistolas septem.' c. lxxxviii.

'Holy Macarius and great Antony.'
George Herbert—*The Church Militant*.

Cf. S. August. *Confess*. viii. 11.

Victorinus—'Romæ Rhetoricam docuit, et in extremâ senectute Christi se tradens fidei scripsit adversus Arium libros,... et Commentarios in Apostolum.' c. ci.

Didymus Alexandrinus—'Captus a parvâ ætate oculis,.... plura opera et nobilia conscripsit.' c. cix.

Aquilius Severus—'Composuit volumen,' &c. c. cxi.

Ambrosius Alexandrinus—'Scripsit adversum Apollinarium volumen.' c. cxxvi.

Dexter—'Clarus apud sæculum, et Christi fidei deditus fertur omnimodam historiam texuisse.' c. cxxxii.

Sophronius—'Vir apprimè eruditus... insignem librum composuit.' c. cxxxiv.

Pachomius—'Monachus vir tam in docendo quam in signa faciendo Apostolicæ gratiæ et fundator Ægypti cœnobiorum... scripsit Regulam utrique generi monachorum aptam quam angelo dictante perceperat.' *Liber Gennadii de Viris Illustribus*, c. vii.

Oresiesis—'Monachus... vir in Sanctis Scripturis ad perfectum instructus, composuit librum divino conditum sale,' &c. c. ix.

Macarius—'Monachus ille Ægyptius, signis et virtutibus clarus unam tantum ad juniores professionis suæ scripsit Epistolam.' c. x. Took priest's orders when forty years old.

Evagrius—'Monachus... scripsit multa monachis necessaria.' c. xi.

Prudentius—'Vir sæculari literaturâ insignis composuit διπτοχαῖον de toto veteri et novo Testamento personis exceptis.' c. xiii.

Commodianus—'Factus Christianus... scripsit mediocri sermone librum adversus Paganos.' c. xv.

Tichonius Afer—'In divinis literis eruditus... scripsit de bello intestino, &c. Composuit et Regulas ad investigandam et inveniendam intelligentiam Scripturarum septem,' &c. c. xviii. De Tichonio sæpius ab Augustino laudato videsis Indices in Augustini opera.

Bachiarius—'Vir Christianæ philosophiæ... edidisse dicitur grata opuscula,' &c. c. xxiv.

NOTE ON P. 103.

Isaac—'Scripsit de Sanctæ Trinitatis tribus personis, et Incarnatione Domini librum.' c. xxvi.

Ursinus—'Monachus scripsit adversus eos qui rebaptizandos hæreticos decernunt.' c. xxvii.

Helvidius—'Scripsit... librum.' c. xxxii. Cf. Lightfoot, *Ep. to the Galatians*, 248 sq.

Evagrius—'Alter scripsit altercationem Simonis Judæi, et Theophili Christiani.' c. l.

Victorinus—'Rhetor Massiliensis... commentatus est in Genesim.' c. lx.

Syagrius—'Scripsit de fide.' c. lxv.

Paulinus—'Composuit de initio Quadragesimæ.' c. lxviii.

Cyrus—'Arte medicus, ex philosopho monachus... scripsit adversus Nestorium.' c. lxxxi.

Victorius—'Calculator scrupulosus... composuit Paschalem censum,' &c. c. lxxxviii.

Boethius, born 475. I must not assume too confidently that he was a Christian—vide Smith's *Dict. of Biography*. But besides the *De Consolatione*, works *De Sanctâ Trinitate, Utrum Pater et Filius et Spiritus Sanctus substantialiter prædicantur*, and others are attributed to him. Dante puts him in Paradise, and he has been canonized by the Roman Catholic Church.

Cædmon, died about 680. The Saxon bard of Whitby, who paraphrased the Book of Genesis and other parts of Holy Scripture.

King Alfred, 849—901. Translator of Bede, and Boethius, the Pastoral of Gregory I, &c.

Dante Alighieri, 1265—1321.

Laurentius Valla, 1406—1457. *Notæ in Novum Testamentum.*

Pico Mirandola, 1463—1494.

Michael Angelo, 1475—1564.
Reuchlin, 1455—1522.
Ludovicus Vives, 1492—1540.
Scaliger, J. J., 1540—1609.
Drusius, John, 1550—1616.
Heinsius, Daniel, 1580—1665. *Exercitationes Sacræ in Novum Testamentum.*
Salmasius, 1588—1653.
Grotius, Hugo, 1583—1645.
Casaubon, Isaac, 1559—1614.
Descartes, 1596—1650.
Pascal, Blaise, 1623—1662.
d'Andilly, Arnauld, brother of the great Arnauld, 1588—1674. Confessions of St. Augustine—Lives of the Fathers, &c.
Nicole, Pierre, 1625—1695. *Perpetuité de la foi.* (Took Holy Orders late.)
Corneille, Pierre, the elder, 1606—1684. Translated the *De Imitatione Christi.*
Tillemont, 1637—1698. Took Holy Orders at forty years of age.
Racine, 1639—1699.
Leibnitz, 1646—1716.
King Henry VIII. De Septem Sacramentis, contra Martinum Luther, Hæresiarcham. (Thence the title of Defender of the Faith, by Brief of Leo X, anno 1521.)
More, Sir Thos., 1480—1534. *Responsio ad convicia M. Lutheri congesta in Henricum Regem Angliæ—De religione Utopiensium.*
Cheke, Sir John, 1514—1557. *De Superstitione,* addressed to Henry VIII. Tutor to Edward VI.
Spenser, Edmund, about 1553—1598. 'Our sage and

NOTE V.   293

serious poet, Spenser, whom I dare be known to think a better teacher than Scotus or Aquinas.'— Milton, *Areopagitica.*

King James I.
Bacon, Lord, 1561—1626.
Selden, John, 1584—1654.
Twysden, Sir Roger, 1597—1672.
Milton, John, 1608—1674.
Hale, Sir Matthew, 1609—1676.
Brown, Sir Thomas, 1605—1682.
Bunyan, John, 1628—1688.
Boyle, Robert, 1626—1691.
Locke, John, 1632—1704.
Newton, Sir Isaac, 1642—1726.
Davies, Sir John, 1570—1626.
Savile, Sir Henry, 1549—1622. Editor of Chrysostom.
Brooke, Fulk Greville, Lord, 1554—1628.
Wotton, Sir Henry, 1568—1639.
Walton, Isaac, 1593—1683.
Falkland, Lord, 1610—1643.
Nelson, Robert, 1656—1715.
Addison, Joseph, 1672—1719.
Lyttelton, George, Lord, 1709—1773.
Southey, Robert.
Coleridge, S. T.
Wordsworth, William.
Knox, Alexander.
Macbride, John David.

NOTE V, p. 109.

Τῶν γὰρ κατὰ τὴν 'Ασίαν πιστῶν πολλάκις καὶ πολλαχῇ τῆς 'Ασίας εἰς τοῦτο συνελθόντων, καὶ τοὺς προσφάτους λόγους ἐξετασάντων καὶ βεβήλους ἀποφηνάντων, καὶ ἀποδοκιμασάντων τὴν αἵρεσιν, οὕτω δὴ τῆς τε ἐκκλησίας ἐξεώσθησαν καὶ τῆς κοινωνίας εἴρχθησαν.—*Ex Anonym. apud Eusebium*, v. 16.

'Aguntur præterea per Græcias illa certis in locis concilia ex universis Ecclesiis, per quæ et altiora quæque in commune tractantur, et ipsa repræsentatio totius nominis Christiani magnâ veneratione celebratur.'—Tertull. *De Jejuniis*, xiii. p. 552.

NOTE W, p. 111.

The uncial Codices A. B. C. (and it may be added ℵ) read καὶ οἱ πρεσβύτεροι ἀδελφοὶ, the reading adopted by Lachmann. Tischendorf in his 7th edition read (with E. G. H. and the majority of cursive MSS.) καὶ οἱ ἀδελφοί. It is to be observed that the corrector of ℵ marked C. introduces the words καὶ οἱ, as a correction, before ἀδελφοί. It is observed by Scrivener (Introduction to the Collation, p. xxiii.) 'that one object of this corrector was to assimilate the Codex to MSS. more in vogue in his time.' Now as his time is supposed to have been about the seventh century, the force of the argument suggested at the foot of p. 111 seems to come out with some clearness.

NOTE X, p. 112.

Εἶτα λοιπὸν κοινὸν τὸ δόγμα γίγνεται· τότε ἔδοξε τοῖς Ἀποστόλοις, καὶ πρεσβυτέροις, σὺν ὅλῃ τῇ ἐκκλησίᾳ, κ.τ.λ. γράψαντες διὰ χειρὸς αὐτῶν τάδε· Ὅρα αὐτοὺς οὐχ ἁπλῶς ταῦτα νομοθετοῦντας· ὥστε δὲ ἀξιόπιστον γενέσθαι δόγμα πέμπουσι τοὺς παρ' αὐτῶν, καὶ ἵνα ἀνύποπτοι ὦσιν οἱ περὶ Παύλου λοιπόν...... ἔδοξεν ἡμῖν γενομένοις ὁμοθυμαδὸν, ἐκλεξαμένοις ἄνδρας, κ.τ.λ. ὥστε δεῖξαι, ὅτι οὐ τυραννικῶς, ὅτι πᾶσι τοῦτο δοκεῖ, ὅτι μετὰ ἐπισκέψεως ταῦτα γράφουσιν.— S. Chrysost. *In Acta Apost.* Hom. xxxiii. vol. ix. p. 254.

NOTE Y, p. 113.

'Nonne et laici sacerdotes sumus? Scriptum est, Regnum quoque nos et sacerdotes Deo et Patri suo fecit. Differentiam inter Ordinem et Plebem constituit Ecclesiæ auctoritas, et honor per ordinis consessum sanctificatur adeo ubi Ecclesiastici ordinis non est consessus, et offers, et tinguis, et sacerdos es tibi solus. Sed ubi tres, ecclesia est, licet laici.' —*De Exhort. Castitatis*, vii. p. 522.

'Dandi quidem (Baptismum) habet jus summus Sacerdos, qui est Episcopus: dehinc Presbyteri et Diaconi, non tamen sine Episcopi auctoritate, propter Ecclesiæ honorem, quo salvo salva pax est. Alioquin etiam laicis jus est: quod enim ex æquo accipitur, ex æquo dari potest: nisi Episcopi jam, aut Presbyteri, aut Diaconi vocantur, discentes. Domini sermo non debet abscondi ab ullo,' &c.—*De Baptismo*, xvii. p. 230.

NOTE Z, p. 113.

'Ad id vero quod scripserunt mihi compresbyteri nostri Donatus et Fortunatus, Novatus et Gordius, solus rescribere nihil potui: quando à primordio Episcopatus mei statuerim nihil sine consilio vestro, et sine consensu plebis, meâ privatim sententiâ gerere.'—S. Cypr. Ep. xiv. *Presbyteris et Diaconis* (p. 33).

'Cui rei non potui me solum judicem dare, cum multi adhuc de clero absentes sint, nec locum suum vel serò repetendum putaverunt, et hæc singulorum tractanda sit et limanda pleniùs ratio, non tantum cum Collegis meis, sed et cum plebe ipsa universa: expensâ enim moderatione libranda et pronuncianda res est, quæ in posterum circà ministros Ecclesiæ constituat exemplum.'—Ep. xxxiv. *Presbyteris et Diaconibus* (p. 68). Cf. Ep. lix. *Cornelio* (p. 137).

'Fecerunt ad nos de quibusdam beati Martyres literas, petentes examinari desideria sua : cum pace nobis omnibus a Domino priùs data, ad Ecclesiam regredi cœperimus, examinabuntur singula præsentibus et judicantibus vobis.'—Ep. xvii. *Fratribus in Plebe consistentibus* (p. 39). Cf. Ep. xliii. and xliv. (p. 85).

'Hoc enim et verecundiæ et disciplinæ et vitæ ipsi omnium nostrum convenit : ut Præpositi cum Clero convenientes, præsente et stantium plebe, quibus et ipsis pro fide et timore suo honor habendus est, disponere omnia consilii communis religione possimus.'—Ep. xix. *Presbyteris et Diaconibus* (p. 42).

On this point the Roman clergy thus reply : 'Quanquam nobis in tam ingenti negotio placeat, quod et tu ipse tractâsti prius : Ecclesiæ pacem sustinendam : (i. e. that the restoration of the lapsed must be deferred :) deinde, sic collatione consiliorum cum Episcopis, Presbyteris, Diaconis, Confessoribus, pariter ac stantibus laicis facta, lapsorum tractare rationem.'—Ep. xxx. *Cypriano Papæ Presbyteri et Diaconi Romæ consistentes* (p. 59).

It is to be observed that St. Cyprian (Ep. lv. *Antoniano fratri*, p. 102) quotes this passage with emphasis : 'Quod etiam Romam ad Clerum tunc adhuc sine Episcopo agentem, et ad Confessores Maximum Presbyterum, et ceteros in custodiâ constitutos, nunc in Ecclesiâ cum Cornelio junctos, plenissimè scripsi. Quod me scripsisse de eorum rescriptis poteris noscere. Nam in Epistolâ suâ ita posuerunt.' (He then cites the words above quoted.)

It is worth adding that Pope Cornelius, elected just after this letter of the Roman clergy was written, 'Factus est

Episcopus de Dei et Christi ejus judicio, de Clericorum pœne omnium testimonio, de Plebis quæ tunc affuit suffragio, et de Sacerdotum antiquorum et bonorum virorum collegio,' &c.— Ep. lv.

NOTE AA, p. 116.

Canon 12. Περὶ τοῦ τοὺς ἐπισκόπους κρίσει τῶν μητροπολιτῶν καὶ τῶν πέριξ ἐπισκόπων καθίστασθαι εἰς τὴν ἐκκλησιαστικὴν ἀρχὴν, ὄντας ἐκ πολλοῦ δεδοκιμασμένους ἔν τε τῷ λόγῳ τῆς πίστεως, καὶ τῇ τοῦ εὐθέος λόγου πολιτείᾳ.

Canon 13. Περὶ τοῦ μὴ τοῖς ὄχλοις ἐπιτρέπειν τὰς ἐκλογὰς ποιεῖσθαι τῶν μελλόντων καθίστασθαι εἰς ἱερατεῖον.

ΒΑΛΣΑΜΩΝ. Καὶ ἀπὸ τοῦ παρόντος κανόνος παρίσταται ὅτι οὐ μόνον ἐπίσκοποι τὸ παλαιὸν ἐψηφίζοντο ὑπὸ τῶν ὄχλων, ἀλλὰ καὶ ἱερεῖς, ὅπερ ἐκωλύθη.

ΖΩΝΑΡΑΣ. Οὐ μόνον ἐπισκόπων ἐκλογὴν οἱ ὄχλοι ποιεῖν ἐκωλύθησαν, ἀλλ' οὐδὲ ἱερεῖς ἐκλέγεσθαι παρεχωρήθησαν.—*Concilia*, Bp. Beveridge.

On the subject of the popular share in election of Bishops, see Beveridge's note on the fourth Canon of the first Nicene Council (vol. ii. p. 97, notes). It is also to be particularly observed, in illustration of the gradual exclusion of the laity from Church authority, how this canon of the first Nicene Council, decreeing the presence of all the Bishops of the province at the election of a Bishop, is quoted in the second Nicene Council, and interpreted as excluding the lay people from all share in such election.

NOTE BB, p. 116.

It seems to me to be important in studying the history of the Reformation, to remember that the real practical settlement of the great question whether the Church should reform itself, and reproduce within its own body and by peaceful means the primitive state of religion, or, by refusing all legitimate reformation, incur the terrible risks of violent disruption, and all the untold losses which such disruption involves, took place not in the sixteenth century, but in the fifteenth. The Councils of Constance and Basle did really determine that the Roman theory, with all its terrible abuses, should be maintained in greater and more exclusive completeness than ever, and that nothing less than an earthquake should liberate any considerable portion of mankind from its tyranny. At Trent there was no longer any question, nor hope. The points were all practically settled. The conclusions were foregone and inevitable. The Tridentine Bishops only put into system the details of the great victory which had been really won in the previous century.

But when Christendom was summoned to meet at Constance in 1414, there really did seem to be some prospect of that real reformation for which the whole Christian world cried out with one voice. The Western Church was indeed at that moment corrupt in many most important ways, corrupted in doctrine, terribly corrupted in morals, full of evil in the corrupt state of the monastic institutions, but nothing had yet been done to make these corruptions indelible, or to prevent the possibility, however great may have been the difficulty, of restoring the Church to a primitive model. The state of the Western Church at that moment may be compared to that of the Eastern at the present: needing much reform in many most important ways, but hitherto uncommitted, hitherto unpledged to maintain unbroken and for ever the very system under which the evils had grown, and with which they were indissolubly united.

NOTE BB.

The state of the Papacy seemed to offer a singular opportunity. Peter di Luna (Benedict XIII), Angelo Corario (Gregory XII), and Balthasar Cossa (John XXIII), all claimed the Popedom. The first two had been deposed by the Council of Pisa, and the third (pirate, tyrant, adulterer, extortioner, violator of nuns) was a man whose detestable and notorious wickedness made it impossible for a Council composed not of creatures of the Roman Court, but of the learned men of Europe, assembled in open consultation, to maintain him in his high position.

Chief among the learned men who took part in the Council were Peter d'Ailly, the Cardinal of Cambray, and his still more illustrious pupil and successor in the Chancellorship of the University of Paris, John Gerson, whose writings, and speeches in favour of reform at the Council of Pisa (1409), had produced a singularly deep and extensive effect. By their efforts (see extracts from the Schedules of the Cardinals of Cambray and St. Mark in Gieseler, iv. 290) others besides Bishops and Abbots,—Doctors, Canonists, even Ambassadors of the great countries of Europe, and Deputies of the Free Cities, took part in the Council.

Nothing could exceed the force, and eloquence, and it may be added, the effect upon the Council, of the leaders of the reform. The sermons and speeches of Peter d'Ailly and Gerson are to be read at length in the collections of Von der Hardt. Their sentiments were in almost every point (I except of course the indefeasible supremacy which they assign to the Bishop of Rome) such as the chief divines of the Church of England have held. It may be worth while to quote a remarkable passage from Gerson's *Opus de modis uniendi, ac reformandi Ecclesiam in Concilio Universali* as illustrating the view taken in these lectures: 'Catholica,

Universalis Ecclesia ex variis membris unum corpus constituentibus est conjuncta et nominata. Cujus corporis, Universalis Ecclesiæ, caput Christus solus est. Cæteri vero, ut Papa, Cardinales, et Prælati, Clerici, Reges et Principes ac plebeii sunt membra inæqualiter disposita. Nec istius Ecclesiæ Papa potest dici nec debet caput, sed solum vicarius Christi, ejus vicem gerens in terris, *dum tamen clavis non erret.* Et in hâc Ecclesiâ, et in ejus fide omnis homo potest salvari etiamsi in toto mundo aliquis Papa non posset reperiri. Hæc Ecclesia de lege currenti nunquam errare potuit, nunquam deficere, nunquam schisma passa est, nunquam hæresi maculata est, nunquam falli aut fallere potuit, nunquam peccavit. In istâ etiam omnes fideles, in quantum fideles sunt, unum sunt in Christo. ... Alia vero vocatur *Ecclesia Apostolica* particularis et privata, in catholica Ecclesiâ inclusa, ex Papâ, Cardinalibus, Episcopis, Prælatis, et viris Ecclesiasticis compaginata. ... Et hæc errare potest, et potuit falli et fallere, schisma et hæresin habere, etiam potest deficere. Et hæc longè minoris auctoritatis videtur esse universali Ecclesiâ :—*et est quasi instrumentalis et operativa clavium universalis Ecclesiæ,* et executiva potestatis ligandi et solvendi ejusdem.' Vid. Gieseler, p. 286.

But the Roman power, with its immense hold upon Christendom, was only in abeyance, and no sooner had the Council in conjunction with the Cardinals (for thirty delegates of the Council took part in the election with twenty-three Cardinals) elected a Pope (Martin V) of respectable character upon whom the various parties could unite, than all hopes of reform were suddenly and absolutely at an end. 'On the day after his election Pope Martin published a Brief confirming all the regulations established by his predecessors, even John XXIII. All the old grievances, Reservations,

NOTE BB. 301

Expectancies, Vacancies, Confirmations of Bishops, Dispensations, Exemptions, Commendams, Annates, Tenths, Indulgences, might seem to be adopted as the unrepealable law of the Church. The form was not less dictatorial than the substance of the decree. It was an act of the Pope, not of the Council. It was throughout the Pope who enacted and ordained : it was the absolute resumption of the whole power of reformation, so far at least as the Papal Court, into his own hands. Whatever he might hereafter concede to the Church in general, or to the separate nations of Christendom, was a boon on his part, not a right on theirs. . . . The Council had given its sanction, its terrible sanction, to the immutability of the whole dominant creed of Christendom, and to the complete, indefeasible hierarchical system.'—*Latin Christianity*, vol. vi. pp. 65, 71 ; see also note on p. 65.

But while the Council of Constance had thus given its entire weight to the Roman system of doctrine and discipline, and vindicated it by the death at the stake of Huss and Jerome of Prague, it did not tranquillize Germany, or materially abate the cry for reform which still resounded in every country beyond the Alps ; and the wonderful successes of the Hussites in the Bohemian war, as they first led to the assembling of the Council of Basle in 1431, so drove the assembled Fathers 'to take more serious views of the absolute and inevitable necessity of reformation in the Church.' But again the hopes of Christendom, less keenly excited after the bitter disappointment of Constance, were frustrated. The internal divisions of the Bohemians, and at last their total overthrow in the battle of Lepan[h], removed the great and pressing urgency which had led to the revival of the subject of reformation ; and the transfer by Pope Eugenius of the

[h] May 30, 1434.—*Latin Christianity*, vol. vi. p. 101.

seat of the Council from Basle to Ferrara and Florence, and the futile efforts under which it continued its sessions at Basle, put an end to whatever prospects there might have been of a large and searching and real Reformation, in which the rights of clergy and laity should alike be fully recognized, and the Church replaced upon a primitive basis. Thenceforward it was clear that the Papal system was to be upheld in every particular, justified in theory, and maintained with the most perfect exclusiveness in practice; and that, by consequence, sooner or later, at least half of the Western Church must be finally lost to the obedience and communion of Rome.

NOTE CC, p. 118.

So speaks Archbishop Manning in his recent volume on the temporal mission of the Holy Ghost :—

'This office of enunciating and proposing the faith is accomplished through the human lips of the pastors of the Church. The pastoral authority, or the episcopate, together with the priesthood and the other orders, constitute an organized body, divinely ordained to guard the deposit of the Faith. The voice of that body, not as so many individuals, but as a body, is the voice of the Holy Ghost. The pastoral ministry as a body cannot err, because the Holy Spirit, who is indissolubly united to the mystical body, is eminently and above all united to the hierarchy and body of its pastors. The episcopate united to its centre is, in all ages, divinely sustained and divinely assisted to perpetuate and to enunciate the original revelation.'

This is, no doubt, the language which, unheard and undreamed of in the early ages of the Church, became the authorized language of strong Ultramontanism from the fifteenth century downwards: rejected as it is by ancient history and the distinct language of the primitive Fathers, rejected by the Gallican Church of Gerson and Bossuet, rejected by the universal voice of Protestant Christendom. That the clergy are the commissioned organs for declaring the truth of the Gospel, I have sufficiently declared in the body of the Lectures; but that 'the episcopate *united to its centre*,' the Pope of Rome, is so divinely sustained and assisted, as to be able to claim the voice of the Holy Ghost for that which they teach, I absolutely deny to be the truth as taught in Holy Scripture and primitive antiquity. I verily believe that in that claim lies the πρῶτον ψεῦδος of debased Christianity, and the real essential cause of the miserable schisms and divisions which afflict the Church.

NOTE DD, p. 122.

See several of the most striking passages of St. Cyprian to this point extracted in Note Z, upon p. 113.

NOTE EE, p. 123.

'First, then, I consider whether all the power that an Œcumenical Council hath to determine, and all the assistance it hath not to err in that determination, it hath it not all from the catholic universal body of the Church and clergy in the Church, whose representative it is? And it seems it hath: for the government of the Church being not monarchical, but as Christ is the head, this principle is inviolable in nature: every body collective that represents, receives power and privileges from the body which is represented; else a representation might have force without the thing it represents, which cannot be. So there is no power in the Council, no assistance to it, but what is in and to the Church. But yet then it may be questioned, whether the representing body hath all the power, strength, and privilege which the represented hath? And suppose it hath all the legal power, yet it hath not all the natural, either of strength or wisdom that the whole hath. Now, because the representative hath power from the whole—and the main body can meet no other way—therefore the acts, laws, and decrees of the representative, be it ecclesiastical or civil, are binding in their strength. But they are not so certain and free from error as is that wisdom which resides in the whole : for in assemblies merely civil or ecclesiastical, all the able and sufficient men cannot be in the body that represents. And it is as possible so many able and sufficient men for some particular business may be left out, as that they which are in may miss or misapply that reason and ground upon which the determination is principally to rest. Here, for want of a clear view of this ground, the representative body errs ; whereas the represented, by virtue of those members which saw and knew the ground, may hold the principle inviolated.

'Secondly, I consider, that since it is thus in nature and in civil bodies, if it be not so in ecclesiastical too, some reason must be given why; "for that body also consists of men ;" those men, neither all equal in their perfections of knowledge and judgment, whether acquired by industry, or rooted in nature, or infused by God ;—not all equal, nor any one of them perfect and absolute, or freed from passion and human infirmities. Nor doth their meeting together make them infallible in all things ; though the act which is hammered out by many together must in reason be perfecter than that which is but the child of one man's sufficiency. If then a general Council have no ground of not erring from the men or the meeting, either it must not be at all, or it must be by some assistance and power upon them when they are so met together; and this, if it be less than the assistance of the Holy Ghost, it cannot make them secure against error.

'Thirdly, I consider, that the assistance of the Holy Ghost is without error. That is no question; and as little there is, that a Council hath it. But the doubt that troubles is, Whether all the assistance of the Holy Ghost be afforded in such a high manner, as to cause all the definitions of a Council in matters fundamental in the faith, and in remote deductions from it, to be alike infallible? Now the Romanists, to prove there is "infallible assistance," produce some places of Scripture; but no one of them infers, much less enforces an infallibility.'

The writer then proceeds to examine the texts John xvi. 13, John xiv. 16, Matt. xxviii. 20, Matt. xvi. 18, Luke xxii. 32, Matt. xviii. 20, Acts xv. 28, and speaks of them in general thus:—

'And for all the places together, weigh them with indifferency, and either they speak of the Church, including the Apostles, as all of them do,—and then all grant the voice of the Church is God's voice, divine and infallible;—or else they are general, unlimited, and appliable to private assemblies as well as general Councils, which none grant to be infallible but some mad enthusiasts;—or else they are limited not simply unto "all truth," but "all necessary to salvation," in which I shall easily grant a general Council cannot err, suffering itself to be led by this Spirit of truth in the Scripture, and not taking upon it to lead both the Scripture and the Spirit. For suppose these places, or any other, did promise assistance, even to infallibility, yet they granted it not to every general Council, but to the Catholic body of the Church itself; and if it be in the whole Church principally, then is it in a general Council but by consequence, as the Council represents the whole. And that which belongs to a thing by consequent, doth not otherwise nor longer belong to it than it consents and cleaves to that upon which it is a consequent, and therefore a general Council hath not this assistance but as it keeps to the whole Church and spouse of Christ, whose it is to hear His word and determine by it. And therefore if a general Council will go out of the Church's way, it may easily go without the Church's truth.'—Laud, *Conference with Fisher*, sect. xxxiii. pp. 252, 266, Anglo-Catholic Library.

NOTE FF, p. 124.

Καὶ παρ' ἑνὸς εὐλαβοῦς καὶ δευτέρου γενόμενον ἔργον πληροφορεῖ ἡμᾶς τῇ συμβουλίᾳ τοῦ Πνεύματος γίγνεσθαι. Ὅταν γὰρ μηδὲν ᾖ ἀνθρώπινον πρὸ ὀφθαλμῶν κείμενον, μηδὲ σκόπῳ οἰκείας ἀπολαύσεως πρὸς τὰς ἐνεργείας ὁρμῶσιν οἱ ὅσιοι, ἀλλ' ὅτι εὐάρεστον τῷ Θεῷ προθέμενοι, δῆλον ὅτι Κύριός ἐστιν ὁ τὰς καρδίας αὐτῶν κατευθύνων. Ὅπου δὲ ἄνδρες πνευματικοὶ τῶν βουλευμάτων κατάρχουσιν, ἕπεται δὲ τούτοις λαὸς Κυρίου ἐν συμφωνίᾳ τῆς γνώμης, τίς ἀμφιβαλεῖ μὴ οὐχὶ τῇ κοινωνίᾳ τοῦ Κυρίου ἡμῶν Ἰησοῦ Χριστοῦ, τοῦ τὸ αἷμα αὐτοῦ ὑπὲρ τῶν ἐκκλησιῶν ἐκχέαντος, τὴν βουλὴν γεγενῆσθαι ;—S. Basil. Ep. 229, vol. iii. p. 510.

NOTE GG, p. 132.

'Superest ad concludendam materiolam, de observatione quoque dandi et accipiendi baptismum commonefacere.

Dandi quidem habet jus summus Sacerdos, qui est Episcopus, dehinc Presbyteri et Diaconi, non tamen sine Episcopi auctoritate propter Ecclesiæ honorem, quo salvo salva pax est. Alioquin etiam laicis jus est : quod enim ex æquo accipitur, ex æquo dari potest, nisi Episcopi jam aut Presbyteri aut Diaconi vocantur discentes. Domini sermo non debet abscondi ab ullo. Proinde et baptismus, æquè Dei census, ab omnibus exerceri potest : sed quanto magis laicis disciplina verecundiæ et modestiæ incumbit? Cum ea majoribus competant, ne sibi adsumant dicatum Episcopis officium Episcopatûs.'—Tertull. *De Baptismo*, c. xvii. p. 230.

NOTE HH, p. 133.

'*Ut in necessitate et fideles baptizent.*—Loco [i] peregrè navigantes, aut si ecclesia proximo [k] non fuerit, posse fidelem, qui lavacrum suum integrum habet nec sit bigamus, baptizare in necessitate infirmitatis positum catechumenum, ita ut si supervixerit ad episcopum cum perducat, ut per manus impositionem perfici [l] possit.'—*Concil. Eliberitanum*, xxxviii.

NOTE II, p. 137.

The passage in St. Augustine (Tract. v. *In Joh. Evang.* c. i.) is a long one. The following extracts will sufficiently exhibit the writer's meaning :—

'Potuit Dominus Jesus Christus, si vellet, dare potestatem alicui servo suo, ut daret baptismum suum tanquam vice suâ, et transferre a se baptizandi potestatem, et constituere in

---
[i] deest ap. Mansi.   [k] in proximo M.   [l] proficere M.

aliquo servo suo, et tantam vim dare baptismo translato in servum quantam vim habeat baptismus datus a Domino. Hoc noluit ideo, ut in illo spes esset baptizatorum a quo se baptizatos agnoscerent. Noluit ergo servum ponere spem in servo.

'Hoc autem Johannes non noverat in Domino. Quia Dominus erat, noverat: quia ab ipso debebat baptizari, noverat: et confessus est quia veritas erat ille, et ille verax missus a veritate: hoc noverat. Sed quid in eo non noverat? Quia sibi retenturus erat baptismatis sui potestatem, et non eam transmissurus, et translaturus in aliquem servum: sed sive baptizaret in ministerio servus bonus, sive baptizaret in ministerio servus malus, non sciret se ille qui baptizaretur baptizari nisi ab illo qui sibi tenuit baptizandi potestatem.

'Non ait, ipse est Dominus; non ait, ipse est Christus; non ait, ipse est Deus; non ait, ipse est Jesus; non ait, ipse est qui natus de virgine Maria, posterior te, prior te: non ait hoc, jam hoc enim noverat Johannes. Sed quid non noverat? Tantam potestatem baptismi ipsum Dominum habiturum et sibi retenturum, sive præsentem in terrâ, sive absentem corpore in cœlo et præsentem majestate, sibi retenturum baptismi potestatem: ne Paulus diceret, Baptismus meus, ne Petrus diceret, Baptismus meus. Ideo videte, intendite voces Apostolorum. Nemo Apostolorum dixit, Baptismus meus. Quamvis unum omnium esset Evangelium, tamen invenis dixisse, Evangelium meum; non invenis dixisse, Baptisma meum.'—Pt. ii. vol. iii. p. 325.

NOTE JJ, p. 139.

'Nec illud te moveat, quod quidam non câ fide ad baptismum percipiendum parvulos ferunt, ut gratiâ spiritali ad

NOTE KK.

vitam regencrentur æternam, sed quod eos putant hoc remedio temporalem retinere vel recipere sanitatem. Non enim propterea illi non regenerantur, quia non ab istis hac intentione offeruntur. Celebrantur enim per eos necessaria ministeria, et verba sacramentorum, sine quibus consecrari parvulus non potest. Spiritus autem ille sanctus qui habitat in sanctis, ex quibus una illa columba deargentata caritatis igne conflatur, agit quod agit per servitutem, aliquando non solum simpliciter ignorantium verum etiam damnabiliter indignorum. Offeruntur quippe parvuli ad percipiendam spiritalem gratiam non tam ab eis quorum gestantur manibus (quamvis et ab ipsis si et ipsi boni et fideles sint) quam ab universa societate sanctorum atque fidelium. Ab omnibus namque offerri rectè intelliguntur, quibus placet quod offeruntur, et quorum sanctâ atque individuâ caritate ad communicationem sancti Spiritus adjuvantur. Tota hoc ergo mater Ecclesia, quæ in sanctis est, facit : quia tota omnes, tota singulos parit.'
—S. August. *Ad Bonifacium,* Ep. xcviii. vol. ii. p. 266.

NOTE KK, p. 140.

'Nemo mihi dicat quia non habet fidem cui mater impertit suam, involvens illi in sacramento, quousque idoneus fiat proprio non tantum sensu, sed et assensu, evolutam puramque percipere. Numquid breve pallium est ut non possit ambos cooperire ? Magna est Ecclesiæ fides. Numquid minor fide Cananææ mulieris, quam constat et filiæ sufficere potuisse, et sibi ? Ideo audivit, *o mulier, magna est fides tua ! sit tibi sicut petisti.* Numquid minor fide illorum, qui paralyticum per tegulas dimittentes, animæ illi simul et corporis obtinuere salutem ? Denique habes, *Quorum fidem ut vidit, ait paralytico, Confide, fili, remittuntur tibi peccata.* Et paulo post : *Tolle grabatum tuum et ambula.* Qui hoc credit, facile huic persuadebitur meritò Ecclesiam præsumere non solum parvulis baptizatis in suâ fide salutem, sed etiam interfectis pro Christo infantibus coronam martyrii.'—S. Bernard, *In Cantica*, Serm. lxvi.

NOTE LL, p. 141.

'Dum per sacratissimum crucis signum vos suscepit in utero sancta mater Ecclesia, quæ sicut et fratres vestros cum summa lætitiâ spiritaliter pariet, nova proles futura tantæ matris, quo usque per lavacrum sanctum regeneratos veræ luci restituat, congruis alimentis eos quos portat pascat in utero et ad diem partûs sui lætos læta perducat: quoniam non tenetur hac sententiâ Evæ quæ in tristitiâ et gemitu parit filios, nec ipsos gaudentes, sed potius flentes....Omnia sacramenta quæ acta sunt et aguntur in vobis per ministerium servorum Dei, exorcismis, orationibus, canticis spiritalibus, insufflationibus, cilicio, inclinatione cervicum, humilitate pedum, pavor ipse omni securitate appetendus, hæc omnia, ut dixi, escæ sunt quæ vos reficiunt in utero, vel renatos ex baptismo hilares vos mater exhibeat Christo.'—*De Symbolo ad Catechumenos*, vi. pp. 575, 555 ; cf. St. Cyril of Jerusalem, *Introd. Lecture*, § 13.

NOTE MM, p. 142.

'Et infantes quidem in brachiis dextris tenentur : majores vero pedem ponunt super pedem patrini sui.'—*Ex S. Gregorii Libro Sacramentorum*, p. 74.

The note on the word 'Patrini' in the Benedictine Edition is as follows : 'Patrini sunt qui offerunt baptizandos eosque baptizatos de sacro fonte suscipiunt, Gallicè *parreins*. Concilium sextum Arelatense, can. 9, *et patroni eos quos de lavacri fonte suscipiunt,* &c. Capitulum Herardi Turonensis Archiep. cap. 27, *ut patres et patrini filios suos et filiolos erudiant et enutriant.* Qui et dicti sunt susceptores Jesse Ambranensis Episc. epist. citatâ *et signent ipsos infantes in frontibus eorum susceptores viri vel fœminæ, id est, patrini vel matrinæ.* Dicuntur et sponsores. Tertullianus lib. de Baptismo : *quid enim necesse sponsores etiam periculo ingeri.* S. Dionysius, cap. 2 et 7, *Eccl. Hierar.* appellat ἀναδόχους, i.e. susceptores.'

NOTE NN, p. 150.

'Cum ergo sint duæ nativitates, ille (sc. Nicodemus) unam intelligebat. Una est de terra, alia de cœlo : una est de carne, alia de Spiritu : una est de mortalitate, alia de æternitate: una est de masculo et fœmina, alia de Deo et Ecclesiâ. Sed ipsæ duæ singulæ sunt : nec illa potest repeti, nec illa.' —S. August. Tract. xi. *In Joh. Evang.* c. 3. vol. iii. pt. ii. p. 378.

NOTE OO, p. 152.

'He that affirms them (infants) to be truly regenerated or sanctified in their infancy must yield to us in this : that such children or infants as have been formerly regenerated in a measure sufficient to their salvation outgrow this measure of regeneration or sanctification after they come to the use of reason, or years of discretion, as they do their apparel or clothes which were fit for them whilst they were infants. And no question but the old man, after we come to the use of reason, grows stronger and stronger in all of us, until we abate his strength, and mortify his members by the Spirit.'— Dr. T. Jackson, vol. iii. p. 101. (bk. x. c. xxvii.)

It is much to be regretted that the works of this writer are so imperfectly indexed. Owing to this, and to the somewhat desultory nature of the argument, they are not nearly so accessible for purposes of reference as they deserve to be. I remember well that many years ago Southey repeatedly recommended me to read the writings of Dr. Jackson as a model of vigorous and genuine English, both in sentiment and style.

NOTE PP, p. 156.

The passage quoted in the text is from St. Augustine, *De Baptismo*, lib. iii. c. 16.

'Primis temporibus cadebat super credentes Spiritus Sanctus ; et loquebantur linguis quas non didicerant, quomodo Spiritus dabat eis pronunciare. Signa erant tempori opportuna. Oportebat enim ita significari omnibus linguis Spiritum Sanctum quia Evangelium Dei per omnes linguas cursurum erat toto orbe terrarum. Significatum est illud et transiit. Numquid modo quibus imponitur manus ut accipiant Spiritum Sanctum, hoc expectatur ut linguis loquantur ? Aut quando imposuimus manum istis infantibus, attendit unusquisque vestrum utrum linguis loquerentur, et cum videret eos linguis non loqui, ita perverso corde aliquis vestrum fuit ut diceret, non acceperunt isti Spiritum Sanctum ; nam si accepissent, linguis loquerentur, quemadmodum tunc factum est ?— Unde cognoscit quisque accessisse in Spiritum Sanctum ? interroget cor suum : si diligit Patrem, manet Spiritus Dei in illo. Non potest esse dilectio sine Spiritu Dei : quia Paulus clamat, Caritas Dei diffusa est in cordibus nostris per Spiritum Sanctum, qui datus est nobis.' See also a beautiful passage on the Holy Ghost regarded as the Soul of the Body of the Church, in the 267th Sermon on the day of Pentecost, vol. v. p. 1090.

NOTE QQ, p. 160.

'Inde est quod exponens nobis Apostolus Paulus hunc panem, Unus panis, inquit, unum corpus multi sumus. O sacramentum pietatis, O signum unitatis, O vinculum caritatis! Qui vult vivere, habet ubi vivat, habet unde vivat. Accedat, credat, incorporetur ut vivificetur. Non abhorreat a compage membrorum, non sit putre membrum quod resecari mereatur; non sit distortum de quo erubescatur; sit pulchrum, sit aptum, sit sanum : hæreat corpori : vivat Deo de Deo : nunc laboret in terrâ ut postea regnet in cœlo.'— S. August. Tract. xxvi. *In Joh. Evang.* c. 6. vol. iii. pt. ii. 499.

NOTE RR, p. 166.

I have often thought it would be useful to embody the mention of these blessings, as given in the Prayer-book, into a prayer, to be used either before communicating, or during the waiting-time in the actual service when there are many communicants. It might be in some such form as this :—

O Lord God Almighty, Who hast given Thine Only-begotten Son, not only to die for us, but also to be our spiritual food and sustenance in the Holy Communion, grant to me grace so to approach Thy blessed feast, that I may spiritually eat the Flesh of Christ, and drink His Blood; that thereby Christ may dwell in me and I in Christ; that I may be made one with Christ and Christ with me. Cleanse my sinful body by His glorious Body; wash my soul by His most precious Blood. Grant me the sacred assurance that Thou still hast favour and goodness towards me; that I am still, sinful and miserable as I have been, a very member incorporate in the mystical Body of

Christ, which is the blessed company of all faithful people; that I am still an heir through hope of Thine everlasting kingdom. And, O merciful Lord God, grant that thus partaking of the Body and Blood of my Lord with all the Church, my body and my soul may be preserved to everlasting life, in Him and through Him Who alone is Life and Resurrection and Salvation, our Lord and Saviour Jesus Christ. Amen.

NOTE SS, p. 171.

'Hoc est sacrificium Christianorum, multi unum corpus in Christo. Quod etiam sacramento altaris fidelibus noto frequentat Ecclesia ubi ei demonstratur quod in eâ re quam offert, ipsa offeratur.'—S. Aug. *De Civ. Dei*, x. 7. vol. vii. p. 243.

Ἀρχιερεὺς ἕκαστος ἑαυτοῦ γίγνεται, ἀποσφάττων τὰς ἐντὸς κακίας καὶ δοκῶν ἀεὶ παρεστάναι τῷ Θεῷ, καὶ κατὰ πᾶσαν πρᾶξιν καὶ ῥῆσιν οὕτω φρίττων, ὡς ὁ ἀρχιερεὺς ὅταν θείῳ θυσιαστηρίῳ παρίσταται.— Theophyl. *Ad Rom.* xii. 1.

NOTE TT, p. 171.

There appears to be considerable diversity in the form of words used by priests in delivering, so to speak, the elements in Holy Communion to themselves. Some supply the first person throughout instead of the second, and say 'The Body (or the Blood) of our Lord Jesus Christ which was given (or shed) for me, preserve my body and soul unto everlasting life. I take and eat this in remembrance that Christ died for me, and feed on Him in my heart by faith with thanksgiving.' 'I drink this in remembrance that Christ's blood was shed for me, and am thankful.'

NOTE TT.

In this, which is, I believe, the most usual practice, there is one signal inconvenience; namely, that the priest professes actually *to do* in his own case, what in the case of all others he desires to be done. The feeding in the heart by faith, and the thankfulness which he solemnly urges upon others, he declares that he himself performs.

I will not argue whether it is right or wrong for a person so to profess and declare about himself. I will only urge that the change of person involves something very different and much more considerable than a mere change of person, and whatever that difference may be, it has no right to be imported where it has no place.

Feeling this inconvenience, some priests omit the latter clause in each case, and retaining the first person in the former one, stop short with the clause of prayer, without proceeding to that of solemn exhortation.

It appears to me that something is lost by the omission, while there is also a clear lack of authority for making it.

For my own part, I can see no difficulty whatever in making use of the words precisely as they stand. The priest is not celebrant only, but he is communicant also, and it is not only right, but very useful and necessary too, that he should act and speak as keeping in mind both these facts. Indeed the whole service requires him to keep them both in mind. The absolutions are spoken just as much, and upon precisely the same terms to himself, as to the congregation. His, no doubt, is the voice, the organic voice, to speak the will of God, and to pronounce the words of delegated power; but in no other point does he differ from all the rest to whom the words are spoken. Even the *form* is not otherwise than analogous to the language of Holy

Scripture, as in the Psalms, 'Praise thou the Lord, O my soul, and all that is within me praise His holy name.' The same consideration may be applied to the *posture* in which the celebrant administers to himself. There seems to be no reason why he should not *stand* to say the words of administration, and '*meekly kneel*' to receive the elements.

NOTE UU, p. 172.

Ὅτι αὐτὸς ὁ Κύριος καὶ ὁ Θεὸς καὶ παμβασιλεὺς ἡμῶν Ἰησοῦς ὁ Χριστὸς τῇ νυκτὶ ᾗ παρεδίδου ἑαυτὸν ὑπὲρ τῶν ἁμαρτιῶν ἡμῶν, καὶ τὸν ὑπὲρ πάντων ὑψίστατον θάνατον σαρκὶ, συνανακλιθεὶς μετὰ τῶν ἁγίων καὶ ἀχράντων καὶ ἀμώμων αὐτοῦ χειρῶν, ἀναβλέψας εἰς τὸν ἴδιον πατέρα, Θεὸν δὲ ἡμῶν καὶ Θεὸν τῶν ὅλων, εὐχαριστήσας, εὐλογήσας, ἁγιάσας, κλάσας διέδωκε τοῖς ἁγίοις καὶ μακαρίοις αὐτοῦ μαθηταῖς, καὶ ἀποστόλοις εἰπὼν [ἐκφώνως] λάβετε, φάγετε.

Ὁ Διάκονος. Ἐκτείνατε.

Ὁ Ἱερεὺς ἐκφώνως,

Τοῦτο γάρ ἐστι τὸ σῶμά μου τὸ ὑπὲρ ὑμῶν κλώμενον, καὶ διαδιδόμενον εἰς ἄφεσιν ἁμαρτιῶν.

Ὁ Λαός. Ἀμήν.

Ὁ Ἱερεὺς λέγει ἐπευχόμενος,

Ὡσαύτως καὶ τὸ ποτήριον μετὰ τὸ δειπνῆσαι λαβὼν, καὶ κεράσας ἐξ οἴνου καὶ ὕδατος, ἀναβλέψας εἰς τὸν οὐρανὸν πρὸς σὲ τὸν ἴδιον πατέρα, Θεὸν δὲ ἡμῶν, καὶ Θεὸν τῶν ὅλων εὐχαριστήσας, εὐλογήσας, πλήσας πνεύματος ἁγίου, μετέδωκε τοῖς ἁγίοις καὶ μακαρίοις αὐτοῦ μαθηταῖς καὶ ἀποστόλοις εἰπὼν [ἐκφώνως] πίετε ἐξ αὐτοῦ πάντες.

Ὁ Διάκονος. Ἔτι ἐκτείνατε.

Ὁ Ἱερεὺς ἐκφώνως,

Τοῦτο γάρ ἐστι τὸ αἷμά μου τὸ τῆς καινῆς διαθήκης, τὸ ὑπὲρ ὑμῶν καὶ πολλῶν ἐκχυνόμενον καὶ διαδιδόμενον εἰς ἄφεσιν ἁμαρτιῶν.

NOTE VV. 317

'Ο Λαὸς. 'Αμήν.
> *Ex Liturgiâ D. Marci, Liturg. Oriental.* Renaudot, vol. i. p. 155. Cf. for St. James's Liturgy, Renaudot, vol. ii. p. 33.

NOTE VV, p. 173.

See for a very full illustration of the statement in the text Mr. Neale's translation of the Liturgies of St. Mark, &c., and the Appendix I of the short formulæ of Institution as they occur in every extant liturgy. The following extract is from that of St. Cyril of Jerusalem (Copto-Jacobite), of which Mr. Neale says, 'St. Cyril's is one of the most valuable of the second class of Liturgies (Hierosolymitan, assimilated to the Alexandrian). From its singular resemblance to, and in some respects its even more singular departure from that of St. Mark, it is *very probably* the real composition, or rather edition, of the Saint whose name it bears.'

For Thine only-begotten Son, our Lord God, the Saviour and Universal King Jesus Christ, in that night in which He gave Himself up that He might suffer for our sins, before the death which by His own free-will He undertook for us all.
People. We believe.
Priest. He took bread into His holy, immaculate, pure, blessed, and quickening hands, and looked up to heaven, to Thee His God and Father, and the Lord of all, and gave thanks.
People. Amen.
Priest. And blessed it.
People. Amen.

Priest. And sanctified it, and brake it, and gave it to His holy Disciples and pure Apostles, saying: Take, eat ye all of it: FOR THIS IS MY BODY WHICH SHALL BE BROKEN FOR YOU, AND FOR MANY SHALL BE GIVEN FOR THE REMISSION OF SINS : do this in remembrance of Me.

People. Amen.

Priest. In like manner also He mingled the Chalice after supper with wine and water, and gave thanks.

People. Amen.

Priest. And blessed it.

People. Amen.

Priest. And sanctified it.

People. Amen.

Priest. And tasted it, and gave it to His glorious holy Disciples and Apostles, saying, Take, drink ye all of it, THIS IS MY BLOOD OF THE NEW TESTAMENT WHICH FOR YOU IS POURED FORTH, AND FOR MANY SHALL BE GIVEN TO THE REMISSION OF SINS : do this in remembrance of Me.

People. Amen.

Priest. For as often as ye shall eat of this Bread, and drink of this Chalice, ye announce My Death, and confess My Resurrection, and keep My memory till I come.

People. We announce Thy Death, O Lord, and we confess Thy Resurrection.

NOTE WW, p. 174.

Μεγάλη ἡ δύναμις τῆς συνόδου, ἤγουν τῶν ἐκκλησιῶν. Σκόπει πῶς μεγάλη ἦν ἡ δύναμις τῆς συνόδου· ἡ τῆς ἐκκλησίας εὐχὴ τὸν Πέτρον ἀπὸ τῶν δεσμῶν ἔλυσε, τοῦ Παύλου τὸ στόμα ἀνέωξεν· ἡ τούτων ψῆφος, οὐχ ὡς ἔτυχε καὶ τοὺς ἐπὶ τὰς πνευματικὰς ἀρχὰς ἐρχομένους κατακοσμεῖ. διάτοι τοῦτο καὶ ὁ μέλλων χειροτονεῖν, καὶ τὰς ἐκείνων εὐχὰς καλεῖ τότε, καὶ αὐτοὶ ἐπιψηφίζονται, καὶ

NOTE XX.

ἐπιβοῶσιν ἅπερ ἴσασιν οἱ μεμυημένοι. οὐ γὰρ δὴ θέμις ἐπὶ τῶν ἀμυήτων ἐκκαλύπτειν ἅπαντα. ἔστι δὲ ὅπου οὐ διέστηκεν ὁ ἱερεὺς τοῦ ἀρχομένου· οἷον ὅταν ἀπολαύειν δέῃ τῶν φρικτῶν μυστηρίων· ὁμοίως γὰρ πάντες ἀξιούμεθα τῶν αὐτῶν. οὐ καθάπερ ἐπὶ τῆς παλαιᾶς τὰ μὲν ὁ ἱερεὺς ἤσθιε, τὰ δὲ ὁ ἀρχόμενος· καὶ θέμις οὐκ ἦν τῷ λαῷ μετέχειν ὧν μετεῖχεν ὁ ἱερεύς· ἀλλ' οὐ νῦν· ἀλλὰ πᾶσιν ἓν σῶμα πρόκειται, καὶ ποτήριον ἕν· καὶ ἐν ταῖς εὐχαῖς δὲ πολὺ τὸν λαὸν ἴδοι τις ἂν συνεισφέροντα...... ἐπ' αὐτῶν πάλιν τῶν φρικωδεστάτων μυστηρίων ἐπεύχεται ὁ ἱερεὺς τῷ λαῷ, ἐπεύχεται δὲ ὁ λαὸς τῷ ἱερεῖ. τὸ γὰρ μετὰ τοῦ πνεύματός σου, οὐδὲν ἄλλο ἐστὶν ἢ τοῦτο. τὰ τῆς εὐχαριστίας πάλιν κοινά. οὐδὲ γὰρ ἐκεῖνος εὐχαριστεῖ μόνος, ἀλλὰ καὶ ὁ λαὸς ἅπας. πρότερον γὰρ αὐτῶν λαβὼν φωνὴν, εἶτα συντιθεμένων ὅτι ἀξίως καὶ δικαίως τοῦτο γίγνεται, τότε ἄρχεται τῆς εὐχαριστίας. καὶ τί θαυμάζεις εἴπου μετὰ τοῦ ἱερέως ὁ λαὸς φθέγγεται, ὅπουγε καὶ μετ' αὐτῶν τῶν Χερουβὶμ, καὶ τῶν ἄνω δυνάμεων, κοινῇ τοὺς ἱεροὺς ἐκείνους ὕμνους ἀναπέμπει; ταῦτα δέ μοι πάντα ἐκεῖνα εἴρηται, ἵνα ἕκαστος καὶ τῶν ἀρχομένων νήφῃ, ἵνα μάθωμεν ὅτι σῶμά ἐσμεν ἅπαντες ἕν, τοσαύτην ἔχοντες πρὸς ἀλλήλους διαφορὰν, ὅσην μέλη πρὸς μέλη, καὶ μὴ τὸ πᾶν ἐπὶ τοὺς ἱερέας ῥίπτωμεν, ἀλλὰ καὶ αὐτοὶ, ὥσπερ κοινοῦ σώματος, τῆς ἐκκλησίας ἁπάσης οὕτω φροντίζωμεν· τοῦτο γὰρ καὶ ἀσφάλειαν πλείονα, καὶ ὑμῖν ἐπιδίδωσι μείζονα κατασκευάζειν πρὸς ἀρετήν.—S. Chrysost. Hom. xviii. in 2 Ep. ad Cor. vol. x. p. 568.

NOTE XX, p. 175.

'Fratres carissimi, tales oportet nos esse cum corpus Christi consecramus, *cum consecratum manducantes, sacrificamus,* cum vobis idem corpus in salutem corporis et animæ porrigimus. Tales etiam vos oportet esse, cum sacrum Sacramentum de manibus nostris accipitis, scientes quod qui corpus Christi indigne accipit, et sanguinem ejus indignè bibit, judicium sibi manducat et bibit. Neque enim credere debemus quod soli sacerdoti supradictæ virtutes sint necessariæ, quasi solus consecret, et sacrificet corpus Christi. Non solus sacrificat, non solus consecrat, sed totus conventus fidelium qui adstat, cum illo consecrat, cum illo sacrificat. Nec solus ligni faber facit domum; sed alius virgas, alius ligna, alius trabes &c. comportat. Debent itaque adstantes habere de suo, sicut et sacerdos, fidem firmam, orationem puram, devotionem piam.'—Guerrici Abbatis, *De Purific. B. Mariæ,* Serm. v. (apud *Opera S. Bernardi,* vol. ii. p. 960.)

Guerricus, from whose Sermons this remarkable passage is extracted, was a pupil and friend of St. Bernard. He is twice mentioned in his letters (Ep. 89, 90): 'Si de fratre Guerrico desideras, immo quia desideras scire, sic currit non quasi in incertum, sic pugnat non quasi aerem verberans. Sed quoniam scit neque pugnantis esse, neque currentis, sed miserentis Dei; ipsum rogat a te orari pro se, quatenus qui jam donavit ei et pugnare et currere, det et vincere et pervenire.' He became Abbot of 'Igniacum' in the diocese of Rheims in the year 1138, and died in 1157.

'Plane quam sanæ verbis doctrinæ fuerit, luculentissimi atque disertissimi et verè spirituales Sermones ejus, quos in solemnitatibus præcipuis in conventibus Fratrum fecit, et a Cantore ejusdem Ecclesiæ excepti sunt, manifeste declarant.'

'Porro ignitum eloquium Domini vehementer quod in sermonibus illis invenitur, ita movet, afficit et accendit legentem, ut durissimus corde sit, qui non ex eorum lectione compunctus ad meliora proficere studeat.'—Preface to the Sermons of Guerricus.

NOTE YY, p. 176.

'Attende igitur, ut prædixi, et semper in mente habe, jugi

memoria retine gratiam tibi singulariter a Deo collatam, quam nec Angelis præstitit, nec ceteris hominibus concessit. Panis enim in manibus tuis in corpus unigeniti Filii Dei transubstantiatur : vinum in sanctissimum sanguinem D. N. Jesu Christi tuâ benedictione convertitur. Multùm ardent Seraphim sanctæ Trinitati præ ceteris cunctis spiritibus loco et caritate conjuncti. . . . Non tamen hoc privilegio prænitent ut Corpus vel Sanguinem Redemptoris nostri in subjecta creatura sanctificent, &c.

'Ipsi enim (sacerdotes) habent claves hujus sacramenti, ipsi sunt veri mediatores inter Deum et hominem, ipsi sunt vox et organum sanctæ Ecclesiæ, ipsi offerunt Deo plebis precationes et referunt propitiationes.'—S. Bernard, *Instructio Sacerdotis*, c. ix. xii. vol. ii. pp. 531, 535.

NOTE ZZ, p. 176.

This statement is borrowed from the note of the Benedictine editor of St. Bernard, who writing upon this passage of Guerricus, after declaring (what we do not doubt) that the priest is the only right and adequate minister for the consecration of the Eucharist, adds, 'Quanquam dici potest, adstantes etiam suo modo sacrificium offerre et conficere per sacerdotem et cum sacerdote, qui populi mediator est et minister. Unde in canone Missæ olim ita legebatur, *et omnium circumstantium, qui tibi offerunt hoc sacrificium laudis,* quibus verbis hæc inserta sunt, *pro quibus tibi offerimus, vel qui tibi offerunt.*'—*Notæ in S. Bernard.* vol. i. p. cxviii.

NOTE AAA, p. 177.

Κοινωνία τοῦ σώματος τοῦ Χριστοῦ ἐστιν· εἶπεν· ἀντὶ τοῦ, ὥσπερ ἐκεῖνο τὸ σῶμα ἥνωται τῷ Χριστῷ οὕτω καὶ ἡμεῖς αὐτῷ διὰ τοῦ ἄρτου τούτου ἐνούμεθα.—Theophyl. ad 1 Cor. x. 16.

Κοινωνία λέγεταί τε καὶ ἔστιν ἀληθῶς διὰ τὸ κοινωνεῖν ἡμᾶς δι' αὐτῆς τῷ Χριστῷ, καὶ μετέχειν αὐτοῦ τῆς σαρκός τε καὶ Θεότητος· κοινωνεῖν δὲ καὶ ἐνοῦσθαι ἀλλήλοις δι' αὐτῆς· ἐπεὶ γὰρ ἐξ ἑνὸς ἄρτου μεταλαμβάνομεν οἱ πάντες ἓν σῶμα Χριστοῦ καὶ ἓν αἷμα καὶ ἀλλήλων μέλη γιγνόμεθα, σύσσωμοι Χριστοῦ χρηματίζοντες.—Joann. Damascen. *Orthod. Fidei,* lib. iv. c. xiv.

NOTE BBB, p. 182.

Ταῦτα οὐχ ἵνα ἁπλῶς μετέχητε λέγω, ἀλλ' ἵνα ἀξίους ἑαυτοὺς κατασκευάζητε. Οὐκ εἶ τῆς θυσίας ἄξιος, οὐδὲ τῆς μεταλήψεως; οὐκοῦν οὐδὲ τῆς εὐχῆς· ἀκούεις ἑστῶτος τοῦ κήρυκος, καὶ λέγοντος, ὅσοι ἐν μετανοίᾳ ἀπέλθετε πάντες. Ὅσοι μὴ μετέχουσι, ἐν μετανοίᾳ εἰσίν. εἰ τῶν ἐν μετανοίᾳ εἶ, μετασχεῖν οὐκ ὀφείλεις. ὁ γὰρ μὴ μετέχων, τῶν ἐν μετανοίᾳ ἐστίν........

Σκόπει, παρακαλῶ· τράπεζα πάρεστι βασιλική, ἄγγελοι διακονούμενοι τῇ τραπέζῃ, αὐτὸς πάρεστιν ὁ βασιλεύς, καὶ σὺ ἕστηκας χασμώμενος;...πᾶς γὰρ ὁ μὴ μετέχων τῶν μυστηρίων, ἀναίσχυντος καὶ ἰταμῶς ἑστηκώς....Εἰπέ μοι, εἴ τις εἰς ἑστίασιν κληθεὶς, τὰς χεῖρας νίψαιτο, καὶ κατακλιθείη, καὶ ἕτοιμος γένοιτο πρὸς τὴν τράπεζαν, εἶτα μὴ μετέχοι, οὐχ ὑβρίζει τὸν καλέσαντα; οὐ βέλτιον τὸν τοιοῦτον μηδὲ παραγενέσθαι; οὕτω δὴ καὶ σὺ παραγέγονας· τὸν ὕμνον ᾖσας, μετὰ πάντων ὡμολόγησας εἶναι τῶν ἀξίων, τῷ μὴ μετὰ τῶν ἀναξίων ἀνακεχωρηκέναι· πῶς ἔμεινας, καὶ οὐ μετέχεις τῆς τραπέζης;—S. Chrysost. *In Ep. ad Ephes.* c. i. Hom. iii. (xi. p. 23). The whole passage is well worth consulting.

NOTE CCC, p. 196.

'Propter ipsam personam, quam totius Ecclesiæ solus gestabat audire meruit, *Tibi dabo claves regni cælorum.*

NOTE DDD.

Has enim claves non homo unus, sed unitas accepit Ecclesiæ. Hinc ergo Petri excellentia prædicatur, quia ipsius universitatis et unitatis Ecclesiæ figuram gessit, quando ei dictum est, *Tibi trado,* quod omnibus traditum est. Nam ut noveritis Ecclesiam accepisse claves regni cœlorum, audite in alio loco quid Dominus dicat omnibus Apostolis suis, *Accipite Spiritum sanctum:* et continuo, *Si cui dimiseritis peccata, dimittentur ei, et si cui tenueritis, tenebuntur.* Hoc ad claves pertinet, de quibus dictum est, *Quæ solveritis in terrâ, soluta erunt et in cælo; et quæ ligaveritis in terrâ, ligata erunt et in cælo.* Sed hoc Petro dixit. Ut scias quia Petrus universæ Ecclesiæ personam tunc gerebat, audi quid ipsi dicatur, quid omnibus fidelibus sanctis: *Si peccaverit in te frater tuus,* &c. Columba ligat, columba solvit; ædificium suprà petram ligat et solvit.'—S. August. Serm. ccxcv. *In Natali Apost. Petri et Pauli,* (v. 1194).

NOTE DDD, p. 198.

I would fain extract the whole of the beautiful passage in which St. Augustine expands the thought here referred to. The following is the conclusion of it:—

'Nemo tamen istos insignes Apostolos separet. Et in eo quod significabat Petrus ambo erant; et in eo quod significabat Johannes, ambo futuri erant. Significando sequebatur iste, manebat ille: credendo autem ambo mala præsentia hujus miseriæ tolerabant, ambo futura bona illius beatitudinis exspectabant. Nec ipsi soli, sed universa hoc facit sancta Ecclesia sponsa Christi, ab istis tentationibus eruenda, in illa felicitate servanda. Quas duas vitas Petrus et Johannes figuraverunt, singuli singulas: verum et in hâc temporaliter ambulaverunt ambo per fidem, et illâ in æternum fruentur ambo per speciem. Omnibus igitur sanctis ad Christi corpus inseparabiliter pertinentibus, propter hujus vitæ procellosissimæ gubernaculum, ad liganda et solvenda peccata claves regni cœlorum primus Apostolorum Petrus accepit, eisdemque omnibus sanctis propter vitæ illius secretissimæ quietissimum sinum, super pectus Christi Johannes Evangelista discubuit. Quoniam nec iste solus, sed universa Ecclesia ligat solvitque peccata; nec ille in principio Verbum Deum apud Deum, et cetera de Christi divinitate et de totius Divinitatis Trinitate atque Unitate sublimia, quæ in illo regno facie ad faciem contemplanda nunc autem donec veniat Dominus, in speculo atque in ænigmate contuenda sunt, quæ prædicando ruebant de fonte Dominici pectoris solus bibit; sed ipse Dominus ipsum Evangelium pro suâ cujusque capacitate omnibus suis bibendum toto terrarum orbe diffudit.'—S. August. Tractat. cxxiv. *In Joh. Evang.* c. 21 (vol. iii. pt. ii. p. 824).

NOTE EEE, p. 200.

Ex Canone I. 'Cum in his omnibus examinatus inventus fuerit plenè instructus, cum consensu clericorum et laicorum, et conventu totius provinciæ episcoporum maximeque metropolitani vel auctoritate vel præsidentia ordinetur episcopus,' &c.

Canon II. 'Episcopus cum ordinatur, duo episcopi ponant et teneant Evangeliorum codicem super caput et cervicem ejus, et uno super cum fundente benedictionem reliqui omnes episcopi qui adsunt manibus suis caput ejus tangant.'

Canon III. 'Presbyter cum ordinatur, episcopo cum benedicente et manum super caput ejus tenente, etiam omnes presbyteri qui præsentes sunt manus suas juxta manum episcopi super caput illius teneant.'—*Concil. Carthag. IV. sive Statuta Ecclesiæ Antiquæ Concilia*, ed. Bruns. p. 141.

NOTE FFF, p. 201.

Καὶ οἱ Ἀπόστολοι ἡμῶν ἔγνωσαν διὰ τοῦ Κυρίου ἡμῶν Ἰησοῦ Χριστοῦ, ὅτι ἔρις ἔσται ἐπὶ τοῦ ὀνόματος τῆς ἐπισκοπῆς. Διὰ ταύτην οὖν τὴν αἰτίαν πρόγνωσιν εἰληφότες τελείαν, κατέστησαν τοὺς προειρημένους, καὶ μεταξὺ ἐπινομὴν δεδώκασι, ὅπως ἐὰν κοιμηθῶσιν διαδέξωνται ἕτεροι δεδοκιμασμένοι ἄνδρες τὴν λειτουργίαν αὐτῶν. Τοὺς οὖν κατασταθέντας ὑπ᾽ ἐκείνων, ἢ μεταξὺ ὑφ᾽ ἑτέρων ἐλλογίμων ἀνδρῶν, συνευδοκησάσης τῆς ἐκκλησίας πάσης, κ.τ.λ.—Clem. Rom. *Ad Corinthios*, c. xliv. (ed. Jacobson, p. 163, where cf. Wotton's note).

NOTE GGG, p. 201.

'Propter quod plebs obsequens præceptis Dominicis, et Deum metuens, a peccatore præposito separare se debet, nec se ad sacrilegi sacerdotis sacrificia miscere : quando ipsa maximè habeat potestatem vel eligendi dignos sacerdotes vel indignos recusandi. Quod et ipsum videmus de divinâ auctoritate descendere, ut sacerdos plebe præsente sub omnium oculis deligatur, et dignus atque idoneus publico judicio ac testimonio comprobetur.......Quod postea secundum divina magisteria observatur in Actis Apostolorum : quando de ordinando in locum Judæ Apostolo Petrus ad plebem loquitur. Surrexit, inquit, Petrus in medio discentium ; fuit autem turba in uno. Nec hoc in Episcoporum tantum et sacerdotum, sed in Diaconorum ordinationibus observasse Apostolos animadvertimus, de quo et ipso in Actis eorum scriptum est : Et convocaverunt, inquit, illi duodecim totam plebem discipulorum, et dixerunt eis. Quod utique idcirco tam diligenter et caute convocata plebe tota gerebatur, ne quis ad altaris ministerium, vel ad sacerdotalem locum indignus obreperet.......Propter quod diligenter de traditione divinâ, et Apostolicâ observatione servandum est et tenendum quod apud nos quoque, et fere per provincias universas tenetur, ut ad ordinationes rite celebrandas, ad eam plebem, cui præpositus ordinatur, Episcopi ejusdem Provinciæ proximi quique conveniant, et Episcopus deligatur plebe præsente quæ singulorum vitam plenissimè novit, et uniuscujusque actum de ejus conversatione perspexit.'—S. Cyprian. Ep. lxvii. p. 171 (*Responsum Synodicum Ecclesiæ Africanæ ad fratres Hispanos in causâ Basilidis et Martialis*).

NOTE HHH, p. 204.

The practice of the Episcopal Church in the United States, and now happily introduced in some of our own Colonial Dioceses, in respect of the election of Bishops, seems to approach more nearly than that of any other portion of the Catholic Church to the primitive model described by Cyprian, as observed 'fere per universas Provincias.' On this subject, I may be allowed to extract an important passage from a letter addressed to me by my valued friend, the Bishop of New York :—

'Our Diocesan Synods or Conventions consist of the Clergy having duly recognized duty, and of a representation of the Laity. There may be three from each Parish. The two orders, on common occasions, vote together; but if a vote by orders be called for, each Parish has but one lay vote. The lay members of the Parish, if there be two or three, must

NOTE HHH. 327

agree or lose their vote. If there be three, two would decide their vote. These lay deputies may be chosen in the Parish by the Vestry, or by the Congregation,—almost always by the former.

'In the election of a Bishop, the two orders vote separately, and must of course concur. In this Diocese they vote *at the same time*, in different parts of the same Church. In some Dioceses the Clergy vote *first, retiring* for the purpose, and they must by a majority nominate a Presbyter before the Laity vote at all; and then they confirm or not the nomination. In one or more of our Dioceses, a majority of two-thirds is required to elect.

'Our *General Convention* consists of two Houses: the House of Bishops, and the House of Clerical and Lay Deputies. The lower House consists of four clerical and four lay Deputies from each Diocese, whether large or small; and these Deputies (clerical and lay) are chosen by the Diocesan Conventions, and their election requires a concurrence of Clergy and Laity.

'Then in each Diocese there is a Standing Committee, four Clergy and four Laymen, elected annually. It is a Council of advice to the Bishop. All candidates for Orders must present papers to the Standing Committee, and are recommended by that Committee to the Bishop, first, in order to be admitted to candidateship, and secondly, at the end of three years, in order to be ordained. In case of death, or disability of the Bishop, the Standing Committee in each Diocese is "the Ecclesiastical Authority" for the time, for all purposes except strictly episcopal acts.

'Then it must be added that in our voluntary system the Laity in the Vestries *call* the Clergy to the charge of the Parish. The Bishop may nominate or recommend, and will usually have much influence, but the final call is from the Vestry. And the Laity pay the minister, as well as supply means for all religious and charitable objects.

'Here, then, we see that—

'1. The Laity call the minister, and pay him.—We have very few endowments.

'2. The Laity in the Diocesan Convention have a veto in the election of a Bishop, and on all canons, resolutions, &c.

'3. The Laity in the Standing Committee have a voice in all admissions to the ministry; and in all cases where the Bishop asks for advice, in legal questions, &c.

'4. The Laity in General Convention have a veto in the election of Missionary Bishops to the Missionary Dioceses (the House of Bishops in these cases first nominating), and also a veto on all canons, changes in the Prayer-book, division of Dioceses, and other work of the General Convention.

'Both the Diocesan and General Conventions include a large number of the ablest Laymen in the country, and these Laymen have always proved themselves cautious and conservative in their action, the great majority of them earnest and sound in their Church feelings and principles. Sometimes when the House of Bishops has acted a little hastily (especially formerly, when it was a smaller body; now it has upwards of forty members), the lower House, with its larger numbers and slower action, and with its able Laymen, has arrested the erroneous action.'

I cannot refrain from illustrating the above by the following extracts from the Journal of the Special Convention of the Diocese of Vermont on the occasion of the election of a Bishop to succeed the late deeply-regretted Bishop Hopkins.

NOTE HHH.

'St. Paul's Church,
Burlington, March 11, 1868.

'This being the place and the time appointed for the meeting of the Special Convention of the Protestant Episcopal Church in the Diocese of Vermont, the Clergy and Laity met at ten o'clock A.M.

'The Convention was called to order by the Rev. JOSIAH SWETT, D.D., President of the Standing Committee; THOMAS H. CANFIELD, of Burlington, Secretary.

'The Secretary then read the Summons of the Standing Committee calling this Convention, which was as follows:—

'DIOCESE OF VERMONT.

'At a meeting of the Standing Committee of this Diocese, held on the 15th day of January, 1868, it was, on motion,

'*Resolved*, That a special Convention of this Diocese be called, as provided in the Canons of the Church, to meet in St. Paul's Church, Burlington, on the 11th day of March next, at 10 o'clock A.M., to elect a Bishop for the Diocese, in the place of the Rt. Rev. JOHN HENRY HOPKINS, D.D., LL.D., D.C.L. Oxon., deceased, and to devise means for his support.

'*Therefore,* I, the President of the Standing Committee, do hereby summon a Special Convention of this Diocese, to meet at the time and place aforesaid; first, to elect a Bishop; and secondly, to provide for the support of the same.

'JOSIAH SWETT.

'*Underhill, January* 16, 1868.

'Eighteen Clergymen being present, and twenty-five Parishes represented by the Laity.

'A quorum, according to the Canons, was found to be

present, and the President then announced that the Convention was duly organized. * * *

'On motion of the Rev. Mr. Smith, the Convention adjourned, for the purpose of attending Divine Service, to meet at three o'clock P.M., to-day.

'Morning Prayers were offered by the Rev. Malcolm Douglass, Rector of St. Paul's Church, Windsor, assisted by the Rev. J. Newton Fairbanks, Rector of St. Thomas's Church, Brandon.

'The Sermon before the Convention was then preached by the Rev. Albert H. Bailey, D.D., Rector of Grace Church, Sheldon, from ST. MATTHEW XXVIII. 20 : "*Lo, I am with you alway, even unto the end of the world.*" * * *

'On motion of Dr. Hicks,

'*Resolved*, That this Convention do now proceed to the election of a Bishop for the Diocese of Vermont.

'After singing the last four verses of the 99th selection of Psalms, some minutes were spent in silent prayer.

'The President then conducted the public devotions of the Convention in the use of the Lord's Prayer and appropriate Collects.

'Mr. Richardson was called to the Chair while the President and Clergy retired to an adjoining room for consultation, and agreeing upon the nomination of a suitable person for Bishop of Vermont.

'On motion of Mr. Walker,

'*Resolved*, That each Lay Delegate when proceeding to the election shall deposit a ballot for the person of his choice.

'Upon the return of the Clergy, the President resumed the Chair, and informed the Convention that the Clergy had proceeded to vote by ballot for a suitable person to be elected Bishop of the Diocese, and that they had unanimously made choice of the Rev. WILLIAM HENRY AUGUSTUS BISSELL, D.D., Rector of Trinity Church, Geneva, of the Diocese of Western New York, and he now in behalf of the Clergy, whose duty it is as required by the Canon to make a nomination, does hereby nominate to the Convention, WILLIAM HENRY AUGUSTUS BISSELL, D.D., for Bishop of the Diocese of Vermont.

'The President then called upon the Laity to prepare their ballots according to the Canons, Messrs. Nichols and Hobart being appointed tellers.

'The ballots having been forwarded and counted, the Rev. WILLIAM HENRY AUGUSTUS BISSELL, D.D., was found to have received upon the second ballotting, fifty-one out of the fifty-six votes cast, whereupon the President announced to the Convention that the nomination of the Clergy was concurred in as required by the Canons.

'On motion of Mr. Nichols,

'*Resolved*, That the Rev. WILLIAM HENRY AUGUSTUS BISSELL, D.D., be, and he hereby is declared to be, duly elected Bishop of the Protestant Episcopal Church in the Diocese of Vermont.

'Which was adopted *unanimously*. The President then announced that the Rev. WILLIAM HENRY AUGUSTUS BISSELL, D.D., having received the requisite number of votes of the Clerical and Lay Delegates of this Convention, as required by the Canons, was, and is hereby declared to be, duly elected Bishop of the Protestant Episcopal Church in the Diocese of Vermont. The whole Convention then arose and joined in singing the *Gloria in Excelsis*.

'The Canonical Testimonial in favour of the Consecration of the Bishop elect was then read and signed by all the members of the Convention, of which the following is a copy:—

NOTE HHH.

'DIOCESE OF VERMONT.

'Testimony from the Members of the Convention.

'We, whose names are underwritten, fully sensible how important it is that the sacred Office of a Bishop should not be unworthily conferred, and firmly persuaded that it is our duty to bear testimony, on this solemn occasion, without partiality or affection, do, in the presence of Almighty God, testify that the Rev. WILLIAM HENRY AUGUSTUS BISSELL, D.D., Rector of Trinity Church, Geneva, of the Diocese of Western New York, is not, so far as we are informed, justly liable to evil report, either for error in religion, or for viciousness of life ; and that we do not know or believe there is any impediment, on account of which he ought not to be consecrated to that holy Office.

'We do, moreover, jointly and severally declare, that we do in our conscience believe him to be of such sufficiency in good learning, such soundness in the faith, and of such virtuous and pure manners and godly conversation, that he is apt and meet to exercise the Office of a Bishop, to the honour of God and the edifying of His Church, and to be a wholesome example to the flock of Christ.'

Signed by eighteen clergy and fifty-eight laymen. * * *

'The Secretary then affixed to the Testimonial his certificate, which is as follows :—

'DIOCESE OF VERMONT.

'Testimony from the Secretary of the Convention.

'I, THOS. H. CANFIELD, Secretary of the Convention of the Protestant Episcopal Church in the Diocese of Vermont, do hereby certify that at a special Convention of the said

NOTE HHH.

Diocese, summoned as the Canon directs, and held in St. Paul's Church, Burlington, on the eleventh day of March, in the year of our Lord one thousand eight hundred and sixty-eight, the Rev. WILLIAM HENRY AUGUSTUS BISSELL, D.D., Rector of Trinity Church, Geneva, of the Diocese of Western New York, was duly and canonically elected to the Office of Bishop of the aforesaid Diocese of Vermont; and that he was announced and declared to be thus elected by the President of the Convention, the Rev. JOSIAH SWETT, D.D.

    'Attest,   'THOS. H. CANFIELD,
'*Burlington, March* 11, 1868.   '*Secretary.*

'On motion of the Rev. Mr. Batchelder,

'*Resolved*, That the Rev. Josiah Swett, D.D., President of this Convention, the Rev. Malcolm Douglass, and Thos. H. Canfield, Secretary of the Convention, be appointed a Committee to inform the Rev. Dr. Bissell of his election to the Episcopate of the Diocese of Vermont.

'On motion of the Rev. Mr. Bliss, it was ordered that the Journal of this Convention, together with the Sermon of Rev. Dr. Bailey, be printed with the Journal of the Annual Diocesan Convention, to be held at Montpelier in June next.

'The minutes of the proceedings of the Convention were then read and approved.

'On motion of the Rev. Mr. Hale,

'*Resolved*, That after the usual religious services, the Convention adjourn *sine die.*

'When after singing the Fortieth Hymn, and prayers and benediction by the President, the Convention adjourned.

      'JOSIAH SWETT,
       '*President of the Convention.*
'THOS. H. CANFIELD, *Secretary.*'

NOTE III, p. 212.

'Homo in baptismo totus abluitur, non præter pedes, sed totus omnino: veruntamen cum in rebus humanis postea vivitur, utique terra calcatur. Ipsi igitur humani affectus sine quibus in hac mortalitate non vivitur, quasi pedes sunt.... Si autem confitemur peccata nostra, qui pedes discipulorum lavit, nobis peccata dimittit usque ad pedes quibus conversamur in terrâ.'—S. August. Tractat. lvi. *In Joh. Evang.*

NOTE KKK, p. 230.

Χριστιανοὶ πόθεν ἡμεῖς; Διὰ τῆς πίστεως, πᾶς τις ἂν εἴποι. Σωζόμεθα δὴ, τίνα τρόπον; Ἀναγεννηθέντες δηλονότι διὰ τῆς ἐν τῷ βαπτίσματι χάριτος. πόθεν γὰρ ἄλλοθεν;—S. Basil. *De Sp. S.* c. x. p. 29.

Πίστις δὲ καὶ βάπτισμα, δύο τρόποι τῆς σωτηρίας, συμφυεῖς ἀλλήλοις καὶ ἀδιαίρετοι. Πίστις μὲν γὰρ τελειοῦται διὰ βαπτίσματος, βάπτισμα δὲ θεμελιοῦται διὰ τῆς πίστεως καὶ διὰ τῶν αὐτῶν ὀνομάτων ἑκάτερα πληροῦται. Ὡς γὰρ πιστεύομεν εἰς Πατέρα καὶ Υἱὸν καὶ ἅγιον Πνεῦμα, οὕτω καὶ βαπτιζόμεθα εἰς τὸ ὄνομα τοῦ Πατρὸς, καὶ τοῦ Υἱοῦ, καὶ τοῦ ἁγίου Πνεύματος. Καὶ προάγει μὲν ἡ ὁμολογία πρὸς τὴν σωτηρίαν εἰσάγουσα· ἐπακολουθεῖ δὲ τὸ βάπτισμα ἐπισφραγίζον ἡμῶν τὴν συγκατάθεσιν.—Ibid. c. xii. p. 32.

NOTE LLL, p. 237.

Νῦν μὲν γὰρ, εἰ καὶ μὴ ἀνακέκραται τοῖς ἀναξίοις ἀλλ' οὖν παρεῖναι δοκεῖ πως τοῖς ἅπαξ ἐσφραγισμένοις, τὴν ἐκ τῆς ἐπιστροφῆς σωτηρίαν αὐτῶν ἀναμένον. τότε δὲ ἐξ ὅλου τῆς βεβηλωσάσης αὐτοῦ τὴν χάριν ψυχῆς ἀποτμηθήσεται.—S. Basil. *De Sp. S.* c. xvi. p. 47.

NOTE MMM, p. 246.

I may perhaps be allowed, in illustration of the expression in the text, to quote a passage from a former work of my own :—

'Thus much only the Scriptures seem to unfold respecting these two sacred Presences' (the Presence of the Second and Third Persons of the Holy Trinity in the Church), 'that the Holy Ghost dwells in the hearts of separate baptized Christians; that Christ dwells in the community of the Church; that the bodies of Christians are, one by one, temples of the Holy Ghost, but that all together are the Temple of Christ; that each Christian is a separate stone instinct with the Holy Spirit, but that all together make up Christ's Temple; that where several have been duly gathered into the Sacred Name (not without the water and the renewing of the Holy Ghost), there is Christ in the midst of them.'— *Sayings of the Great Forty Days*, ii. p. 84.

NOTE NNN, p. 249.

Had the translators of the Bible in King James's reign foreseen the extent to which their work would have become the great standard of the English language in future times, they might perhaps have ventured on introducing occasionally a new word where no English one existed to supply the full meaning of the original, or to change the meaning of one already in use. It might have been a very bold thing to use the 'soul' to express the Greek $\psi\nu\chi\dot{\eta}$, in both its senses (I mean as signifying both the immaterial, immortal part of man's nature, as distinguished from the mortal body = the immortal soul, and the specifically called $\psi\nu\chi\dot{\eta}$, which (equally immaterial) is contradistinguished from the πνεῦμα or spirit, and is occupied with the desires and interests of this mortal life), but we should in all probability have become accustomed to such an usage, and been spared the extreme inconvenience which results from having to translate ψυχή by the word 'life,' as is the case now in a great number of places in the Gospels,—eminently in Matt. x. 39; xvi. 25; Luke xiv. 26; John x. 11, &c.; xii. 25 So too with the word παράκλητος. From the fact of its being translated 'Comforter' in the Gospel and 'Advocate' in St. John's Epistle a great doctrine is obscured, and English readers have to be informed, as of a new thing, that the word is the same in the original language, and that both the words by which it is translated are really applicable in both books to both the Holy Persons to whom they appear to be applied separately. Had the translators ventured to keep the word 'Paraclete,' introducing a new word into the language to signify a new combination of ideas, this inconvenience would have been avoided.

I might make the same observation with respect to the word διαθήκη, which, translated almost indifferently by the words 'covenant' and 'testament' (see especially the strange way in which these words are interchanged in the ninth and tenth chapters of the Hebrews), and capable from its connexion with διατίθημι of being translated equally well by the word 'dispensation' (cf. Luke xxii. 29; Acts iii. 25; Heb. viii. 10; x. 16), produces a perpetual difficulty in interpretation, while the English reader is left to discover for himself that it is but a single word in the original which is rendered in so various, and apparently irreconcileable ways.

The word παράκλητος may be regarded (1) as a word of classical Greek, in which case it means (see Liddell and Scott's Lexicon) one called in; an advocate, called in to speak, or plead, as before a magistrate. In the passage of St. John's Epistle this is clearly its leading meaning, and, if it were not for the other passages which combine another shade of meaning with this, there would be no fault to find with the word 'Advocate' as the translation of it.

(2) But it is also a word which is modified by the later use of the Alexandrian Greek. Παρακαλέω is used in the New Testament in the two senses of '*to beseech*' and '*to comfort.*' (It never occurs in St. John's Gospel.) The two senses occur in close juxtaposition in Acts xvi. 39 and 40. Of these two senses the first is much the most common; the second is used, almost exclusively, in the passive voice. (Matt. v. 4; Luke xvi. 25; Acts xx. 12.) In the LXX it is used in the active (παρακαλείτε, παρακαλείτε τὸν λαόν μου, λέγει ὁ Θεός. ἱερεῖς λαλήσατε εἰς τὴν καρδίαν Ἱερουσαλήμ, παρακαλέσατε αὐτήν, κ.τ.λ. Isa. xl. 1, 2; cf. Ps. cxix. 50; Gen. xxxvii. 35, &c.); so also in those remarkable verses (2 Cor. i. 3—7) in which the idea of 'comfort' is in various shapes repeated not less than ten times in four verses.

Παράκλησις occurs twenty-nine times in the New Testament, twenty-one times in the sense of 'comfort;' cf. Nahum iii. 7; Isa. lvii. 18. Παρακλήτωρ is used in the Book of Job for a comforter (Ὑπολαβὼν δὲ Ἰὼβ λέγει, Ἀκήκοα τοιαῦτα πολλά, παρακλήτορες κακῶν πάντες, Job xvi. 2). So also παρακαλῶν, 2 Sam. x. 3: cf. Ps. lxix. 20; Eccl. iv. 1; Lam. i. 9, 16; Isa. li. 12.

The word παράκλητος is quoted from Philo in Grinfield's Editio Hellenistica; but in the classical sense as an advocate only.

Thus the word *Paraclete* may be understood to have the sense of 'one called in' (I suppose that the fundamental form must be passive) in order to *plead*, to *exhort*, and to *comfort*.

'Hinc patet,' as is well said by Corn. a Lap., 'quod Christus quoque fuerit apostolorum et fidelium Paracletus; id est primò advocatus, intercessor, orator, juxtà illud Pauli' (Johannis?) '*Advocatum habemus apud Deum Patrem, Jesum Christum*, ait S. Aug. Secundò, exhortator, incitator, impulsor: Tertiò, consolator, ut vertit Syrus: hæc tria enim significat Græcum παράκλητος. Sed abiens Christus misit alium Paracletum, sc. Spiritum Sanctum, qui in his tribus Christo successit. Ipse enim primò est advocatus fidelium, quia *postulat pro nobis gemitibus enarrabilibus*, Rom. viii. 26. Ipse pariter est noster exhortator et consolator, quæ duo hic (sc. Joh. xiv. 6) maximè spectat Christus, q. d. Ego huc usque vos, o discipuli mei, docui, rexi, consolatus sum, ac proinde ob instantem meum discessum contristamini; sed animos erigite, et confidite. Ego enim mei loco vobis submittam alium Paracletum, qui vos non ad modicum tempus, ut ego, sed totâ vestrâ vitâ, doceat, incitet, consoletur, et protegat.'

www.ingramcontent.com/pod-product-compliance
Lightning Source LLC
Chambersburg PA
CBHW030255240426
43673CB00040B/980